An Awkward Partner

An Awkward Partner

Britain in the European Community

Third edition

STEPHEN GEORGE

OXFORD UNIVERSITY PRESS

*This book has been printed digitally and produced in a standard specification
in order to ensure its continuing availability*

OXFORD
UNIVERSITY PRESS

Great Clarendon Street, Oxford OX2 6DP

Oxford University Press is a department of the University of Oxford.
It furthers the University's objective of excellence in research, scholarship,
and education by publishing worldwide in

Oxford New York

Auckland Cape Town Dar es Salaam Hong Kong Karachi
Kuala Lumpur Madrid Melbourne Mexico City Nairobi
New Delhi Shanghai Taipei Toronto
With offices in
Argentina Austria Brazil Chile Czech Republic France Greece
Guatemala Hungary Italy Japan South Korea Poland Portugal
Singapore Switzerland Thailand Turkey Ukraine Vietnam

Oxford is a registered trade mark of Oxford University Press
in the UK and in certain other countries

Published in the United States
by Oxford University Press Inc., New York

ISBN 978-0-19-878223-0

Preface to the Third Edition

ALTHOUGH the nature of this book is explained in the Introduction, it is perhaps worth underlining that it is intended to be an initial overview of a topic that had not previously been surveyed in book form at the time that the first edition appeared.

Chapters 1 to 7 of this edition remain exactly as in the second edition. Chapter 8, which in the second edition went up to the beginning of 1994, has been substantially extended to take the story of the Major Government through to its end in the 1997 general election. There have also been some small changes to the text of Chapter 9 to reflect the lessons from the experience of the last years of the Major Government.

Since the first edition was produced, various memoirs of politicians who were involved in the events have appeared. I decided not to rewrite the text of the second edition to incorporate reference to these, especially as they contain nothing that encouraged me to change the judgements expressed in the first edition. For the same reason, and for consistency, I have not drawn on them in those chapters which have been added since the first edition. Readers might like to compare for themselves the version of events presented here with that given in memoirs by Margaret Thatcher, Geoffrey Howe, Nigel Lawson, *et al.*

I will repeat here a clarification that appeared in the Prefaces to the previous two editions: I have throughout the text referred to 'Britain' as an international actor. This is a double simplification. First, the state referred to is properly 'the United Kingdom of Great Britain and Northern Ireland', for which 'Britain' is simply a convenient and instantly recognized abbreviation. Secondly, it is obvious that states do not literally act: only individuals can do that, so references to 'Britain' doing something or other are a shorthand for an action taken on behalf of the state by an authorized individual.

As in previous editions, I would like to thank Nigel Ashford for permission to quote from his Ph.D. thesis, and the University Association for Contemporary European Studies for permission to reproduce in Chapters 5 and 6 material which previously appeared as UACES Occasional Paper 4, *The British Government and the European Community since 1985* (London, 1987).

As the analysis in the Conclusion indicates, I am hopeful that this may prove to be the definitive edition of this book, in the sense that it might no longer be accurate to describe Britain as an awkward partner in the future, and I shall have to continue the story in another book which will be called something along the lines of *New Labour, New Europe*.

STEPHEN GEORGE

October 1997

Contents

Abbreviations

ASTMS	Association of Scientific, Technical, and Managerial Staffs
BBC	British Broadcasting Corporation
CAP	Common Agricultural Policy
CBI	Confederation of British Industry
CEEC	Committee for European Economic Co-operation
CIEC	Conference on International Economic Co-operation
COCOM	Co-Committee of NATO (to monitor trade with the East)
CSCE	Conference on Security and Co-operation in Europe
EC	European Community
ECSC	European Coal and Steel Community
Ecu	European currency unit
EDC	European Defence Community
EEC	European Economic Community
EFTA	European Free Trade Association
EMS	European Monetary System
EMU	Economic and Monetary Union
EPC	European Political Co-operation
ERDF	European Regional Development Fund
EU	European Union
Euratom	European Atomic Energy Community
EUREKA	European Research Co-ordinating Agency
FBI	Federation of British Industry
FDP	Freie Demokratische Partei Deutschlands
FRG	Federal Republic of Germany
GATT	General Agreement on Tariffs and Trade
GNP	Gross National Product
HMSO	Her Majesty's Stationary Office
IEA	International Energy Agency
IGC	inter-governmental conference
IMF	International Monetary Fund
MEP	Member of the European Parliament
NATO	North Atlantic Treaty Organization

NEC	National Executive Committee
NHS	National Health Service
OECD	Organization for Economic Co-operation and Development
OPEC	Organization of Petroleum Exporting Countries
SDI	Strategic Defence Initiative
SDP	Social Democratic Party
SNP	Scottish National Party
SPD	Sozialdemokratische Partei Deutschlands
TUC	Trades Union Congress
UACES	University Association for Contemporary European Studies
UNICE	Union of Industries in the European Community
UTC	United Technologies Corporation
VAT	Value Added Tax
WEU	Western European Union

Introduction

On 1 January 1973 Britain became a member of the European Communities, twenty-two years after the first of those Communities had been created without British participation. Within a year of achieving membership, Britain was already regarded as something of an awkward partner, a reputation that has remained through to the time of writing.

After a brief review of the relationship between Britain and the Communities prior to membership, this book concerns itself with the basis for that reputation. It is intended to be an overview of the field, a presentation of the record more than a detailed analysis of the reasons for the awkwardness, but it is not possible to separate explanation from account totally, and the elements of explanation that are emphasized here are political. They stress the influence of external circumstances and domestic political considerations in moulding the attitudes of successive British Governments to developments within the Community.

The chapters are ordered chronologically and divided according to the succession of British Prime Ministers, except for Chapters 5, 6, and 7 which divide the Thatcher Governments into three periods determined by developments at the EC level. For thematic unity Chapters 5 and 6 overlap a little, so that some events that occurred during the 1979–84 period are actually recounted in Chapter 6, since they are more relevant to the theme of new directions for the Community, which became the dominant theme of British policy after June 1984, than to that of settling Britain's dispute over its contributions to the Community's budget, which is the main theme of Chapter 5.

Each chapter begins with an outline of the international context within which the events described in the chapter occurred and of the domestic political and economic situation during the period in question. Some of the relevance of this is brought out explicitly in the rest of the chapter; otherwise the purpose is to set the development of British policy within the Community in a wider frame of reference, and simply to remind the reader that these developments were taking place against a specific background.

One other piece of background information that may assist the reader to follow the story concerns the nature of the European Community itself. The outline that follows offers only the barest bones of the constitutional and institutional structure of the Community: no more than is needed to understand the references in the main text. More detail may be found in Chapter 1 of this same author's *Politics and Policy in the European Community* (Oxford, 1984).

The European Community/Communities

Already in this introduction the terms 'European Communities' and 'European Community' have both been used, perhaps causing a degree of confusion. Strictly speaking the first remains the correct term.

There are three Communities: the European Coal and Steel Community (ECSC), the European Atomic Energy Community (Euratom), and the European Economic Community (EEC). They remain legally separate entities, but in 1967 the institutions of the three were merged, and since then it has become common, and logical, to speak of the European Community (EC) in the singular.

In Britain, perhaps another example of awkwardness, the usage is less common than in the rest of the Community, and the most common abbreviated term is still 'EEC', even where the reference is to powers or functions proper to one of the other Communities. In the United States usage is even looser, and it is not uncommon to come across the abbreviation 'ECM' for 'European Common Market', a term that has no legal basis and does not accurately represent the scope of the EC.

In this book the term European Community and its abbreviation EC are used except where reference is specifically to one of the three Communities, or to the period prior to merger in 1967, or where other writers are being quoted.

The Institutions of the European Community

The main institutions of the EEC are the Commission, the Council of Ministers, the European Council, the Court of Justice, and the European Parliament.

The Commission consists of a body of international civil servants working under the guidance of a small group of Commissioners. There is one Commissioner from each member state, plus a second one from each of the larger states (Britain, France, West Germany, Italy, and Spain). These Commissioners are nominated by their national Governments, but are sworn not to take instructions from any national Government during their tenure of the post. They are appointed for a four-year, renewable term. One of their number acts as President during each four-year period, and by convention the nationality of the President rotates between the member states. The functions of the Commission are to make formal proposals for Community legislation, and to monitor the implementation of measures that have been agreed by the Council of Ministers.

The Council of Ministers consists of representatives of the Governments of the member states. The actual representative varies according to the subject under discussion, so that when agricultural matters are being considered the representatives will be national Ministers of Agriculture, or their nominees, whereas when trade matters are under consideration the national Ministers for Trade, or their nominees, will attend. In this book the different Councils are distinguished by referring to them as the Council of Agriculture Ministers, the Council of Trade Ministers, etc.

According to the original Treaties, the highest level of the Council of Ministers is Foreign Minister level, but the institutionalization of meetings of Heads of Government (plus the French President, who officially is a Head of State) has added a new top layer to the structure, which was formally recognized in the Single European Act of 1986, and is known as the European Council. Journalists and others still refer to meetings of the European Council as 'European summit meetings'.

The Court of Justice is the supreme Court of the EC. It consists of one judge from each member state, although during periods when there has been an even number of member states (as at present) a second nominee from one state, on a rotating basis, has ensured that there would always be a clear majority decision when the judges were divided. The Court rules on all questions of the interpretation of Community law, and on breaches of obligations under the Treaties or under EC legislation.

The European Parliament has been directly elected since 1979. Before that it consisted of national parliamentarians who were nominated by their parties to sit in it as a second job on top of their national parliamentary duties. It used to be known as the European Parliamentary Assembly, and many British politicians continued to refer to it as the 'European Assembly' even after it became a directly elected body: indeed, some persist in doing so to this day, presumably to emphasize that its powers are strictly limited, and that it is more an advisory assembly than a legislature.

1. The Background: Britain and Europe, 1945–1973

BRITAIN came late to membership of the European Communities. When the negotiations began in 1950 that led to the creation of the ECSC, forerunner of the present EC, the British Labour Government of Clement Attlee was invited to participate, but declined. When the six states that had formed the ECSC started to discuss extending the common market in coal and steel into a general common market, the British Conservative Government of Sir Anthony Eden initially took part in the discussions, but withdrew when unable to convince the Six to be less ambitious in their plans.

As a consequence of this refusal to become founder members, the British found themselves outside a highly successful economic grouping which, as their own economic problems grew and their independent influence in the world declined, it proved impossible for them to ignore. Within a few years of the setting-up of the general common market the Conservative Government of Harold Macmillan was opening negotiations to see whether a basis could be found for British membership. But, because of French resistance, it took until 1973, and two further applications, before membership was actually achieved.

This delay in achieving membership meant that Britain did not participate in the most successful period of the history of the Communities, and only managed to become a member as world economic conditions ushered in a period of recession. As a result, membership did not come to have the popular positive connotations in Britain that it had in the founder states. Also, during the years when Britain was not a member, the Communities took on a shape that suited the original six member states far better than it suited Britain.

The International Context

The alliance of Britain, the United States, and the Soviet Union that had been victorious over Hitler had been under strain before the end of the war, and broke apart soon after it. In March 1946 the British wartime leader, Winston Churchill, spoke of an iron curtain that was descending across Europe from the Baltic to the Adriatic.[1] This line marked the division between the states of Eastern Europe, which were in the Soviet sphere of influence and on to which the USSR imposed a communist form of government, from the states of Western Europe which lay beyond the influence of the Soviet Union, but in some cases only precariously so. By the end of 1946 co-operative relations between the Soviet Union and its former allies had effectively broken down, and a condition of hostility falling short of armed conflict had emerged. This condition came to be called the Cold War.

Within the capitalist world the United States was undoubtedly the dominant state. It had the strongest economy, and the greatest military potential, including possession of the atomic bomb. In contrast to the healthy position of the US economy, the states of Western Europe were in a parlous condition as a direct consequence of the war. In June 1947 US Secretary of State George Marshall announced a European Recovery Program, under which the United States between 1948 and 1952 was to give $17 billion in grants to the states of Western Europe to help them to rebuild their economies. Marshall Aid was offered to the Soviet Union and the states of Eastern Europe, but with little hope that it would be accepted. When Soviet Foreign Minister Molotov walked out of talks on the aid programme in Paris, the seal was set on the division of Europe into two ideologically opposed camps. In 1949 the division was graphically symbolized by the creation of two separate German states, the Federal Republic in the west and the Democratic Republic in the east, and by the election of the anti-communist Konrad Adenauer as first Chancellor (Prime Minister) of the Federal Republic.

There followed a period during which the leadership of the United States within the capitalist world was unchallenged, even if in some quarters it was resented. The threat that Stalin's USSR appeared to present to the West fostered unity behind the strongest capitalist state. The signing of the North Atlantic Pact, which instituted the North Atlantic Treaty Organization (NATO), in April 1949 marked the formal commitment of American troops to

[1]   In a speech in Mar. 1946 in Fulton, Missouri.

the defence of Western Europe. As if to underline its necessity, the invasion of South Korea by the communist North in 1950 appeared to confirm the inherent expansionism of the USSR: the parallel between a divided Korea and a divided Germany reinforced the unity of the leaders of Western Europe behind US leadership.

The price that the West Europeans paid for US protection and economic assistance was the acceptance of a world economic order based on a US blueprint. That meant accepting a commitment to multilateral world free trade, and an international monetary system based on the dollar. It was a system that gave certain privileges to the United States, such as allowing it to run a balance of payments deficit without having to introduce domestic deflationary measures to correct it; but it also assisted the recovery of the European states, some of which in the 1950s began to outstrip US rates of economic growth.[2] This new prosperity was partly, though, based on the investments that had been made in Western Europe by US multinational corporations, which was resented in some quarters, particularly in France.

There was also resentment in France of the political dominance of the United States, highlighted in 1956 when a joint Franco–British force attempted to repossess the Suez Canal from Egypt, whose President Nasser had nationalized it, only to be prevented by US opposition. The incident also caused a deterioration of Franco–British relations, because it was the British who bowed to US pressure to halt the operation when the French wanted to go on.[3]

A turning-point in relations between the United States and Western Europe was the return to office in France of General Charles de Gaulle, the man who had led the Free French forces during the war, and the first Prime Minister after the liberation of the country. Unsympathetic to the liberal and socialist parties that dominated the first elections, and without a political party of his own to back him, he resigned as premier in 1946, but remained active in politics, condemning the political manœuvring that was a prominent feature of the Fourth French Republic. In 1958 he was swept back to office when an army rebellion in Algeria, against

---

[2] For more detailed accounts, see Stephen George, *Politics and Policy in the European Community* (Oxford, 1985), chs. 4 and 5; E. A. Brett, *The World Economy since the War: The Politics of Uneven Development* (London, 1985), chs. 3 and 5; Joan Edelman Spero, *The Politics of International Economic Relations* (3rd edn., London, 1985), ch. 1.

[3] See David Carlton, *Britain and the Suez Crisis* (Oxford, 1988).

moves to end French rule, raised fears of a civil war. De Gaulle, with his military background and conservative credentials, seemed the only man able to salvage the situation. His price for doing so was the dissolution of the Fourth Republic and the installation of a Fifth Republic which rapidly developed into a presidential regime. As President, de Gaulle reserved foreign affairs in particular to himself.

One basis of de Gaulle's foreign policy was anti-Americanism. His own experience of US attempts to unseat him as leader of the Free French during the war gave personal commitment to this policy, but it drew its strength from tapping a latent resentment of US domination that stretched across the French political spectrum. In its first phase the policy centred on developing the Communities into an organization with a joint foreign policy, under French leadership. When this approach collapsed in the face of resistance from the smaller member states, de Gaulle dispensed with the backing of the rest of the Communities, although accepting the economic necessity of continued French membership, and contented himself with acts of defiance against the United States. He visited Moscow in 1964, and signed trade agreements with the Soviet leadership; he withdrew French forces from the integrated NATO command structure in 1966, and expelled NATO headquarters from French soil; and in the later 1960s he conducted a concerted campaign to undermine the dollar by converting dollars from France's foreign currency reserves into gold, thus precipitating a serious monetary crisis.[4]

By the end of the 1960s US leadership was no longer unquestioned elsewhere in Western Europe. A relaxation of tensions between East and West, that developed gradually under Stalin's successors Khruschev and Brezhnev, encouraged dissent to become more open. Following the demise of Adenauer in the Federal Republic, a momentum began to build for a diplomatic opening to the East, which in 1969 brought into office the Social Democrats under Willy Brandt, who was committed to an *Ostpolitik* of improved

---

[4] On de Gaulle's foreign policy in general, the best book is Edward L. Morse, *Interdependence and Foreign Policy in Gaullist France* (Princeton, 1973); on the policy of exchanging dollars for gold, see Henrik Schmieglow and Michele Schmieglow, 'The New Mercantilism in International Relations: The Case of France's External Monetary Policy', *International Organization*, 29 (1975), 367–92.

relations with the communist bloc.[5] Throughout Western Europe a generation of young people who did not remember the war, or the fears of Soviet invasion that followed it, campaigned against US involvement in Vietnam, and put pressure on politicians to repudiate US leadership.

Although still the strongest single economy in the world, the United States no longer dominated the capitalist system as it had immediately after the war. West European states and Japan had caught up with and were overtaking US levels of productivity and wealth. By the beginning of the 1970s the United States was running a balance of trade deficit with Japan, and becoming increasingly concerned about its relative performance. At the same time it was becoming irritated with allies that criticized it but made little contribution to ensuring the stability and maintenance of the capitalist world system from which they were benefiting. By the end of the 1960s the post-war international system was about to reach a major turning-point.

The Domestic Context

Between the end of the war and the start of the 1970s the Labour and Conservative Parties alternated in office. To the surprise of many people, who expected that Winston Churchill's wartime leadership would produce a Conservative victory, Labour won the first general election in 1945 with a substantial majority, and proceeded to put through a programme of economic and social reforms that included the nationalization of key sectors of industry and the creation of a National Health Service. The popularity of this programme is indicated by the extent to which it was accepted by the Conservatives, and became the basis of a broad consensus on domestic policy that lasted through to the 1970s.

But the Labour Government also necessarily presided over a period of economic restraint which was an inevitable consequence of the dislocation caused by the war; and the weariness that this produced in a people who had suffered for too many years contributed to such a drastically reduced majority for Labour in February 1950 that another election had to be held in September

[5] On *Ostpolitik*, see Willy Brandt, *A Peace Policy for Europe*, trans. Joel Carmichael (London, 1969); Michael Kreile, '*Ostpolitik* Reconsidered', in Ekkehart Krippendorf and Volker Rittberger (eds.), *The Foreign Policy of West Germany: Formation and Contents* (London, 1980), ch. 4.

1951. This time, by courtesy of Britain's electoral system, the Conservatives won, despite polling fewer votes than Labour, and so were in office in time to claim credit for the effects of the world economic boom that was just beginning. On this basis they held office for the next thirteen years, under four Prime Ministers: Churchill until 1955, Anthony Eden from 1955 to 1957, Harold Macmillan from 1957 to 1963, and Alec Douglas-Home briefly from Macmillan's resignation to the general election in 1964.

During these thirteen years there was first a recovery in national self-confidence, then a steady decline. The Suez crisis of 1956 is often seen as a turning-point: it emphasized the relative weakness of Britain in world affairs, and sparked a bout of national self-examination which extended beyond matters concerned with foreign and defence policy to a questioning of the performance of the economy.

British rates of economic growth in the 1950s were extremely high by historical standards, but the sense of well-being that this generated was gradually undermined by the realization that other European states were performing better. Balance of payments crises became a recurrent problem, as imports expanded faster than exports, and inflation rose more rapidly than in the economies of Britain's competitors. Governments found themselves trapped into a 'stop–go' cycle, expanding the economy through the stimulation of demand only for the balance of payments to plunge into deficit so that demand had to be reined back to avert a sterling crisis.

By 1960 concern was such that the Government, under pressure from the Federation of British Industry (FBI), decided to embark on a programme of modernization of the economic structure. But this implicit admission that all had not been as well as it had been portrayed during the previous decade played into the hands of the Labour Party, which presented itself as a more dynamic modernizing force and, helped by scandals that undermined the moral authority of the Government, won the 1964 general election with a very narrow majority.

Labour, under the leadership of Harold Wilson, consolidated its victory and increased its majority substantially in 1966. Elected on a programme that stressed the need for Britain to undergo a technological revolution, it soon found itself grappling with intractable obstacles. One was the balance of payments, which, because of the weak export performance of the British economy, continued in chronic deficit. Eventually the pound sterling had to be devalued in 1967, but only after a long and costly struggle to hold the parity against the dollar in the interest of keeping the City of London an attractive home for international capital. The other problem was the resistance of the trade unions to the modernization programme.

Britain has a long history of trade unionism, and, unlike the position in some other European states, it had not been broken by fascism. When the economic expansion began in the 1950s, British industry soon began to experience labour shortages. Where other European states were able to supply industry's demand for labour through the displacement of workers from agriculture, British agriculture was already relatively efficient and a small employer. The labour shortages increased the bargaining power of the trade unions, who felt able to pursue bigger wage increases in the 1950s than did their counterparts in the rest of Western Europe, thereby contributing to the lower competitiveness of British exports. There was also resistance from British workers to the introduction of the work-routines that were the basis of the high productivity of industry in competitor states, which again contributed to poor competitiveness, and hindered adaptation of the nineteenth-century industrial structure to the post-war world.

Officially the trade unions supported the modernization strategy of the Labour Government, but the rank and file of the union movement did not necessarily agree with the leadership, a circumstance which produced a certain schizophrenia in the reactions of the unions' leaders to the measures taken by Labour, and led to a large increase in unofficial industrial stoppages. It was the failure of the Wilson Government to deal with industrial militancy which finally undermined its authority and led to the narrow Conservative victory in 1970. Wilson's attempt to bring industrial relations under the rule of law foundered on the outright rejection by the leaders of the trade unions of any legal regulation; a wave of strikes in 1969 led to highly inflationary wage settlements, and blew apart the Government's prices and incomes policy that was designed to keep down inflation. 'Economic disorder set in long before the June 1970 election transferred the damnable inheritance to a Conservative administration.'[6]

---

[6] Keith Middlemass, *Politics in Industrial Society* (London, 1979), 442.

British Foreign Policy and World Order

According to writers who adopt what is called a 'realist' approach to international politics, states formulate their foreign policies on the basis of the pursuit of national self-interest. Clearly there is a lot of truth in such a view. The problem is that what constitutes 'the national interest' is far from being clear-cut. The national interest of a state may be defined in a variety of ways, and the way in which it is defined will depend on several factors, including the perceptions and habits of mind of the policy-makers.

British national interests in the post-war world tended to be defined in rather broader terms than were the national interests of some other West European states, reflecting the legacy of Britain's role as the dominant state in the international system of the nineteenth century, and its status as an imperial power.

From the end of the Napoleonic Wars to the outbreak of the First World War, Britain, largely because of its early industrialization, had been the dominant state in the international system. It had used this dominance 'to usher in the age of free trade',[7] and had then acted to maintain the system against any threat to its stability.

So for over a century British policy-makers had been in the habit of looking at British external policy, including economic policy, in terms of how it would contribute to the maintenance of world order. This global perspective was reinforced by Britain's imperial role. As the rulers of an empire 'on which the sun never set', the makers of British policy had to consider the whole of the world in their calculations of what constituted the national interest. They could not afford to concentrate only on European affairs; indeed, European affairs held a relatively minor position in their perceptions, except when continental European states threatened to disrupt the world order set up and maintained by Britain.

British policy towards Europe throughout the nineteenth century and into the early twentieth century was to promote a balance of power on the Continent, such that no one state could dominate. If there were a threat of that balance being irrevocably tilted in one direction, the British counterweight was thrown into the other pan of the scale, as it was against Napoleonic France, and against Germany in both 1914 and 1939.

---

[7] Robert Gilpin, *The Political Economy of International Relations* (Princeton, 1987), 73.

For some historians, the story of the two world wars is the story of an attempt by Germany to end Britain's position of dominance within the international system, and of British resistance to this.[8] The outcome of the First World War was determined by the entry of the United States, which in terms of wealth and industrial strength was already ahead of Britain and Germany.

On this view of history the inter-war years represent a period when Britain had already ceased to be strong enough to justify it playing the role of the dominant world power, but, because of the withdrawal of the United States from participation in the international system, and because of the defeat of Germany, there was no barrier to Britain continuing to play the role.

This background predisposed British policy-makers, politicians and civil servants alike, to think of Britain as occupying a special position in world affairs, a tendency reinforced by Britain's experience in the Second World War as the only European state not to be invaded. Again the issue was largely settled by the entry of the United States into the war, but British leaders were key participants at the conferences of the allied powers that decided on the post-war settlement.

After the Second World War most states in Western Europe were concerned primarily with their own economic recovery, and with rediscovering a sense of national identity after the trauma of a war that had resulted in defeat and national humiliation for the Germans, and that had involved the division of almost all the other nations of Western Europe between fascists and anti-fascists, collaborators and resistance fighters. While these states were formulating their foreign policies in line with such objectives, Britain continued to formulate its foreign policy in global terms.

Partly this represented the fact that Britain did indeed retain world responsibilities. It remained an imperial power; it assumed responsibility for territories that had been colonies of, or had been occupied by, the defeated states, and were not immediately in a position to take their independence; and, under agreements with the United States and the Soviet Union that had been concluded at Yalta in 1945, it had responsibility for seeing the restoration of civilian government in a clearly defined 'sphere of influence'.

---

[8] See, for example, Geoffrey Barraclough, 'From the European Balance of Power to the Age of World Politics', in his *An Introduction to Contemporary History* (Harmondsworth, 1967), ch. 4.

Partly, though, the adoption of the global perspective was a matter of the way in which the policy-making élites thought about foreign policy. It represented a long-held habit of mind that proved difficult to break. Britain had always held a special place in ordering the affairs of the world, and, despite its reduced position when compared with the United States and the Soviet Union, its statesmen and diplomats continued to assume that it would still play such a role.

Because of this it has been suggested by writers using hindsight that the political and administrative élites in Britain were suffering from an 'illusion of grandeur'. Such a charge seems less than fair. All the indications are that the Foreign Office was perfectly aware that Britain was incapable of resisting the strength of the United States, or of the Soviet Union once it had recovered from the depradations of war; and from late 1946 onwards the Soviet Union increasingly came to be seen as the major threat to the stability of the capitalist world.[9]

In order to counteract the influence of the USSR it was seen in the Foreign Office as essential that the United States be kept in the system as a significant actor. After the First World War the United States had withdrawn from the international system, and it was this withdrawal that had led to Britain having to continue to assume responsibility for the maintenance of world order itself. Its failure had resulted in the Second World War. Preventing a further withdrawal of the United States into isolation became a major preoccupation of British foreign policy after the war.

It was probably for this reason that Winston Churchill made the special relationship with the United States the first of the three spheres of influence for Britain that he identified in a famous analysis of the country's position in the world. The other two spheres were the Commonwealth and, definitely in third place, Europe. Although he presented this analysis when he was the leader of the opposition, there is little doubt that it represented the consensus view of the Conservative and Labour leaderships, and of the Foreign Office.

The idea of a special relationship with the United States was based on the belief that the Americans would need guidance in how to conduct themselves in international affairs, and would be

[9] Elisabeth Barker, *The British between the Superpowers, 1945–50* (London, 1983), especially her comments in the Preface, p. x.

prepared to accept such guidance from another English-speaking nation which had lately played the role of dominant power in the world. This belief managed to survive growing evidence that the United States had little intention of listening to the British advice. When successive US Administrations supported the movements for West European unity, this was seen by the British as a mistake which simply proved that the Americans needed British guidance. Suggestions from Washington that Britain might join the European Communities that were being formed were seen in the same light.

So, despite the support of the United States for British participation in the European Communities, the maintenance of the belief in a special Atlantic relationship acted as a psychological barrier to Britain's policy-makers seeing the need for such participation.

The same argument can be applied to the second of Churchill's three spheres of influence, the Commonwealth. This relationship had several implications that worked against Britain seeing itself as a possible participant in the European Communities. The first was that British policy-makers appear to have believed that its leadership of the Commonwealth would allow Britain to speak with a louder voice in international affairs than could other European states. The assumption that Britain would lead the Commonwealth, despite the rhetoric of equality between sovereign nations, appears arrogant in retrospect, but was perhaps understandable at the time.

The second aspect was purely commercial. In 1948 Britain sent 40 per cent of its exports and re-exports to the Commonwealth.[10] Whole sections of the British economy were dependent for their prosperity on this trade. So it could be seen as being in the interest of the British economy as a whole to cultivate the special links as far as possible. It also meant that there were influential pressure groups with an interest in maintaining the links. Any move into a preferential trading relationship with other West European states would be seen as jeopardizing this other trading relationship; it was largely on these grounds that the Board of Trade consistently opposed British membership of the European Communities.

Finally, the Commonwealth had a special resonance in terms of domestic politics: it was an idea to which the British public was strongly attached. Empire had been a powerful unifying idea in Victorian England, and the Commonwealth inherited the force of

[10] Kenneth O. Morgan, *Labour in Power, 1945–1951* (Oxford, 1984), 391–2.

this idea that had been implanted in millions of minds at school. But, beyond that, British people had relatives in parts of the Commonwealth, particularly Australia, New Zealand, Canada, and South Africa, and it was these former dominions that most British people continued to think of when they thought of the Commonwealth.[11] The Commonwealth, then, had considerable economic and political importance for Britain, but it became a real barrier to co-operation with the six states that eventually came together to form the European Communities. As with the special relationship with the United States, the existence of the Commonwealth as a perceived British sphere of influence deterred British policy-makers from seeing any need to be part of a 'narrow' European grouping. The existence of vested economic interests opposed to close links with any other group of states lest it jeopardize the profitable (for them) relationship with the Commonwealth, combined with a popular sentiment that could easily be mobilized in favour of 'kith and kin' in the Commonwealth and against 'foreigners' in Europe, proved to be a considerable political obstacle even when the slow evolution of British policy did come round to a more favourable view of membership.

That point was not reached until the beginning of the 1960s, ten years after the initial steps were taken in creating the first European Community, with an invitation being extended to Britain to join in at the outset of the experiment—an invitation that was declined.

British and French Policy towards Europe

During the post-war period a division steadily emerged between Britain and France over the future of Europe. An early indication of this division appeared in 1947 when the British and French took the initiative in convening a conference of all European states interested in receiving aid from the United States under the plan proposed by Secretary of State George Marshall. They first held talks in Paris with the Soviet Union, but, after Soviet Foreign Minister Molotov

[11] As late as 1974 the Social Policy Centre found that amongst the 59% of respondents who thought that Britain should have forged stronger links with the Commonwealth rather than with the EC, 36% when pressed to be more precise mentioned Australia, 34% New Zealand, 27% Canada, and no more than 2% mentioned any other Commonwealth country, although 17% mentioned the United States (Robert Jowell and Gerald Hoinville (eds.), *Britain into Europe: Public Opinion and the EEC, 1961–75* (London, 1976, 59)).

walked out and made it clear that the East European states would be refusing the offer of Marshall Aid, the French and British proceeded together with the fourteen other states that were interested, and a Council for European Economic Co-operation (CEEC) was created. This Council reported to the United States in September 1947 on the members' joint plans for utilizing the promised aid. The document indicated a good deal of agreement, but on one issue there was disagreement. The formation of a customs union had been proposed by the French, but the British had declined to be involved in such a project.[12]

Ideas for customs unions and economic unions had been high on the agenda of discussions between continental European states since before the end of the war, the most concrete result being the Benelux customs union between Belgium, The Netherlands, and Luxemburg. In Algiers in 1944, before the liberation of France, schemes emerged from officials serving the Free French grouping under de Gaulle for a North-West European coal and steel area and for a West European economic union.[13] Such ideas became the basis for post-war France's European policy. They were championed in particular by the influential civil servant Jean Monnet, who emerged at the end of the war as the head of the Economic Planning Commission charged with organizing France's economic recovery. For Monnet, the objective of pursuing West European unity was 'to create a huge continental market on the European scale'.[14] He recognized that France was too small an economy to be able to compete effectively in international terms, and that a wider domestic market was necessary if European companies were to be fostered which would match the Americans in size and scale.

This approach was rejected by the British Government. In response to the proposal made in the CEEC for a customs union, the British representatives argued, on what were to become familiar grounds, that the problems of Europe were global problems, and that an exclusive trading block would be no solution. It did appear that Ernest Bevin, the British Foreign Secretary, was actually quite favourably disposed towards a customs union,[15] as were some economists within the Foreign Office, but here the economic

[12] Elisabeth Barker, *Britain in a Divided Europe* (London, 1971), 78–9.

[13] John W. Young, *Britain, France and the Unity of Europe* (Leicester, 1984), 5–7.

[14] Jean Monnet, 'A Ferment of Change', *Journal of Common Market Studies*, 1 (1962), 205.   [15] Young, *Britain, France . . .*, p. 67.

ministries were more influential, particularly the Board of Trade, which at that time remained a firm defender of Britain's Commonwealth links. The universalist views expressed by the British delegation within the CEEC were, therefore, in defence of a particular and very conservative view of Britain's economic interests. It was not long, though, before Bevin and the Foreign Office came round to rejecting later revivals of similar suggestions by the French, for strategic reasons. The growing perception of a threat to Western Europe from the Soviet Union convinced the Foreign Secretary that the continued commitment of the United States to the defence of Western Europe had to be Britain's highest policy objective, and the existence of sentiments in France that were less than enthusiastic about the involvement of the United States in European affairs convinced British policy-makers that they must oppose the formation of the sort of regional grouping that the French favoured lest it contribute to a schism with the Americans.

Ironically, the United States supported the idea of a customs union in 1947, and continued to give backing to French schemes for West European regional organizations. Although the thrust of US policy was towards the creation of a multilateral system of free trade, it was the view of the State Department that the defence of Western Europe against communism was its major objective, and that could be more effectively achieved by a unified West European bloc than by a collection of separate states. This remained a consistent position throughout the negotiation of the various European Communities, which brought the United States repeatedly into conflict with the British view.

What most worried the British was the appeal that ideas for a European customs union had for those within France who also favoured the idea of Europe as a 'third force' between the Soviet Union and the United States. A similar idea had appealed to elements of the British Labour Party immediately after the war, but was abandoned by them following the Hague Congress of April 1948, an event designed to further the cause of European unity at which 'Labour observers noted that the attendance was overwhelmingly representative of Conservative and capitalist groups'.[16] Indeed, the star British speaker was Winston Churchill, which was a sure reason for Labour members to be suspicious of the unity movement.

[16] Morgan, *Labour in Power*, p. 392.

There was a difference, though, between the 'third forcism' of British Labour Party members and that of many French politicians, including figures such as the conservative Georges Bidault, who as Foreign Minister in 1946 had proposed an Anglo–French treaty around which Western Europe could unite independently of the United States and the USSR. For the Labour members there was an ideological motivation: a desire to find a middle way between the capitalism of the United States and the communism of the USSR. Although such ideas did exist in France, for many French politicians the motivation was national pride. France did not relish being subordinate to the United States. Without the special relationship that the British believed they had with the United States, independence seemed the only alternative to inferiority. It was widely accepted, though, that independence could only be achieved through co-operation with other West European states. The vision of France leading a united Western Europe emerged most explicitly with the return to power in France of General de Gaulle in 1958; but it was present as an underlying theme of French policy throughout the Fourth Republic.

Here, then, were the main lines of British and French policy towards Europe. For Britain, the security of Western Europe and the capitalist world had to be based on the unchallenged leadership of the United States; this was the obvious position for Britain to take, given its own experience as a dominant world power, its historical and cultural sympathy for the United States and its conviction that it could enjoy a special relationship with the new dominant power. For France, worried by the prospect of US domination, the key to balance in Europe was to build up Western European unity under French leadership. This approach was rejected by a Britain suspicious of the third forcism inherent in the project. The solution suggested by the United States, that Britain should itself take the leadership of the movement for West European unity, was rejected because of an unwillingness to compromise British sovereignty, and because of the strength of commitment to the economic link with the Commonwealth.

The Schuman Plan

When, on 9 May 1950, the French Foreign Secretary Robert Schuman proposed the pooling of French and West German supplies of coal and steel, and invited the participation of any other European states that wished to associate themselves with the experiment, he was making public a scheme that had been hatched by Monnet and his associates in the French Economic Planning Commission. It was a step towards Monnet's ideal of a large European economic unit, but it was a small step. The British were not the only ones to have doubts about surrendering sovereign economic decision-making. There was opposition in France too, which was why proposals for economic unions had met with no success. Now Monnet was proposing a lateral approach to the problem. Integration of two sectors of the modern industrial economy would provide a practical start on a process that Monnet hoped would lead eventually to a full economic union.[17]

The British reaction to the proposal was negative, as Monnet had expected. Coal and steel were well-chosen sectors for a first experiment in integrating continental West European economies: both sectors were plagued by problems which supranational co-ordination might solve. But they could not have been less well chosen to appeal to the British Labour Government, which had just completed the nationalization of these two industries. Having campaigned over years for nationalization, the Labour Party was hardly likely to surrender control once it had been attained. Even if the leadership had been inclined to do so, the rank and file of the Party would not have tolerated it. As Herbert Morrison put it to Kenneth Younger, 'It's no damn good—the Durham miners won't wear it.'[18]

The way in which the French Government handled the announcement of Monnet's scheme suggests perhaps it did not even want British participation. Ernest Bevin was personally annoyed because he was given no forewarning of the announcement, although US Secretary of State Dean Acheson was. Acheson had a meeting with Bevin shortly after being given the information by Georges Bidault in Paris, but said nothing about it. This led Bevin to see a Franco–American plot to seize the initiative away from Britain in the formulation of plans for Western Europe.

To add to the Foreign Secretary's personal annoyance, the French

[17] For a description of this process, see Ernst B. Haas, 'The Expansive Logic of Sectoral Integration', in his *The Uniting of Europe: Political, Social and Economic Forces, 1950–1957* (2nd edn., Stanford, California, 1968), ch. 8.

[18] Quoted in Morgan, *Labour in Power*, p. 420, and Young, *Britain, France . . .*, p. 156.

insisted that all those who wished to participate in the scheme must accept the principle of surpranationalism. Attachment to the principle of national sovereignty had not been undermined in Britain by the war, as it had been in the countries that accepted the French invitation (the Benelux states, West Germany, and Italy); and the French, who continued to display a strong sense of national identity themselves, must have realized that this would be a difficult condition for any British Government to accept.

The demand for a commitment to supranationalism was not immediately rejected, however. Instead the French were told that the British Government must know the full extent of the surrender of sovereignty that was being suggested, and its effects. Similar responses were to become a feature of Britain's relationship with the EC in the future. Always the British want to know precisely what is meant by grand-sounding but vague phrases such as 'supranationalism' and 'European union'. To the other Europeans, as to the French on this occasion, such a response is usually seen as a sign of Britain being awkward, and adopting a delaying or even wrecking tactic. To the British it seems a prudent and pragmatic course to adopt before entering into commitments.

After some three weeks of inconclusive discussions of the implications of supranationalism, Schuman announced on 1 June that the principle was non-negotiable, and that any state that wanted to be involved in the negotiations must accept it by 8.00 p.m. on 2 June. This condition was immediately rejected by the British Cabinet as impossible. Nevertheless, civil servants continued to examine the proposals.

The Foreign Office expressed concern at the neutralist, and third-force implications of the scheme, and wondered if Britain might make some economic sacrifice to join in order to ensure that developments in such a direction did not occur. The economic ministries, however, were uniformly opposed to membership, arguing that it would be damaging for the British steel industry and would hinder the search for a global multilateral approach to economic problems. There was also opposition from the champions of the Commonwealth link, who believed that British membership would 'work against the Commonwealth relationship: Britain's policy of selling steel at an export premium, from which Commonwealth countries were dispensed, would no longer be possible'.[19]

[19] Morgan, *Labour in Power*, p. 419.

The position taken by the economic ministries was strengthened by the hesitancy of the Foreign Office, where the prevailing view was scepticism about the prospects for success of the venture. There were voices arguing the importance of the initiative. Sir Oliver Hardy, the British ambassador in Paris, believed that the plan represented 'a turning point in European and indeed in world affairs',[20] but this assessment may have been partially discounted because Sir Oliver was consistently in favour of European integration. Nevertheless, the Cabinet, after discussing the reports of officials on 22 June, did decide to consider the strategic and Commonwealth implications of the plan further. However, this intention was overtaken by the Korean war, which broke out on 24 June. From then on the attention of the Foreign Office and the Government was concentrated outside Europe.

From Schuman to Pleven

The failure of the British Labour Government to come to terms with the Schuman plan in 1950 was compounded by the Conservative Government which succeeded it in 1951. Despite Churchill's protestations of his commitment to the ideal of European integration whilst in opposition, once he became Prime Minister he disappointed those on the Continent who had expected his return to office to signal a change of attitude. Macmillan later ascribed this to Churchill's unwillingness 'to press the issue against the hostility of the Foreign Office and the indifference of the Treasury'.[21]

Most civil servants and politicians failed to grasp what was happening within the ECSC. The success of the Community in dealing with the problems of the coal and steel industries led the six participating states to think of further co-operation, but British policy-makers missed the significance of this growing sense of common destiny amongst the Six. Three factors appear to have contributed to this blindness of officials.

First, there was a preoccupation with sorting out the country's wider world role. As it slowly became obvious that the Commonwealth would not unquestioningly back British diplomatic initiatives, and as differences with the United States increased, so more and more attention was paid to the difficulties in these two spheres of

[20] Ibid. 418.
[21] Harold Macmillan, *Riding the Storm, 1956–1959* (London, 1971), 65.

influence at the cost of a lack of detailed attention to what was happening in Western Europe.[22] Here can be seen the force of prior assumptions. Difficulties in the first two spheres might have led to greater interest in the third, but the presumption held fast that the Commonwealth and Atlantic axes were more important than Europe, and produced the opposite effect.

Secondly, there was growing concern about the performance of the British economy. At first this was diagnosed predominantly in terms of internal conditions rather than in terms of external alignments and trading relationships. In the early 1950s economists and governments concerned themselves with the effect of full employment in bidding up wage rates to what were believed to be internationally uncompetitive levels. It was this diagnosis which led to the adoption of the 'stop–go' policies of the 1950s in an attempt to rein back on the rate of increase of wages, and which later led to the policy of wage freezes. It was only in the mid-1950s that attention started to be paid to any external factors, and then it was the need to reduce defence expenditure which dominated attention. Finally, in the late 1950s it began to dawn on economic analysts and policy-makers that there might be some problem in the pattern of British overseas trade, and it was only at this point that the economic concern stopped being a barrier to an awareness of developments in Western Europe and instead started to focus attention on those developments.[23]

The third factor that may have obscured a proper British appreciation of the success of the enterprise of the Six was that the second attempt to form a Community was a resounding failure. In 1950 René Pleven, the French Prime Minister of the day, proposed a European Defence Community (EDC) which would pool the military resources of the six states in the same way as the ECSC had pooled their resources of coal and steel. After a stormy history, the idea eventually collapsed when the Treaty that would have set up the new Community failed to receive ratification in the French National Assembly.

The European Defence Community and Western European Union

Monnet, the originator of the concept of integration by sectors,

[22] Barker, *Britain in a Divided Europe*, p. 102.   [23] Ibid. 148.

always had severe doubts about the chances for success of the EDC proposal.[24] The whole point of his approach was that it did not challenge sovereignty seriously in the early stages. The habit of co-operation, it was hoped, would be built up gradually in non-controversial areas. Defence was therefore the least suitable sector to be integrated at such an early stage in the process. As Monnet feared, the hostile reaction that resulted from the suggestion of pooling national armies overwhelmed the idea, and caused its collapse.

It was circumstance which put defence on the agenda. The invasion of South Korea by communist North Korea led the United States into a large military commitment to the defence of the South. In the face of the high costs of such an operation, and in an atmosphere in which many Europeans and Americans seriously believed that the Korean move was only a prelude to a similar invasion of West Germany from East Germany, the United States demanded that the West Europeans make a larger commitment to their own defence. In particular they demanded that West German troops be deployed in the defence of their own country.

The suggestion that the German army be reconstituted caused dismay in France, and Pleven's proposal was presented as a way to meet the US demand whilst avoiding allowing a German army to come into existence. The EDC would involve all the participating states in supplying troops, but all except Germany would also be allowed to maintain a national army for deployment outside the European arena. Germany, however, would only supply troops to the European army, and would have no separate force of its own. The German troops would also be under non-German command within the European army.

This plan was initially greeted with some scepticism by the United States, American officials doubting its chances of success. The British Labour Government was predictably negative. There were some hopes, though, that there would be a change of policy when the Churchill Government was elected. That hope was destroyed by Anthony Eden, Churchill's Foreign Secretary, at a NATO Council meeting in Rome in November 1951, when he told a press conference that British units would not participate in EDC. According to Lord Kilmuir, who as Sir David Maxwell Fyffe was

[24] In Jean Monnet, *Memoirs*, trans. Richard Mayne (London, 1978), 343, he simply says of the launching of the plan for the EDC, 'We had no choice.'

Home Secretary at the time and was known as a supporter of European unity, Eden's dismissal of the possibility of British participation was 'the single act which above all others destroyed Britain's name on the continent'.[25]

Eden for his part maintained that his declaration was actually designed to allow the EDC experiment to proceed with a greater chance of success, and that he had the support of the United States for his line. He reports in his memoirs that, although the United States supported British participation in EDC in principle, by the time that the Conservatives came to office the US Administration had decided that a move by Britain to be associated at that stage would 'complicate the budgetary and other technical arrangements and would delay rather than hasten the final solution'.[26] This is what Eden reported to Churchill as the outcome of discussions that he had with Eisenhower in Rome on the day before the press conference mentioned above. But he went on in his memoirs to imply that this was not the real reason for rejecting British participation when he said, 'It was now clear that the policy which we preferred could be pursued in full accord with them.'[27] In other words, the British preferred not to be involved with the EDC, and Eisenhower's statement gave them an excuse to follow that preference.

Eden also appears to have assumed from an early stage that the EDC scheme would fail. When it did exactly that in September 1954, he had already given a lot of thought, together with his officials, to what alternative could be proposed. He was thus in a position to suggest that the Brussels Treaty of 1948 be expanded and a Western European Union (WEU) formed. West Germany and Italy would be invited to join Britain, France, and the Benelux states in the Union, which would be a confederal organization, but all except Britain would accept WEU verification of their agreed level of armaments and forces. This would allow a close check to be kept on German remilitarization, whilst not insulting the new German Government by singling it out for exceptional treatment.

The creation of WEU may have been Eden's greatest achievement as Foreign Secretary, but it was not to develop into a significant European institution: NATO remained the major forum for

---

[25] Quoted in Anthony Sampson, *Macmillan: A Study in Ambiguity* (London, 1967), 90.
[26] Anthony Eden, *Memoirs: Full Circle* (London, 1960), p. 32.   [27] Ibid. 33.

defence collaboration. When France withdrew from the NATO command structure in 1966, WEU might have provided a means for European discussion of defence, but there was no development in that direction until the 1980s.

What did come out of the EDC/WEU experience was a reinforcement of the British conviction that the Community method of promoting European collaboration was misconceived and doomed to failure. The lesson that British policy-makers took from the episode was the wisdom of their own preferred pragmatic approach to European co-operation, which did not involve any abrogation of national sovereignty.

The Messina Negotiations

Because it was convinced that the failure of the EDC demonstrated the futility of the whole Community approach, the British foreign policy establishment was unable to take seriously the prospects for success of the Messina negotiations which resulted from a Benelux proposal that the common market in coal and steel be extended to a general common market and a simultaneous French proposal for a European atomic energy community. As Macmillan put it: 'The official view seemed to be a confident expectation that nothing would come out of Messina.'[28]

This viewpoint worried Macmillan, who at the time was Chancellor of the Exchequer. He wrote to Sir Edward Bridges, the Head of the Treasury, expressing his concern that Britain was being too complacent and negative. If Messina did produce fruit, Macmillan 'did not like the prospect of a world divided into the Russian sphere, the American sphere and a united Europe of which we were not a member'.[29]

The United States supported the new scheme. Eden, now Prime Minister, and Selwyn Lloyd, his Foreign Secretary, visited Washington in February 1956 and returned to report that the Americans were as enthusiastic for the Messina project as they had been for the EDC. Even Macmillan appears to have found this surprising given the experience over defence, and he records in his memoirs that the Americans 'were equally ignorant of all the difficulties in the new plan . . . the risks of the creation of a high-tariff group in Europe, inward-looking and self-sufficient'.[30]

[28] Macmillan, *Riding the Storm*, p. 73.   [29] Ibid. 74.
[30] Ibid. 74–5.

In fact the British were wrong to believe that the failure of the EDC indicated that the EEC proposal would also fail. Instead it seems to have acted as a spur to the Six to make the EEC succeed. As the Messina negotiations made rapid progress, the British eventually had to come to terms with their likely success, although there was no question at this stage of Britain applying for membership of an organization that ran counter to all British prejudices on how European co-operation ought to be handled. Instead, Britain launched a proposal of its own for the creation of a European free-trade area, within which the Six could if they wished have a greater degree of economic unity than existed between the other states. The major differences from the EEC were that there was no aspiration for the free-trade area to develop into a deeper form of economic integration, and it would have no common external tariff against the products of the rest of the world. It would be simply an agreement by the participating states to remove tariffs on trade between themselves.

The motivation for the free-trade proposal had several aspects. There was a growing realization in the economic ministries that it would be damaging for Britain to be outside a common tariff barrier that might be erected around the Six; at the same time there was an equal concern not to exclude Commonwealth trade. But the British hostility to the common external tariff also paralleled the concern of the United States. It was this aspect of the EEC which the Americans liked the least, and Britain risked appearing therefore as the mouthpiece of the United States in this respect.

The negotiations over a possible free-trade area dragged on for over a year, then finally collapsed when General de Gaulle acceded to office in France. The French were already hostile to the British suggestion, not least because agriculture, the main French export industry, was definitely excluded from the British plan. Franco–British relations also deteriorated over the Suez affair. Britain's decision to abort the operation in the face of US opposition annoyed the French, who were more keen than the British to displace Nasser, whom they blamed for many of their troubles in Algeria. The British action was interpreted as subservience to the United States, and suspicions of the extent to which Britain was acting as a US agent in trying to prevent the creation of an economic grouping with a common external tariff were increased.

The difficulty for France in ending the free-trade negotiations was a certain sympathy for the idea on the part of West Germany. De Gaulle overcame this barrier by exploiting the alarm caused in Bonn by Britain's apparent willingness to negotiate over a Soviet demand in November 1958 that allied troops be withdrawn from West Berlin. De Gaulle promised the Federal German Chancellor, Konrad Adenauer, French support over Berlin in return for West German support for the ending of the free-trade negotiations. The agreement was reached on 26 November 1958, twelve days *after* France had unilaterally announced to the Press that an agreement on a free-trade area without a common external tariff would not be possible: the precedent for de Gaulle's later unilateral vetoes of British membership of the European Communities was thereby set.

Perversely, what the free-trade negotiations achieved above all else was to ensure that the EEC would go beyond what Britain hoped to see. The British emphasis on the unacceptability of the EEC idea irritated the French, who had initially been somewhat cautious about the Benelux proposal, and pushed them into accepting more far-reaching agreements than might otherwise have been the case. By the time that the negotiations finally collapsed, Britain had isolated itself from the Six and what is more had lost the argument over what shape West European unity ought to take.

This situation was to persist into the 1960s, when Britain finally came to apply for membership of the very Communities the creation of which it had resisted for so long. As Miriam Camps says in her study of the period from 1955 to 1963, 'the British Government had lost the initiative and was reacting to European situations created by others; it was not itself setting the pace'.[31]

The First British Application

When Britain did come to apply for membership of the Communities, it was for a mixture of political and economic reasons. Already by the late 1950s economists both inside and outside government were coming to the conclusion that the economic problems that Britain was experiencing were due in good part to the pattern of British trade, which continued to be oriented much more to the Commonwealth than towards Western Europe at a time when the fastest growth in world trade was between

[31] Miriam Camps, *Britain and the European Community, 1955–63* (London, 1964), 505.

industrialized states. It was perhaps because this fact had already begun to impress itself on the minds of civil servants in the economic ministries that there was support from the Treasury and the Board of Trade for the negotiation of an agreement on a free-trade area with the Six states that decided to form the EEC.

At the time of these negotiations, the Foreign Office was opposed to Britain becoming a full member of the emerging Communities, but it would probably be most accurate to describe the attitude of the Foreign Office during the negotiations on the free-trade area as one of indifference. By the beginning of 1960, though, there was some evidence that the Foreign Office was beginning to take an interest in the problems of Britain's relations with the Six, most notably a speech by Selwyn Lloyd, the Foreign Secretary, to the Council of Europe in January 1960, in which he suggested that it had perhaps been a mistake for Britain not to join the ECSC, that the British wished the EEC well, and still considered themselves to be part of Europe.[32]

This interest arose initially from the deterioration of relations that followed the breakdown of the free-trade negotiations, but it increased as evidence emerged that the Six were discussing ways of moving beyond economics to some form of political co-operation, particularly in the field of foreign affairs.

An inter-departmental committee of senior civil servants was set up in 1960 to consider Britain's relations with the Six, and it came to the conclusion 'that on political grounds—that is, to ensure a politically stable and cohesive Western Europe—there was a strong argument for joining the Common Market'.[33] The economic case was seen as less important. The argument did not represent enthusiastic conversion to membership. On the contrary, it was built on the premiss that British strategy with respect to Europe remained correct, but that the unfortunate appearance of the EEC meant that the objectives could probably not be achieved without membership. Also very important in the thinking of the committee was the worry that, if the EEC were successful, and particularly if political co-operation were added to economic integration it might become the main partner of the United States displacing Britain.

At this stage the Cabinet was not quite ready to accept such a

[32] Barker, *Britain in a Divided Europe*, p. 168, and Camps, *Britain and the European Community*, p. 280.
[33] Barker, *Britain in a Divided Europe*, p. 171.

major step as applying for membership of the Communities, and the majority view appears to have been that some form of association short of full membership was still obtainable, and was preferable to full membership. But Macmillan, now Prime Minister, seems to have been convinced by the arguments of the committee of civil servants. There were also signs of a more general change of mood in élite circles: the serious Press was beginning to argue for membership, with the *Financial Times* leading the way in April, to be followed shortly after by the *Guardian*, the *Observer*, and *The Times*.

An important development in this change of mood was the proposal made by President de Gaulle of France on 31 May 1960, in a radio broadcast, for political co-operation between the states that constituted the EEC. There were two particularly significant points about this proposal, which was later formalized in 1961. The first was that de Gaulle talked of 'organised cooperation between states'.[34] There was no suggestion of supranationalism, or the development of a European super-state, which meant that Britain was able more easily to live with the idea of being part of such a scheme. Secondly, de Gaulle included defence as well as foreign policy co-ordination in the remit, and no mention was made of NATO. This alarmed the British, whose whole policy for Western Europe was predicated on the necessity of keeping the United States fully involved in the defence of the Continent. This gave Britain an incentive to be involved in any such system of political co-operation in order to prevent Western Europe drifting even further from the British idea of its future and proper role.

Perhaps because of this development, Macmillan seems already to have been preparing some initiative towards the Communities in the summer of 1960, when he moved pro-Europeans into key positions in the government. Duncan Sandys was moved from Aviation to the Ministry for Commonwealth Relations, which was likely to be a source of opposition to any move towards the Communities; Christopher Soames was made Minister of Agriculture, again taking charge of an area of potential opposition; and Edward Heath became Lord Privy Seal and Foreign Office Minister with special responsibility for European affairs.

The policy of the United States around this time may have been a crucial factor in Macmillan's decision to apply for membership.

[34] Ibid. 180.

British proposals to develop the Organization for European Economic Co-operation into an Atlantic economic organization were rejected by the US Administration of Eisenhower, which made no secret of its support for the EEC. When Eisenhower was succeeded by Kennedy in 1961, Macmillan went to Washington in April for talks to establish, amongst other things, whether there would be any change of attitude by the new Administration on the central issue of British membership of the EEC. He was left in no doubt that there would be no change. Indeed, if anything the new Administration seemed even keener to press Britain into membership. The influential Under-Secretary of State for Economic Affairs, George Ball, was a close friend of Jean Monnet, and had developed the view that Britain outside the Community remained a disruptive factor preventing the success of the experiment in European unity. Kennedy himself left Macmillan in no doubt that a British application would be welcomed by the United States. Anthony Sampson, in his biography of Macmillan, quotes Arthur Schlesinger Jr. as saying:

Kennedy fully understood the economic difficulties British entry would bring to the United States. But these were in his mind overborne by the political benefits. If Britain joined the Market, London could offset the eccentricities of policy in Paris and Bonn; moreover, Britain, with its world obligations, could keep the EEC from becoming a high-tariff, inward-looking white man's club. Above all, with British membership, the Market could become the basis for a true political federation of Europe.[35]

These arguments seem to have weighed heavily with Macmillan. As Camps put it:

The reflection that the shortest, and perhaps the only, way to a real Atlantic partnership lay through Britain's joining the Common Market seems to have been a very important—perhaps the controlling—element in Mr Macmillan's own decision that the right course for the United Kingdom was to apply for membership.[36]

Other writers have seen different factors as crucial. F. S. Northedge has argued that the enforced departure of South Africa from the Commonwealth in 1961 was a turning-point in British attitudes towards membership of the Communities. The opposition to continued South African membership of the

[35] Quoted in Sampson, *Macmillan*, p. 224, from Arthur M. Schlesinger Jr., *A Thousand Days: John F. Kennedy in the White House* (London, 1965).
[36] Camps, *Britain and the European Community*, p. 336.

Commonwealth following the Sharpeville massacre[37] was led by the black and Asian members. Britain took the traditional line that the internal affairs of member states were not a matter of relevance for the other members, however much they might deplore the regime or its actions. But on this issue Britain did not prevail, and the idea that Britain could exercise diplomatic influence out of proportion to its size by its leadership of the Commonwealth received a severe, possibly fatal blow.[38]

The effective expulsion of South Africa from the Commonwealth against British wishes may have caused some reassessment of the importance and utility for British foreign policy of the Commonwealth link. Yet, as Northedge himself accepts, 'Macmillan must have given wide-ranging thought to . . . a British application to join the EEC before making that application in June 1961',[39] and the South African affair really came too close to the application to have been a decisive, rather than a reinforcing factor in the decision.

Sampson summarizes the situation convincingly when he says: 'Several streams converged to generate a strong tide towards Europe, and it would have been hard for any prime minister to go against it.'[40] Sampson singles out particularly the attitude of the senior Departments of State, the Treasury and the Foreign Office, and also that of big business interests, represented by the FBI, which by 1961 was pressing strongly for entry for economic reasons.

The picture that emerges, then, is of a gradual official realization of the danger that the EEC might become an economic and political embarrassment to Britain. Economically, against the expectations of most British civil servants and politicians, the Community was working, and was working well enough for its members to be threatening to outstrip Britain in rates of economic growth. Politically, the long-term British strategy, which gave a central place to keeping the United States involved in the defence of Western Europe, was threatened by the neutralist and third-force tendencies that were being displayed by France under the leadership

---

[37] On 21 Mar. 1960 black South Africans who were protesting peacefully against the pass laws that required them to carry identity papers were fired upon by police at Sharpeville and dozens were killed, most of them shot in the back.

[38] F. S. Northedge, 'Britain and the EEC: Past and Present', in Roy Jenkins (ed.), *Britain and the EEC* (London, 1983), ch. 2; p. 28.

[39] Northedge, 'Britain and the EEC', p. 28.

[40] Sampson, *Macmillan*, p. 209.

of de Gaulle, and that threatened to involve the rest of the EEC Six through the political co-operation plans that were under discussion. As Elisabeth Barker points out, throughout the 1960s the debate about British entry to the European Communities was also a debate about a possible autonomous European defence stance, and this factor loomed very large in Foreign Office assessments of the need for membership.[41]

The political and strategic aspects of the decision were those which Macmillan stressed when, at the end of July 1961, he announced to the House of Commons the intention of his Government to apply for membership of the Communities. The tone of the announcement was very cautious, however, and had no ring of enthusiasm about it. The implication was that Britain recognized the necessity of making this move, but was far from welcoming it. To some observers the Prime Minister appeared to be trying to 'back into Europe', and this was likely to have unfortunate consequences. The *Guardian* commented:

The plunge is to be taken but, on yesterday's evidence, by a shivering Government . . . All that Mr Macmillan said is correct. But his approach is so half-hearted that it must diminish the chances of success in the negotiations. He has made a depressing start . . . We must show that we believe in the ambition of a politically united Europe. This is just what Mr Macmillan has not done . . .[42]

This was a perceptive argument, for, when eventually the French President rejected the application, he quoted as his main reason that Britain had not yet accepted a European vocation. The caution of the Prime Minister also meant that there was no real attempt to convert the British public to enthusiasm for the Communities, which stored up trouble for the future.

The most likely reason for Macmillan's caution was his appreciation of the problems that his own party would have in swallowing the new orientation. The strong emotional attachment to the Commonwealth within the Conservative Party was a particular problem.

The Commonwealth aspect of the question overshadowed all others . . . [and the] emotional aspect of the problem was, and continued to be, the most difficult aspect . . . It could be demonstrated . . . that the Commonwealth was not an economic alternative to the Common Market . . .

[41] Barker, *Britain in a Divided Europe*, chs. 17–19.
[42] Quoted in Elisabeth Barker, *The Common Market* (rev. edn., Hove, 1976), 76.

Nevertheless, there was a nagging doubt that, since the Commonwealth relationship was being changed, it was probably being changed for the worse.[43]

The pro-Conservative Press naturally picked up on this issue. The *Daily Telegraph* supported the application, but stressed that 'Membership of the Common Market is a bigger issue for Britain than for any major Continental Power. That is . . . because of the Commonwealth and the vast role that the Commonwealth plays in our trade, our investment and our ways of political, social, legal and cultural thought.'[44]

It was, though, Lord Beaverbrook's *Daily Express* which acted as the mouthpiece of those sections of British capital that had a vested interest in the maintenance of a special trading relationship with the Commonwealth, coming out unequivocally against the application, and accusing the Prime Minister of putting 'Europe ahead of the Commonwealth'.[45] The influence of this line of argument meant that Macmillan had to cover his back when negotiations began, by demanding from the Six wide-ranging special treatment and exemptions for almost all of the Commonwealth countries.

Despite the problems of accommodating these extensive British demands, the negotiations made good progress until January 1963, when President de Gaulle announced a unilateral French veto on British membership. His fundamental reason, as already noted, was that he did not consider that Britain had accepted a European vocation; ironically, he quoted the same doubts as had been expressed in conservative quarters in Britain: 'England in fact is insular, maritime, bound by her trade, her markets, her supplies, to countries that are very diverse and often very far away . . . How can England, as she lives, as she produces, as she trades, be incorporated in the Common Market?'[46]

The other factor that de Gaulle picked out was Britain's continued attachment to the United States. The actual incident that he pointed to as evidence of Britain's lack of a European vocation was the Nassau agreement of December 1963, by which Macmillan accepted President Kennedy's offer of US Polaris missiles to act as the delivery system for British nuclear warheads, following Britain's abandonment of its own Skybolt missile which had proved too

---

[43] Camps, *Britain and the European Community*, p. 339.
[44] Quoted in Barker, *The Common Market*, pp. 76–7.
[45] Quoted in ibid. 78.   [46] Quoted in ibid. 79.

expensive to develop. This was, however, more in the nature of an excuse than a reason for the veto.

In 1963 de Gaulle would probably have vetoed the British Government's application to join the EEC whether or not the Nassau deal had been made. De Gaulle detested this apparent revival of the special relationship, but his opposition to Britain joining the EEC was mainly based on his determination that France should dominate it. However, Macmillan, by making the realisation of a British nuclear deterrent a political priority and reducing Britain's application to join the EEC to second place, provided de Gaulle with a pretext.[47]

So the British application ended in the same way as had the attempt to set up the free-trade area, with a French veto. The conflict between French and British views of the future of Europe emerged again. The French President, more overtly nationalist and third forcist than the Prime Ministers of the Fourth Republic, believed that the influence of Britain within the Communities would work in a different direction, to give a more Atlantic orientation to policy than he wished to see. He made no secret of his view that, if admitted, Britain would act as the US 'Trojan horse' within the Communities. To prevent that development he was prepared to risk the ire of his partners, particularly the Benelux states, which remained staunch advocates of British membership.

The British Government was philosophical about the veto, declaring that it would not turn its back on Europe, and leaving open the prospect of a renewal of the application at a later date. In the event, that renewal came under a Labour Government in 1966.

From Veto to Veto

Being refused entry probably made membership a more readily accepted objective within the Conservative Party: there was an insult to be overcome. But it was the Labour Party which won the 1964 general election, albeit with a very slender majority. Although Labour contained some supporters of membership of the Communities, there had been a clear majority in the Party in the country against entry. The Labour attachment to the ideals of the Commonwealth and the special relationship with the United States was, if anything, even stronger than that of the Conservative Party.

---

[47] Anthony Verrier, *Through the Looking Glass: British Foreign Policy in an Age of Illusions* (London, 1983), 166.

The supporters of the Commonwealth link tended to be on the left of the Party, and the supporters of the relationship with the United States more to its right, but in both cases the Communities were seen as rival attractions to the preferred foreign policy orientation. In addition, the left condemned the Communities as a conservative, Catholic, and capitalist club, an attitude that dated back to the disillusionment of many on the left of the Party with the idea of a united Europe in the late 1940s, when they had hoped to see it as the basis for a third force, only to find that the European movement was dominated by anti-communist elements.

Harold Wilson, who became Prime Minister in 1964, appeared to share the view that British membership of the Communities was not desirable. In any case, there was no question of any major foreign policy initiative being taken in the first two years of the Labour Government, when its slender parliamentary majority meant a concentration on the more popular pieces of domestic legislation in order to prepare the way for another election at which Labour could hope to gain a more clear-cut victory.

Yet already by 1965 Barbara Castle, a left-wing member of the Cabinet who was at that time hostile to the Communities, was becoming concerned at the secrecy in which foreign policy was wrapped, complaining that Foreign Secretary Michael Stewart's reports to Cabinet were 'perfunctory', and worrying about news-paper reports that 'we were more interested now in going into the Common Market'[48] although 'Most of us simply did not know'.[49] On 26 May 1965 she recorded in her diary that Douglas Jay, another leading Labour opponent of membership of the Com-munities, 'warned that we must watch the Party's drift into the Common Market. The pressures that way were unrelenting, not only on the part of officials but also of George Brown who, despite the PM's warnings about talking to the press, had given a long interview to the *Guardian* implying that revisions of policy were going on.'[50]

George Brown, the deputy leader of the Labour Party, had been narrowly beaten in the leadership ballot by Wilson. His ideas on economic reconstruction were based very much on the French experience. It was Brown who advocated the creation of an economic planning body outside the Treasury, and he who headed

---

[48] Barbara Castle, *The Castle Diaries, 1964–70* (London, 1984), 18.
[49] Ibid. 20.   [50] Ibid. 33.

this Department of Economic Affairs in the Wilson Government. The idea was modelled closely on the Economic Planning Commission that Monnet had set up in France. Following the same logic as Monnet, Brown was also a believer in the necessity for a wider economic zone than the nation-state to become the basis for future prosperity. He also appears to have shared to some extent the French attraction for a third force in world politics, stating in his memoirs that he saw a united Europe as a way 'to stop the polarisation of the world around the two superpowers'.[51]

In order to secure Brown's full backing and support, Wilson seems to have made some kind of commitment to him on membership of the Communities,[52] and the renewal of the application figured prominently in the manifesto for the 1966 election. The realities of office may also have contributed to convincing Wilson that membership was necessary, in much the same way as they had convinced Macmillan before him; the influence of the Foreign Office, now convinced of the necessity of membership, may well have helped him to this conclusion. Yet, as with Macmillan, Wilson's conversion was hardly marked by enthusiasm. The 1966 manifesto spoke of Britain being ready to enter the Communities 'provided essential British and Commonwealth interests are safeguarded'.[53]

In 1967 the negotiations were less liable to be complicated by demands for special treatment for Commonwealth states. Since the first entry negotiations both Britain and many Commonwealth states had found their trade with the Communities growing more rapidly than with one another. The Commonwealth states had less to fear from British membership as the importance to their own economies of trade with Britain declined. Wilson committed himself on only two points: to secure favourable terms for exports of cane sugar from the Caribbean into the EEC, and to obtain special terms for New Zealand lamb and dairy produce.

But the problem the first time around had not been in negotiating an agreement: it had been de Gaulle's veto. So it proved the second time around. Indeed, de Gaulle refused to accept the new British

---

[51] Quoted in Avi Shlaim, Peter Jones, and Keith Sainsbury, *British Foreign Secretaries since 1945* (Newton Abbot, 1977), 212.

[52] Alfred F. Havinghurst, *Britain in Transition: The twentieth century* (4th edn., Chicago and London, 1985), 521.

[53] Quoted in Shlaim *et al.*, *British Foreign Secretaries*, p. 196.

application, a move that Britain counteracted by tabling its application at a meeting of the WEU in July 1967. But in November 1967 the French President announced that he still did not see Britain as being ready to join what was now the EC (the merger that was agreed in 1965 having taken place). Before de Gaulle could agree to entry, Britain would have to make 'very vast and deep changes'. The Labour Government left its application on the table, but by now it seemed clear that there would be no progress until de Gaulle's departure from office.

After de Gaulle

In 1969 de Gaulle resigned from office after failing to secure the 'yes' vote for which he had asked in a referendum on constitutional reforms. The referendum was presented to the French people as a vote of confidence in the President, and they refused to give that vote. De Gaulle's longest-serving Prime Minister, Georges Pompidou, was subsequently elected as his previous master's successor.

The Labour Government immediately moved to reactivate its application for EC membership, and at a summit meeting in The Hague in 1969, that was called at Pompidou's insistence, the Six agreed to proceed with the negotiations for British entry.

They also agreed to complete another major item of unfinished business from the era of de Gaulle. In 1965 de Gaulle had withdrawn France from participation in the work of the Council of Ministers of the Communities in a dispute over the methods that would be used to finance the Communities' budget. Although France had returned to the Council in January 1966, definitive arrangements for financing the budget were still not in place. The arrangements which were agreed were to cause problems for Britain in the future. The Labour Government asked to be involved in the discussions on the issue, but France refused to allow this. The outcome was agreement on a system of financing which made it almost certain that Britain would have to bear a financial burden out of proportion to its relative wealth.

Here was a new complicating factor in the negotiations for British entry, which were eventually renewed by a Conservative Government at the end of June 1970, the Labour Party having rather surprisingly lost the general election that was held in that month. The outcome of these negotiations was agreement on the

terms of British entry to the Community, and they set the context
for British policy within the EC following membership.

Conclusion

The picture that emerges of Britain's relationship with the
European Communities up to 1970 is of slow adjustment to a
changed reality. The British political and administrative élites
emerged from the Second World War seeing their country as
occupying a special position amongst European states. The
Churchillian doctrine of the three spheres of influence was the
prevalent view: Britain was a global power, and only incidentally a
European power. Both of the major Departments of State, the
Treasury and the Foreign Office, took a globalist view of Britain's
responsibilities, and formulated policy accordingly. Although there
was a clear recognition that Britain was no longer the dominant
power in the world, its position was seen as being at the right hand
of the new dominant power, the United States, acting as a sort of
first lieutenant. There were differences on the most desirable world
order, but these were far less than the agreement on the need for
multilateral free trade and strong US military leadership in the face
of the commonly accepted threat from the Soviet Union.

The attitude of the makers of British policy towards other West
European states was condescending, and at times almost contemp-
tuous. France in particular was considered to be politically and
economically unstable. This in turn led to the serious under-
estimation of the prospects for success of the ECSC and then of the
EEC. It also reinforced British reluctance to become involved in
ventures that would tie the fortunes of the British economy, seen as
fundamentally strong, to those of European economies that were
seen as weak and liable to crisis.

When policy did change, with Macmillan's application for
membership of the Communities in 1961, it was more a tactical
than a strategic change. The strategic objectives of British policy
remained the pursuit of multilateral free trade and the organization
of the defence of the capitalist world under US leadership. The
application for membership was a recognition that these objectives
were threatened by the development of the Communities without
Britain. In effect, Macmillan seems to have been responding to
consistent US advocacy of British membership, 'to go in there and

dominate it on behalf of joint British and American concerns'.[54] This was precisely what de Gaulle suspected the British of attempting to do, and was the grounds for his veto.

At the economic level, the threat to British trade of an EEC from which Britain was excluded was a subsidiary theme of the Macmillan application, but one that became stronger in the Wilson application as the tremendous success of the member states of the Communities compared with the rather modest performance of the British economy had to be recognized. The post-war view that the British economy was fundamentally stronger than any other in Western Europe had to be abandoned in the face of the evidence. Underlying this narrow self-interested motive for pursuing member-ship, though, there was always another theme, which was the need to steer the Communities away from becoming an inward-looking trading bloc that would be damaging to the British belief in an open world economy as the best basis for prosperity.

In applying for membership of the Communities, under both Macmillan and Wilson, Britain was pursuing its consistent view of how Europe ought to relate to the rest of the world. There was no conversion to the ideal of European union that was espoused by the leaders of the founder states; there was no attempt to sell the idea of British membership in anything other than pragmatic terms to the British electorate; there was no abandonment at either official or popular level of a commitment to a strong sense of national identity, which remained the basis for the electoral appeals of politicians in all parties; there was no abandonment of the attachment to the special relationship with the United States, or of the commitment at both official and popular levels to the Atlantic Alliance as the basis of international stability.

All of these elements were to emerge and re-emerge as themes in the history of Britain's relationship with the EC after 1970. The failure of the British to embrace the ideal of European union has continually led to differences with other member states. The unpopularity of the EC with much of the electorate for much of the time has influenced the approach to negotiations by statesmen (and women), who are also politicians who have to win elections. The strong sense of national identity has made it difficult for Britain's

[54] Richard Neustadt, quoted in Michael Charlton, 'How (and Why) Britain Lost the Leadership of Europe (II): A Last Step Sideways', *Encounter*, 57/3 (Sept. 1981), 28.

representatives in the Council of Ministers of the EC to put the interests of Europe before those of Britain where a clash occurs.

Most importantly of all, though, the relationship between the EC and the United States, and the relationship of the EC to the wider world order, have been frequent sources of disagreement with the Community, in which Britain has often been seen as the US Trojan horse, or at least as the awkward partner.

2. The Heath Government, 1970–1974

EDWARD HEATH was Prime Minister during a difficult period domestically, when the cumulated problems from Britain's past were compounded by adverse international circumstances. The years from 1970 to 1974 saw the collapse of the post-war international system, which had been under strain for some time, and the shock waves blew both the British economy and the EC seriously off course.

The first year and a half of Heath's premiership were devoted to getting Britain into the EC; the rest to an attempt to make a success of membership and to define a new course for the Community itself. The achievement of the first objective was Heath's most positive contribution to the future of Britain. The failure of the second also left its legacy for his successors.

The International Context

Disturbances in the international economy, particularly in the monetary system, began in the late 1960s. These became considerably worse during the early 1970s, with the collapse of the system of fixed exchange rates that had been set up after the war, and a rapid rise in the price of raw materials, culminating in a massive increase in the price of oil.

In March 1968 the US dollar came under sustained speculative pressure. The link between the dollar and gold that was the basis of the whole monetary system was only retained by inventing a two-tier market for gold, with central bankers promising to deal at $35 per ounce regardless of the market price prevailing for private buyers. The crisis of confidence in the dollar was a combination of two concerns, about the ratio of dollars to US reserves of gold, and about signs that the US economy was not as strong as it needed to be to carry the burden of managing the world's monetary system. The ratio of dollars to US gold reserves had deteriorated considerably in the post-war period, as the United States printed more and more dollars to finance deficits on its balance of payments; so, whereas there had been more than enough gold in the United States to meet any actual demand from holders of dollars immediately after the war, by the end of the 1960s the ratio was hopelessly inadequate to withstand any run on the dollar. This in itself was not important so long as confidence in the strength of the US economy remained high; but by 1968 the United States was not only continuing to run an overall deficit on its balance of payments, it was also experiencing a heavy trade deficit with Japan and having difficulty in maintaining its surplus with Western Europe.

None of the central bankers who devised the scheme considered the two-tier price for gold to be a very adequate solution to the 1968 crisis. Although the immediate problem was overcome, by 1971 the United States was forced to accept the inevitable, and end the formal convertibility of the dollar into gold. At the same time President Nixon imposed a 10 per cent surcharge on those imports into the United States that were already subject to duties, amounting to approximately 50 per cent of total US imports. These measures, which were accompanied by the introduction of a wage–price freeze to tackle domestic inflation, sent shock waves through the whole of the capitalist world.

An attempt was made to patch up the structure of fixed exchange rates at a meeting at the Smithsonian Institute in Washington in December 1971. The attempt did not survive long. By March 1974 the world had entered an era of floating exchange rates; but even before that, in June 1972, the pound sterling had to be floated on the international exchanges as intense speculative pressure against it made it impossible for the Bank of England to hold its Smithsonian parity.

These disruptions severely damaged business confidence throughout the capitalist world, and there was an international slide into recession in the winter of 1971–2, to which governments responded by·introducing reflationary budgets in the spring of 1972. The Heath Government in 1972 presented 'the most expansionary budget in British history',[1] but this was in line with what was happening elsewhere. The cumulative consequence of these separate but coinciding reflationary efforts was a new twist to the spiral of

[1] Nick Gardner, *Decade of Discontent: The Changing British Economy since 1973* (Oxford, 1987), 37.

inflation and in particular a marked rise in the price of raw materials for industry, as demand rose.

The increase in the price of commodities encouraged the oil-producing states in their efforts permanently to increase their export earnings. To this end they had formed the Organization of Petroleum Exporting Countries (OPEC) in September 1960, but it had been relatively ineffective until the late 1960s, when the new Libyan regime of Colonel Gaddafi showed that a determined approach, coupled with the threat to limit production if prices were not raised, could produce results. OPEC had successfully adopted the same tactics in January–February 1971. The five-year agreement then reached with the oil companies, adjusted to take account of the floating of the dollar, was still in force in 1972; the rise in the price of oil that occurred as a result of rising demand in 1972 therefore benefited the companies and not the producing states. In new negotiations, in October 1972, the companies insisted that they had a five-year agreement which ought to be respected; but events were rapidly running beyond their control as a result of the war in the Middle East that had broken out just two days before the negotiations began.

The Arab–Israeli war of 1972 increased considerably the self-confidence of the OPEC states. The Arab members of OPEC, finding unity in their opposition to Israel, unilaterally announced a doubling in the price of their oil. They also imposed a ban on deliveries of oil to states that supported Israel in the conflict. Although the oil companies managed to get around the complete embargo on the supply of oil to specific countries, the reaction of the governments of the major industrialized states showed just how dependent they were on oil, and how lacking in unity in response to concerted action from the producers. This success encouraged OPEC to double the price of oil again in late December 1973.

These increases in the price of a commodity that was absolutely fundamental to industrial production tripped the whole of the capitalist world into deep recession, and at the same time gave a sharp twist to the inflationary spiral. The effects on every capitalist state were profound, but they were particularly far-reaching in Britain, which already had higher rates of inflation and unemployment than its competitors. Although the aftermath of the December 1973 decision had largely to be handled by Heath's Labour successor, the turbulence that accompanied the buildup to the storm made Heath's job in piloting the ship of state incomparably more difficult. The economic squalls also blew the EC seriously off course, and contributed to the difficulty that Britain experienced in fitting into the convoy that it had only just managed to join. At the same time, international political developments actually brought Britain closer to the other member states of the EC in defining a European identity towards the rest of the world. The attitude of the Nixon Administration towards Western Europe during 1971–2 was one of neglect. Attention in Washington was focused on extracting the United States from the Vietnam war, which was a drain on the already troubled economy, and then on developing *détente* with the Soviet Union in an attempt to pave the way for agreements on limiting nuclear armaments, which was also seen as a means of helping the US economy by allowing a reduction in the large budgetary deficit. In these efforts, the Administration failed to consult with its European allies, which caused considerable concern within Western Europe, where fears grew of a US–Soviet condominium that would exclude any influential role for Europe in determining its own future.

Growing European concern about US policy eventually made itself felt in Washington, and in April 1973 Henry Kissinger, the US Secretary of State, announced that the United States had decided to make this 'The Year of Europe', and called for the conclusion of 'a new Atlantic Charter' that would cover defence, monetary, and trade matters. He also suggested that Japan should be associated with this initiative.

Reaction in the EC to the speech was not favourable. There had been no prior consultation with the Europeans about the initiative, which underlined what they saw as the arrogance of the Administration; there was resentment that Kissinger explicitly allocated to Europe a regional role in contrast to the global role envisaged for the United States; there was concern at the deliberate linkage of defence with economic issues, which suggested that the United States wanted concessions on trade and monetary affairs in return for a continued commitment to the defence of Western Europe; and there was mystification at the inclusion of Japan in the Atlantic community (a reaction shared by the Japanese).

Although the Europeans did not feel that they could ignore the initiative, and efforts were made to draw up 'Declarations of Principles' on economics and defence, the US response to European concern actually served to make relations worse than they were before. So did the Middle East war. The US Secretary of State believed that *détente* had to be accompanied by a resolute resistance to any attempt by the USSR to extend its influence in the world. Because the Soviet Union supported Egypt, the main Arab combatant, the war was interpreted by the United States in terms of East–West relations. The response of the EC states, prompted by the threat of an Arab embargo on their supplies of oil, was interpreted by the United States as a failure of allies to give it support in the struggle to hold the line against Soviet expansionism. For their part the EC states resented the lack of any consultation with them about diplomatic moves to end the war, and particularly the lack of any warning when, in the course of the conflict, the United States decided suddenly to declare a world-wide strategic alert.

It was against this background of a disintegrating international economic system and an increasingly difficult relationship between the United States and its European partners that Britain finally entered the EC, at the third try, and attempted to establish itself as a leading member of the club from which it had been excluded for so long.

The Domestic Context

In opposition to the 1964–70 Labour Governments, the Conservative Party adopted a new leader and a new economic programme. The leader, Heath, was the first to be elected rather than to emerge from discussions in private between leading members of the Party. His election was a surprise: he was hardly in the traditional mould of leaders of the Conservative Party, being of comparatively humble origins. It was to the son of a carpenter, rather than to a traditional Tory or an inheritor of wealth, that the Conservatives looked for the electoral charisma that they felt they were lacking.

The new economic programme was based on a radical rejection of state intervention in the economy, a commitment to the free market that was the product of an intellectual counter-revolution that went on within the Conservative Research Department under the guidance of Lord Blake between 1945 and 1951, but that had no opportunity to assert itself during the years when first Churchill, then Eden, then Macmillan ruled the Party and the country.[2]

[2] Patrick Cosgrave, 'Heath as Prime Minister', *Political Quarterly*, 44 (1973), 435–46.

Heath himself was not committed to this analysis, which argued that Britain's problems were the consequence of state intervention in the economy, and that the solution lay in the withdrawal of the state so far as practicable; for him it was an approach that was useful in electoral terms, because it distinguished the Conservatives very clearly from the Labour Party. He certainly believed that the problems of the British economy lay in a lack of efficiency and enterprise, and that the problem of militant trade unionism needed to be tackled as an urgent priority. But in terms of methods for encouraging efficiency and fostering economic growth he was a pragmatist. Indeed, he was very much in the mould of Macmillan, the Prime Minister with whom he had worked very closely as Conservative Chief Whip and then as chief negotiator for Britain's first application for membership of the EC.

Nevertheless, Heath was elected in 1970 on the basis of a 'new style of government' which would 'reduce public expenditure, cut income tax, reform industrial relations, strengthen competition, and give overriding priority to bringing inflation under control (without, however, the use of a statutory incomes policy)'.[3] Yet during its first two and a half years in office the new Government abandoned or reversed almost all of its policies. Its determination not to use public money to support inefficient firms ('lame ducks') was abandoned to save Rolls Royce from bankruptcy, and aid that had been withdrawn from the Upper Clyde Shipbuilders was restored; public expenditure rose to record heights; and in 1972 a phased prices and incomes policy was introduced to combat inflation. This reversal of the free-market policies on which the Government had been elected was partly a response to the realities of economic management in a rapidly changing world situation, and partly a retreat from the politically unacceptable consequences of the original policies. The free-market approach would not have been abandoned so quickly, however, had the Prime Minister had a commitment to it in its own right. For Heath it was no more than a possible means to other ends: a useful electoral programme, and an economic experiment worth trying. As Gamble explains: 'The highest priority was given to the achievement of sustained economic growth; at first free market policies were attempted, but when these failed to work they were replaced or supplemented by

---

[3] Gardner, *Decade of Discontent*, p. 87.

interventionist policies which went beyond anything tried in the previous decade.'[4]

The policy to which Heath was most strongly personally committed (other than membership of the EC) was trade-union reform. Here Heath saw a fundamental role for the state, and he picked out of the wastepaper basket the plans that Wilson had scrapped for bringing industrial relations under the framework of legal regulation. His Industrial Relations Act ran into determined and predictable opposition from the trade unions, but Heath pressed ahead with it because he saw it as such a fundamental part of any programme for solving Britain's economic problems. However, the 'abrasive and aggressive stance'[5] that he took towards the working class led to industrial turmoil, helped to undermine the popularity of his Government, and strengthened the position of the left within the Labour Party, a factor that was to have consequences for Britain's industrial relations, and for Britain's attitude towards the EC, once Heath gave way to Wilson in 1974.

The two policies of reform of industrial relations and membership of the EC, both of which Wilson had embraced before Heath, and both of which were necessary parts of any strategy for the modernization of the British economy, might have 'easily become the basis of a new political and social consensus in the 1970s', but instead they 'became the main issues around which the political and social divisions crystallized'.[6]

Ultimately Heath was to lose a general election in 1974 on essentially this issue of the relationship between government and trade unions. Following a damaging strike by Britain's miners in the winter of 1973–4, Heath asked the country to choose who was to rule: the trade unions or the elected government. The electorate voted for a quiet life, hoping that a Labour government would be able to work with the unions, as Wilson maintained that it would, and bring an end to the industrial strife that was a marked feature of the Heath years.

Before that stage had been reached, Heath had already abandoned the free-market policies with which he had come into office, in

---

[4] Andrew Gamble, *Britain in Decline: Economic Policy, Political Strategy and the British State* (London, 1981), 126.
[5] Joseph Frankel, *British Foreign Policy, 1945–1973* (London, 1975), 311.
[6] Ibid. 32.

what the Press christened a 'U-turn'. The failure of Heath, and his
defeat 'at the hands of the miners' as it was seen, reinforced the
position within the Conservative Party of the ideological proponents
of the free market, who were able to claim that it was this
abandonment of the original economic programme which was
responsible for the failure. What this analysis ignored was that the
retreat from the policies of the free market was a response to the
realities of an economic situation that deteriorated rapidly as a
consequence of changes beyond the control of any government. It
was certainly a pragmatic response from a non-ideological Prime
Minister, but any understanding of what went wrong for the Heath
Government must take into account the upheavals through which
the world economy was passing in this period.

Faced with an accelerating collapse of both the international and
domestic frameworks for his policy towards the Community, it is
hardly surprising that even a Prime Minister as committed to
membership of the EC as Heath should have found it difficult to
sustain the momentum of his policy in that direction.

The Third Attempt

Edward Heath is the only British Prime Minister to date to have
been fully committed to the idea of the EC. His personal record of
commitment goes back to his early days in politics. He made his
maiden speech in Parliament on the necessity for European unity,
and the desirability of Britain joining in the negotiations on the
Schuman plan; he was a member of Jean Monnet's Action
Committee for the United States of Europe; and he was the chief
negotiator for Macmillan's application for membership.

During the 1970 election campaign it was made clear that a
priority of the Conservatives, if elected, would be to secure
membership for Britain. When victory was achieved, the new
Government lost no time in reopening negotiations with the
Community.

The renewed application took place against a background of
some considerable volatility in the attitude of the British public to
the exercise. A Gallup poll in April 1970 showed 59 per cent of the
electorate disapproved of the Government even applying for
membership, with only 19 per cent in favour.[7] This substantial

[7] Simon Z. Young, *Terms of Entry: Britain's Negotiations with the European
Community, 1970–1972* (London, 1973), 19.

opposition continued into the beginning of 1971, but had changed to support by the autumn of 1971. Ashford suggests that the shift was due to a number of factors:

The perception of the negotiated terms as satisfactory, the attraction of a strong Government with a clear policy, distrust of what was seen as unprincipled opposition by the Labour Party and confused signals to Labour voters, the massive information and propaganda campaign, and that many voters only then gave serious attention to the issue with the clear possibility of membership, all contributed to public endorsement of entry by October 1971.[8]

Although Ashford identifies a clear perception that the terms negotiated were satisfactory, there were major problems that resulted from Britain's late arrival at the negotiating table. The terms which were actually negotiated may have been the best available, but they were by no means entirely favourable to Britain.

The Terms of Entry

Negotiations concentrated on a number of issues: sterling, the Commonwealth, agriculture, and the size of British contributions to the Community's budget were the most important. Of these it was the last which was to prove the most difficult issue to resolve.

The position of sterling as an international reserve currency, and the existence of the 'sterling balances', were raised by the French Finance Minister, Valéry Giscard d'Estaing, as a potential barrier to the British currency joining in the efforts of the EC to move towards an economic and monetary union. Sterling's role as a reserve currency was a legacy of the era when Britain was the dominant economic power in the capitalist world. Since the end of the war, sterling had taken second place to the dollar. But there were still large quantities of sterling held as part of the foreign-currency reserves of other states. Also, during the war Britain had secured financial assistance from the rest of the British Empire in the form of deposits made in sterling in London: these were the sterling balances. The obligations that arose from the special position of its currency meant that it was very difficult for the British Government to devalue sterling without precipitating a massive removal of funds from London, which would have had disastrous effects on its

[8] Nigel Ashford, 'The Conservative Party and European Integration, 1945–1975', Ph.D. thesis (Coventry, 1983), 304–5.

economy. When the pound was devalued in 1968, the holders of sterling balances were given a special assurance, under the Basle Agreement, that the value of their deposits would be guaranteed in dollars should a further devaluation become necessary. This agreement was renewed even while the negotiations for EC entry were going on.

Giscard sought an assurance that the position of sterling would be brought into line with that of the other currencies of the Community, and in particular that the sterling balances would be run down by a phased programme of repayment. The British Government indicated that it appreciated the problem, and that it would be tackling it, but refused to agree to any externally imposed timetable, and insisted that the issue could not form part of the official negotiations on entry.

On the Commonwealth the position was much less complicated than it had been in 1961. Changes in the patterns of trade of Commonwealth countries had left only two outstanding issues: Caribbean sugar and New Zealand dairy produce. Both, however, proved to be difficult because in both cases the British were asking for privileged access to the Community for agricultural products that were in direct competition with the produce of Community farmers; more pertinently, French farmers were major producers of cheese and sugar beet.

On agriculture generally, it was clear that it would not be easy for Britain to adapt to the Common Agricultural Policy (CAP) that the Six had created. All states followed some sort of protectionist and interventionist policy for agriculture. The traditional British system was one of deficiency payments. Food prices were allowed to find their own level, and farmers were compensated for any shortfall in their incomes by payments directly from the Government. The system managed to keep food prices low while ensuring stability of farmers' incomes, and it allowed the Government to bring pressure to bear on individual farmers to improve their efficiency. The subsidy came from the taxpayer, and, as the British tax system placed the emphasis on progressive income tax, this meant that the richer citizens paid more towards the subsidy than the poorer.

The system that had been adopted by the Community was one based on guaranteed prices. Every year national Ministers of Agriculture decided on the level of prices for the agricultural products covered by the CAP. If prices fell below the agreed levels, the Commission would intervene in the market to buy up surplus produce, which was then placed into storage. If prices were above the level prevailing in world markets, subsidies were paid to farmers who exported their produce to bring their receipts up to the level that they would get if they were selling in the Community market.

This arrangement caused two problems for Britain. One was that it implied a large increase in the general price of food in the country. The second was that Britain, as a net importer of food, stood to gain little from the agricultural fund, which dominated payments from the Community's budget.

The first problem was one that the Heath Government accepted as insuperable. The CAP had to be accepted if membership was to be achieved. In any case, the British system was proving to be a cause of financial difficulty, and as early as 1960 Christopher Soames, then Minister of Agriculture, had advised Macmillan that some change, putting more of the cost on to the consumer, seemed essential irrespective of any move to join the EC.[9] The negotiators therefore concentrated on achieving a satisfactory period for phasing in the full effects of the policy on prices, and on getting agreement to special concessions on certain particularly sensitive items like butter.

The second problem was one half of what ultimately proved to be the most intractable issue on the agenda of the negotiations: the size of British contributions to the Community's budget.

The Issue of Budgetary Contributions

General de Gaulle did not only block British entry to the Community. In 1965 he precipitated a crisis over the Commission's proposals for financing the budget, which was the final piece of the jigsaw needed to bring the EEC to the end of its first phase. Until his departure the budget continued to be funded by national contributions that had to be agreed each year.

President Pompidou soon indicated his willingness to consider the reopening of negotiations on British entry, but made it clear

---

[9] Michael Charlton, 'How and Why Britain Lost the Leadership of Europe (I): "Messina! Messina!" or, The Parting of the Ways', *Encounter*, 57/2 (Aug. 1981), 8–22.

that he first wanted agreement on the other outstanding issue from the de Gaulle years, the funding of the budget. Presumably the reason for this order of priority was that, before British entry, the French wanted to see a system put in place that the British would be obliged to accept as part of the price for membership, and that would benefit France. The proposals that had been made by the Commission would incidentally also disadvantage Britain. It is not suggested that Pompidou wished to install the system deliberately to make Community membership more expensive for the British, but he presumably reckoned that, if the British had a say in what system of financing was adopted, they would argue for a system that would be less unfavourable to them, and that as a result would almost certainly be much less favourable to France.

So in 1970 agreement was reached on a financial structure that would earmark as the Community's own resources all revenues from levies on imported food and receipts from the common external tariff on industrial goods (except for 10 per cent which would be retained by the member states to cover collection costs), plus a proportion not exceeding 1 per cent of national revenues from the Value Added Tax (VAT).

This was a system that would disadvantage Britain because it imported far more food and industrial goods from outside the Community than did the other member states. This meant that there would be much larger payments to be made into the budget, whilst the domination of the budget by the CAP, from which Britain stood to benefit little, meant that Britain faced the prospect of becoming one of the largest net contributors to the budget.

At the opening of negotiations in Luxemburg on 30 June 1970,

Anthony Barber made a statement which . . . went to the heart of the matter: the impact of the new agreement of the Six on Community finance. He pointed out that the Labour Government had hoped to take part in negotiating it, in which case, no doubt, fair provision would have been made for Britain as for the other members. But Britain had not been there. In 1967 the Brussels Commission had said that the existing financial arrangements, if applied to Britain, would 'give rise to a problem of financial burdens'. The new decisions, Barber said, had made that problem of balance even more severe.[10]

Much discussion took place on the actual size of the contributions

[10] Barker, *Britain in a Divided Europe*, p. 247. Anthony Barber was at that stage the British chief negotiator; he was soon to become Chancellor of the Exchequer and be replaced as chief negotiator by Geoffrey Rippon.

to the budget that Britain would be liable to make under the formula. From the outset, though, the Government appears to have recognized, as it admitted in its 1971 White Paper, 'that it would not be possible to seek to make fundamental alterations in the system of providing funds for the Community'.[11]

The conclusion on both sides, after much swapping of estimates, was that the actual size of contributions was impossible to estimate for any distance ahead, because there were too many variables involved. For example, part of the problem arose because of the high British propensity to import goods from outside the Community; it was confidently anticipated that membership would lead to some degree of trade diversion, so that Britain might soon be expected to be importing more from its Community partners and less from the outside, thereby incurring lower contributions to the budget in the form of levies and tariffs; but nobody could predict how far or how fast this process would go.

At the outset of the negotiations on entry, the British and French positions were widely divergent. The French were insisting that Britain should begin paying its full share into the budget from the first day of membership. The British, worried about the implications for their balance of payments, which was precariously in surplus as a result of strenuous efforts by the Labour Government and considerable sacrifices by the country over the preceding few years, were asking for a long transitional period during which there would be a phased buildup to the full level, starting at 3 per cent of the total budget in the first year of membership, against the 21 per cent that was their estimated full contribution.

The Heath–Pompidou Summit

By the spring of 1971 negotiations in Brussels had reached an impasse. The British Government was unsure whether the French were genuinely wanting to find a way of allowing Britain into the Community or were looking for an excuse to prevent entry yet again. The French for their part seem to have been unsure of British intentions: whether the British Government was just trying to gain access in order to rearrange the Community from the inside into the sort of outward-looking free-trade area that its predecessors had

[11] HMSO, *The United Kingdom and the European Communities*, Cmnd. 4715 (London, 1971), para. 91.

always appeared to favour, or whether the change of Prime Minister really meant a change of heart.

Christopher Soames was at that time the British ambassador in Paris. He had been appointed by the Labour Government in August 1968, and in February 1969 had been given an extraordinary audience with de Gaulle, who had expounded to him his views of the future of the Community and had suggested that the way forward for Britain lay in bilateral negotiations with France prior to any further formal application for membership. That episode had ended in a deterioration of Anglo–French relations when the British Government chose to release reports of the meeting to the other member states of the EC. However, Soames decided in 1971 to take up de Gaulle's suggestion, and, in consultation with Michel Jobert, then secretary-general at the presidential Elysée Palace, set in motion arrangements for a bilateral summit between Heath and Pompidou.

The summit took place in May 1971, and was a 'very, very good meeting'.[12] The two men, who had only met once or twice before, struck up a good working relationship: 'They did not become chummy, or relax easily in each other's company . . . But they evidently felt not only a certain political sympathy . . . but also— perhaps even more important—impressed each other as solid, down-to-earth, trustworthy men able to deliver the goods.'[13] The meeting was enough to break through the distrust that had bedevilled the negotiations in Brussels, and to give them a new momentum. It took only a month to reach agreement on the outstanding issues, and in late June a series of agreements was signed in Luxemburg that paved the way to British entry to the Community.

Helped by the West German decision of May 1971 to float the Deutschmark, which upset the French and set back hopes for further progress towards economic and monetary union, the problem of sterling was allowed to disappear altogether. At a meeting in early June, Giscard, to the surprise of delegations from the other member states, accepted a British assurance that the sterling balances would be run down in an orderly manner and measures would be taken to bring sterling into line with other currencies. This went no further than earlier statements, but in the

---

[12] Uwe Kitzinger, *Diplomacy and Persuasion: How Britain Joined the Common Market* (London, 1973), 119.   [13] Ibid. 121.

aftermath of the bilateral summit the French were this time prepared to believe the assurances.

Arrangements were agreed on the phasing of British implementation of the common external tariff and the removal of British tariffs against other member states, on the introduction into Britain of the CAP, and on the phased introduction between 1973 and 1980 of British contributions to the Community budget. On this issue the French gave a good deal of ground from their original demand that the full contribution be made from the start. On the other hand, the British accepted that the problems that they anticipated once the transitional period was finished should be left for future discussion. The British Government set a great deal of store on an assurance that, if unacceptable situations should arise, 'the very survival of the Community would demand that the institutions find equitable solutions'.[14]

In fact, Heath's strategy on this, as on other issues including New Zealand butter and Caribbean sugar, was not to allow them to prevent rapid completion of the entry negotiations, but to defer the problems, which were recognized by the Government as very real problems, for later negotiation. In particular, on the issue of budgetary contributions, he appears to have hoped that the problem could be solved by an enlargement of the budget to end its domination by the CAP, and to introduce new common spending policies, particularly a regional policy, from which Britain would benefit. Thus, although its gross contributions would increase, Britain would start to receive more back from the budget than it was paying in, thus becoming a net beneficiary.

This seems, even in retrospect, to have been a sensible approach in the conditions of the times. As Young pointed out, in any subsequent negotiations 'the original Six will no longer hold what was their strongest card in the entry negotiations—the ability simply to deny admittance to a British Government plainly very anxious to enter'.[15] To gain entry, and then sort out any difficulties, was the approach taken by the Heath Government.

The Paris Summit: October 1972

The participation of the Heath Government in the work of the

---

[14] HMSO, *The United Kingdom*, para. 96.
[15] Young, *Terms of Entry*, p. 211.

Community began before formal membership on 1 January 1973. In October 1972 a summit meeting was held in Paris of the Heads of Government (for France, the Head of State) of all the members of the enlarged Community. This conference 'functioned as a kind of constitutional convention',[16] mapping out the areas of priority for common action. Heath had a very high profile at the meeting. He showed his determination to push the EC forward in directions that would be beneficial to Britain. Aware that he faced a sceptical public at home, he put at the top of his priorities for Community action the creation of a European Regional Development Fund (ERDF), which he saw as essential to redress the balance in the Community's budgetary arrangements between agriculture and industry, and to provide rapid and tangible benefits to convince the British people of the merits of membership. Commitment to the ERDF occupied a prominent place in the final communiqué of the conference.

Two further areas were added to the final communiqué largely as a result of the importance attached to them by the British Prime Minister. The first was agreement to pursue a joint approach to trade talks with the United States, which were scheduled to begin the following year within the context of the General Agreement on Tariffs and Trade (GATT). Here Britain was in harmony with France in wanting a hard line to be taken. Heath appears to have been no admirer of the way in which Richard Nixon, the US President, had handled international economic affairs. Heath was keen that non-tariff barriers to free trade should be included on the agenda alongside tariff barriers, something to which the United States was opposed, and that a deadline be set for the start of the talks. These arguments were presented, however, in the context of a commitment to multilateral free trade, which meant avoiding protectionist sentiments and keeping the Community open to trade with Japan and the United States.

On this issue it was West Germany that acted as the more sympathetic partner to the United States, and persuaded the others not to set a deadline that it might be politically impossible for the US President to keep, given the pressure Nixon was facing from protectionist elements in the US Congress. The argument for a joint negotiating position, that would put non-tariff barriers on the

[16] Ross B. Talbot, *The European Community's Regional Fund* (Oxford, 1977), 197.

agenda, was accepted, despite the fact that it 'touched on central issues of the industrial policy of national governments, including government purchasing, which presented serious problems for the liberalization of trade not only with non-Community partners but even within the Community area of tariff-free trade itself'.[17]

The second issue that Britain got included in the final communiqué was the need for the Community to negotiate a joint policy on energy. British officials admitted that this was something about which Heath had 'a bee in his bonnet'.[18] Ironically, energy was the very issue that was soon to put the British Government in the dock, accused of being an awkward partner. At the time it was not seen as particularly important by the other member states, but international developments were soon to change that.

Two other agreements at this summit were less welcome to the British Government: on the adoption of a programme of measures in the areas of industrial, scientific, and technological policy; and on the formulation of a common social policy.

The agreement to set January 1974 as a deadline by which agreement would be reached on the first of these areas marked the concern within the Community that the EC should take advantage of its size to make advances in technological research and development, and even to get ahead of the United States and other commercial rivals. The British Government tried to get agreement that priority should be accorded to the harmonization of company law, which would facilitate cross-border mergers, and to the elimination of non-tariff barriers to trade by harmonizing food, pollution, and health rules. It was less keen on positive steps to create joint research programmes and a common industrial policy. These attitudes were consistent with the position that Heath had adopted in his Godkin Lectures given at Harvard University in 1967.[19]

German priority for the formulation of a common social policy, including worker participation in the management of firms, the harmonization of social security measures, and the promotion of dialogue between trade unions and employers at the Community level through the strengthening of the recently created Standing Committee on Employment, reflected the policy orientation of the

[17] Roger Morgan, 'Can Europe Have a Foreign Policy?', *World Today*, 30 (1974), 43–50.   [18] *The Economist*, 28 Oct. 1972.
[19] Edward Heath, *Old World, New Horizons: Britain, The Common Market and the Atlantic Alliance* (London, 1970).

coalition Government of Social Democrats (SPD) and Free Democrats (FDP) in Bonn, but it also reflected West German national interests. The harmonization of social security benefits in particular had important implications for rates of taxation, and therefore for industrial costs. It was also a measure that was favoured by other member states though not by Britain. Measures proposed by the Commission to advance this objective were to be blocked repeatedly by successive British Governments in the years to come, causing an underlying irritation, culminating in 1986, when Thatcher's Government took advantage of its six-month tenure of the presidency of the EC to try to wipe such issues off the Community's agenda once and for all.[20]

Primary emphasis in the final communiqué, though, was given to Economic and Monetary Union (EMU), with a view to its completion not later than 31 December 1980. The objective of EMU had been argued at an earlier summit, which had also acted as a sort of constitutional convention, in The Hague in 1969. This had been the summit at which it had been agreed to reopen negotiations on British entry, as one part of a three-part plan for progress. Enlargement had been linked with 'completion' of the first stage of integration, which produced the 1970 agreements on financing the Community budget, and 'deepening' of the level of integration, which meant primarily moves to achieve EMU.

There had been some disagreement on how to advance towards this agreed objective. The French had wanted to see monetary integration lead the way. That would have implied tying the exchange rates of national currencies together, and central banks agreeing to assist each other in holding those parties against speculative movements of funds across the international exchanges. The Germans had seen this as a recipe for allowing France to follow inflationary policies while not having to worry about the effect on the international value of the franc because the German Bundesbank would support it from its ample reserves of foreign currency. Unwilling to undertake such support operations, the Germans had tried to insist that the priority should be given to the co-ordination of economic policies. The compromise had been to attempt to advance on both fronts simultaneously.[21]

---

[20] This is covered in Ch. 7 below.
[21] See Loukas Tsoukalis, *The Politics and Economics of European Monetary Integration* (London, 1978).

The exercise remained a particularly important priority for the French, and at the Paris summit President Pompidou pressed for a European monetary fund to be set up by April 1973 as the first stage of a process that would lead to full monetary union by 1980. The Germans agreed, stressing the need for anti-inflationary measures to be taken simultaneously. In the context of the turmoil in international monetary markets that had followed the ending of the convertibility of the dollar in August 1971, the Germans had fallen into line with the French because they were anxious to establish a zone of monetary stability in Europe.

EMU was generally supported by the original Six. The ERDF, on the other hand, had been an objective only of Italy prior to enlargement. Now the Italians were joined by the British and Irish, who also had an interest in the creation of such a redistributive fund. The Germans again were apprehensive, because, as with monetary union, they expected to have to pick up the bill for any such development. Nevertheless, they were prepared to see the issue put on the agenda, recognizing that it would be difficult for the British in particular to make positive steps towards economic union without some guarantee of support for the less prosperous regions of the United Kingdom. It is probably fair to assume, though, that at this stage the French and Germans saw a direct trade-off between their agreement to the ERDF and British participation in the attempt to achieve EMU.

Gaining a Reputation

At this stage in the story there was no reason to think that Britain would not prove to be a co-operative member of the Community. Certainly there was no doubt that the Government would stand up vigorously for British national interests within the EC. This was no less than was expected of every member. The important point was that Heath seemed to interpret British national interests in a way that coincided with the interests of the Community in an advance towards closer unity.

The Government was 'on record as aspiring to the evolution of a closely-knit community with a common currency and a common economic policy which would exercise real influence upon the international system'.[22] There appeared to be backing for this

[22] Frankel, *British Foreign Policy*, p. 173.

approach from significant interest groups within the British state. The City of London, always influential on the thinking of the Treasury, and previously rather divided and ambiguous in its attitude, had rallied to the idea of membership following the dollar crisis of August 1971: 'The dollar crisis led those in charge of the City's strategy to rethink London's place in the international financial world. Europe, they became convinced, provided the direction for the City's flight forward: London would find a new role as the "financial growth pole" for Europe.'[23]

In addition, entry to the EC was a central component of Heath's strategy for industrial regeneration in Britain, a strategy based on the promotion of competition.

Heath . . . wants to replace the old, comfortable class-ridden Britain by a tougher, more competitive society with better rewards for the able . . . Part of his enthusiasm for entry into the Common Market derives from his belief that intensified competition will stimulate those worthy of survival and purge the incompetents.[24]

The bases for Britain's future reputation as an awkward partner can nevertheless be discerned even at the time of entry. In particular, the Labour Party came out in opposition to entry on the terms negotiated by the Conservative Government. The story behind this stance is told in the next chapter: it was to cause tremendous problems for the future relationship of Britain with the Community once a Labour Government returned to office in 1974.

Yet even before that Britain had managed to achieve a reputation for being awkward and uncooperative that had scarcely been anticipated when the Treaty of Accession was signed on 22 January 1972. There were three grounds for the complaint.

First, the newcomers had a strong line on what was necessary in order for the Community to become an effective actor in international affairs. The British pursued a campaign to have as many of the Community's institutions as possible concentrated in Brussels, and for the size and quality of the staff of the Commission to be increased. This position, defended as the pursuit of EC objectives, upset the Commission because it implied that it was not efficient (a view that British officials certainly appear to have held); it upset the French, who had long argued against the centralization of the Community in Brussels; it upset Luxemburg, and France

[23] Henk Overbeek, *Global Capitalism and Britain's Decline* (Amsterdam, 1988).

[24] Andrew Roth, *Heath and the Heathmen* (London, 1972), 5.

again, because it implied that they would lose Community institutions that were situated on their soil; and it seemed to all of the original members to be impertinent for a new member to be lecturing them on the structure and functioning of their institutions. Secondly, the British pursued their national objectives vigorously, stressing on issues such as the ERDF, reform of the CAP, and the opening of negotiations with the African, Caribbean, and Pacific states that these coincided with the interests of the Community as a whole, as laid down at the Paris summit; but they were equally vigorous where their interests did not coincide with those of the Community, as on their right to continue to give national regional aids to areas that on EC definitions would not be eligible for assistance. And they were also prepared to block progress in fields that did not fit in with their national view of what were appropriate areas of activity. One such was technological co-operation. Commission proposals for a substantial commitment of funds to Euratom research over a five-year period met with stiff opposition from Britain on the grounds that too much money was being committed for too long a period. Eventually a compromise was reached that gave more to the Commission than to the British position, but the high profile adopted by a newcomer on the issue caused some offence, particularly to Italy, which had the biggest commitment to the programme, and within the Commission.

Thirdly, the British appeared awkward to their new partners because they refused to accept any linkages between issues. The process of linking issues together in package deals that gave something to everyone had served the Community of Six well. Now the British arrived pressing for progress on those areas that suited them, and refusing to make concessions in other areas in return. This, and the other complaints, were well illustrated by the three big issues that occupied the attention of the Community during this period: EMU, energy policy, and the ERDF.

Economic and Monetary Union

EMU was one of the first issues on which Britain began to earn a reputation as an awkward partner in the EC. It was accepted that there would be problems about sterling entering the joint float of European currencies because of its special position as a former international reserve currency, which had left it with a responsibility to service the debts known as the sterling balances. Nevertheless, there was great disappointment when the British Government would not attempt to put its currency into the joint float unless the Community as a whole took responsibility for underwriting its value. The German Economics Minister, Helmut Schmidt, indicated his willingness to underwrite the sterling balances themselves, but Anthony Barber, his British counterpart, insisted that the commitment must be more far-reaching.

What added to the sensitivity of the issue was that Italy had also taken the lira out of the joint float, and was using British non-participation as an excuse for not re-entering. There was also great resentment that Britain was making demands for the ERDF, from which it would benefit, without being prepared to make even an effort to put sterling into the float.

The suspicion existed that on this issue Heath would have been prepared to accept the German offer, and to take sterling into the system, but that he gave way to pressure from the Treasury. He was also insisting that other policies—particularly the setting-up of the ERDF—should not be conditional on sterling's participation, thus breaking a connection that was important to the states that were trying to make the joint float work. For Germany, which would pick up most of the bill for the ERDF, the main justification for agreeing to it was as part of the price to keep the Community together; yet the British were not prepared to come together with the others on this important aspect of progress towards EMU.

Insult was added to injury when the British began to press for the European reserve bank, that was proposed for the next stage of the EMU experiment, to be placed in Brussels; most of the other member states were prepared to agree that it should be in Luxemburg. This reflected Heath's strongly held view that the institutions of the EC should be concentrated in Brussels so far as possible, to increase their efficiency and effectiveness. But it looked bad for him to be standing out against the rest of the Community on an issue in which his Government was not actually involved.

Even worse, British Treasury officials made little secret of their belief that there was a lamentable lack of competence on monetary affairs in Brussels. They made it known that they believed the Community would not be able to overcome the obstacles and pitfalls that lay in its path unless its monetary directorate-general was beefed up, both in size and in quality. An unsuccessful attempt was made by the Government to displace the Italian director-general, Ugo Mosca, with a Briton. When that failed, an equally unsuccessful attempt was made to get a British nominee placed as deputy to Mosca.

The British view was that the Organization for Economic Co-operation and Development (OECD) and the International Monetary Fund (IMF) were both more dynamic and more competent bodies than the Commission when it came to monetary affairs. It was the IMF which had helped to sort out the monetary chaos that followed runs on the major currencies in 1969; and the OECD which had unscrambled the monetary chaos of 1971, when President Nixon ended the convertibility of the dollar into gold. On both occasions Raymond Barre, the French Commissioner for monetary affairs, had 'put his head firmly in the sand'.[25]

On this issue, as on several others, Heath pressed a line that he believed was good for the EC. He had a clear view of where the Community ought to be going, and British officials stated that view very firmly. This did not go down well with the original members, nor with the Commission, particularly because it involved telling some painful home truths about the effectiveness of the operation that the Commission was running at that time. There was perhaps a lack of a fine diplomatic touch at work here. On the other hand, there can be no doubt that the tasks that faced the Community were not only important, they were also urgent. Perhaps Heath felt that they were too urgent to allow a more leisurely approach.

Energy Policy

When Heath raised the issue of a common policy on energy at the Paris summit, it was in the context of attaining an agreement on the external stance to be taken by the EC. He believed that it was necessary to have a unified policy towards the producer states, which, already before the Arab–Israeli war, were acting as a cartel. But the crisis over the supply of oil that was brought about by the war persuaded most of the other member states to support the view of France, that an agreement on internal regulation of the Community market in oil was necessary.

When an attempt was made to get agreement on the form of a

[25] *The Economist*, 31 Mar. 1973.

common policy in May 1973, it failed because the French insisted that internal regulation of the market was a prerequisite to an external policy. This was rejected by the British, West German, and Dutch Governments. On the eve of the outbreak of the Middle East war these positions still remained much the same, although there had been some modification of the British position in the light of growing shortages of refined oil products in Europe. But Britain was still not prepared to accept the French idea that Brussels should supervise the choice of suppliers for private oil companies. Since its attitude ran so strongly counter to the general French line of wanting to minimize the role of the Commission in making important strategic decisions, the suspicion grew that France was pressing the point in order to block the formulation of a common external stance, in opposition to Britain's argument that the Commission should negotiate with the United States and the oil producers on behalf of the Community as a whole.

The outbreak of the Arab–Israeli war and the consequent shortages of oil led to a change in these alignments. The Germans, who had previously opposed a policy for controlling the supply of oil internally within the Community, now became keen on reaching such an agreement, as did the Dutch, who suffered the most from the Arab embargo.

But the British position hardened. Although Britain was not at that time a producer of oil, the reserves of oil in the North Sea were known, and domestic political opinion saw the new pressure for an internal policy on energy as an attempt by the rest of the EC to get its hands on 'our oil'; sections of the Press threatened to blow the issue up into something of an anti-EC campaign. In the face of this sort of domestic political opposition, Heath, who had enough domestic political problems to be contemplating calling an election at any favourable moment, simply could not concede the point. Again, as so often in this history, domestic political constraints hindered the evolution of British policy within the Community and prevented concessions being made that might have achieved corresponding concessions on issues important to Britain.

The most important such issue was the setting up of the ERDF, which had become almost the centre-piece of Heath's campaign to make the EC acceptable to the British people, and to resolve the increasingly obvious problem of British budgetary contributions.

The Regional Development Fund

Heath made a good start in his campaign to have a substantial ERDF when he got the objective written into the communiqué of the Paris summit. He achieved a second important step when he managed to get a British Commissioner, George Thomson, appointed to the relevant portfolio. Although a member of the Labour Party, Thomson was a pro-Community figure who had negotiated with the EC on behalf of Wilson's Government, and who had publicly stated that Wilson's rejection of the terms of British entry negotiated by Heath was hypocritical because he knew that the Labour Government would have accepted the same terms had they been offered.

There were two issues concerning the proposed fund that were crucial. One was its size in absolute terms. Too small a fund would produce no tangible benefits for Britain, and would do nothing to reduce the domination of the budget by the CAP. The other was the distribution of the money available. If the principle were adopted that every member state must get something out of the ERDF, even a large fund would do less to redress the imbalance in economic prosperity within the Community than would one that concentrated the resources on the very poorest regions, wherever they were situated.

The British Government made it known publicly that it was looking for a fund of approximately 3 billion units of account over three years, and this was precisely the amount that Thomson proposed to his fellow Commissioners. This amount was reduced during discussion within the Commission to 2.4 billion units of account, and it was on the basis of that figure that negotiations began within the Council of Ministers.

The response of the West German Government to the proposal was ambiguous. Chancellor Brandt seemed favourably disposed to the amount proposed, seeing it as a price worth paying for consolidating British membership of the EC. On the other hand, his Finance Minister, Helmut Schmidt, one of the strongest figures within the SPD, was unhappy about the amount, feeling that the German budget could not stand to make such a commitment.

France was less concerned about the absolute size of the fund than with ensuring that the distribution of the money involved was organized in such a way that France should obtain some benefit, and should not be a net contributor to the budget as a whole.

The energy crises of 1973 had a direct and damaging effect on the negotiations about the ERDF. The economic difficulties that followed the cut-back in deliveries of Arab oil to Europe strengthened the hand of that faction within West Germany that felt that the country could not afford a large fund. This reaction was compounded by Heath's refusal to accept an agreement on pooling and sharing energy resources within the Community. The economic problems also hardened the French attitude on the distribution of money from any fund that might be set up.

At Paris in 1972 the agreement had been to set up a fund by the end of 1973. Ross B. Talbot, who made a detailed study of the negotiations on this issue, argues that:

a European Regional Development Fund (ERDF) would have been established prior to 31 December 1973, if the Arab–Israeli (Yom Kippur) War had not intervened, followed by the OPEC . . . strategy of a quadrupling of oil prices. The OPEC strategy was directed towards different objectives, but there was a vital crossing point; the monopoly politics of oil became dominant over the EEC politics of redistribution. The Regional Fund issue was the temporary victim of power politics within the EEC, involving Great Britain, Western Germany (FRG) and France.[26]

Instead of meeting at Copenhagen to celebrate the completion of the tasks they had set in Paris, the Heads of State and Government found themselves engaged in an emergency summit dominated by oil. Not only the ERDF, but also progress on EMU had been thrown off course by the shock waves from an event external to the Community. Discussion at the summit indicated a continuing refusal of the British to accept the need for joint EC measures to combat the crisis, accompanied by a continuing insistence on the need for the member states to adopt a common stance towards the outside world. The latter position sat rather uneasily alongside the British response to the crisis, which was to follow France in concluding bilateral deals with oil-producing states.

The summit did produce a Declaration on Europe's identity, that had been held up by several months of negotiation. But the weakness of the statement was evident to any impartial observer. In a leading article *The Economist* criticized Heath for pushing for an intangible common foreign policy while not realizing that a common energy policy within the Community was an essential prerequisite for an external stance that would be credible to either

---

[26] Talbot, *The European Community's Regional Fund*, p. 216.

the United States or the Arabs.[27] Although this criticism ignored the domestic political obstacles to agreeing to Community regulation, and the strength of opposition from the oil companies, it had logical validity.

Whatever the reasons for Heath's obduracy on this matter, there is no doubt that it contributed to bringing Anglo–German relations to a post-war low. Although a renewed commitment was made at the summit to setting up the ERDF, it became obvious that the West Germans were likely to agree only to a much smaller fund than Heath was committed to obtaining. However much the British might feel that Brandt was going back on his apparent willingness of a few months earlier to pay for the size of fund proposed by the Commission, the British really did play into the hands of those members of the German Government, especially Schmidt, who had all along argued for a more limited exercise.

When, three days after the summit, negotiations reopened on the ERDF, with the Germans stating their hard line, the British contributed to their growing reputation for being awkward partners by their response. A telephone call to the Prime Minister produced a dramatic statement from the British delegation that their Government intended to veto progress on other issues, including energy, unless the Germans would agree to pay more than they were now offering. This approach ran entirely counter to the previous refusal of Britain to accept cross-issue linkages in negotiations. It also was reminiscent of the way in which de Gaulle used to treat the Community; but, as John Lambert pointed out at the time, 'Edward Heath is not de Gaulle'[28] and the move backfired, simply contributing to a hardening of the German line.

It proved impossible to reach agreement on an ERDF before the Heath Government left office in February 1974, and the Wilson Government that succeeded it showed little interest in this specific issue, being committed to a total renegotiation of the terms of British entry. Eventually a fund was set up by a decision of the Paris summit in December 1974. It was both smaller and later than had been hoped, and it certainly was too small and too late to perform the task that Heath had expected of the ERDF, which was to prove

[27] *The Economist*, 22 Dec. 1973.
[28] John Lambert, 'European Ideals Fade in the Oil Scramble', *Sunday Times*, 27 Jan. 1973.

tangible benefits from Community membership for Britain and thereby to legitimate entry in the eyes of the electorate.

Conclusion

The Heath Government entered the EC with high aspirations and positive plans. In some ways, it may have entered with too much enthusiasm. The plans that Heath had for the future of the EC were perfectly justifiable, but they were perhaps a little too far-reaching not to be slightly resented by the original member states. This resentment was enhanced by the vigour with which the British Government pressed its own national interests on issues such as the classification of regions eligible for aid, reform of the CAP, and subsidies for butter. To achieve concessions in these areas the British 'trod with heavy feet'.[29]

At the same time as pressing these particular interests, the British loudly urged the Community to adopt a common external policy stance towards the United States, particularly over the scheduled GATT round and over energy. Yet on issues that were perceived by the Six as being directly complementary to this, moves towards monetary union and the formulation of an internal policy on energy, the British refused to co-operate.

It seems that there was a certain amount of hypocrisy over the issue of British participation in the joint float of the Community's currencies. Up to the end of 1973 the German and French Governments were officially putting pressure on Britain and Italy to reintegrate their currencies into the snake; but it was reported that Finance Ministers were privately discouraging fixing of parities.[30] Tsoukalis suggests that the public stance was probably an excuse to continue blocking the regional fund.[31]

The linkage that was made by France between agreement on an internal energy policy and adoption of a common external stance on the issue was also probably using one as an excuse to block the other, as was the later linkage made by the Germans between agreement on the internal energy policy and agreement on a substantial ERDF.

[29] *The Economist*, 4 Aug. 1973.
[30] Ibid., 21 July 1972.
[31] Tsoukalis, *The Politics and Economics of European Monetary Integration*, p. 153.

In this light it may be that Britain was not particularly the awkward partner in the EC during 1973. All the partners were being awkward for one reason or another. What does appear obvious, though, is that the French and Germans were, understandably, much more adept at playing the Community game in such a way as to appear to be *communautaire*. Even if the linkages with policies favoured by Britain were deliberately forged, it does seem as though the British Government played into the hands of the other member states. Perhaps this is partly explained by the pressure that Heath was under on the domestic front.

Whatever the reasons, the year that began with great harmony and optimism in the Community ended with tension between Britain and her partners. Despite the good intentions of the Prime Minister, Britain had gained a reputation for being difficult to work with. Strong pursuit of national interests had not been paralleled by any recognition of the need for compromise and package deals. The pursuit of effectiveness within the Commission had bruised susceptibilities within that body. The fact that Britain and the United States appeared at times not to be working in harmony did not entirely allay a suspicion that Britain was acting as de Gaulle had anticipated, playing the US Trojan horse. British efforts to ensure that the EC was not an inward-looking body, which might be more accurately interpreted as a reflection of the traditional policy of internationalism, were seen as evidence of Britain trying to tie the EC to the United States, a perception that was strengthened by the positive British response to the US proposal for a conference of consumers of energy in Washington following the December increases in the price of oil.

Overall, Britain during its first year or so of membership established a reputation for being an awkward partner that was to be considerably increased by the approach of the Labour Government that succeeded Heath to office in February 1974.

3. The Wilson Governments, 1974–1976

THE Labour Government that was elected in February 1974 had no overall majority in Parliament. It was the largest single party, but until a second election in October 1974 was dependent on minor parties to secure a majority for its legislation. Even after October, its majority was only three seats. With this slender margin of parliamentary manœuvre it had to tackle a difficult domestic political situation, and an economic crisis of major proportions, against a background of continuing international turbulence. Although the Government was to become increasingly involved in initiating economic summits between the major powers, and in promoting international monetary reform, that phase of its activity mainly came after Harold Wilson's resignation in March 1976, and is dealt with in the next chapter. For the two years of Wilson's premiership the struggle was to stabilize the domestic front, and in that process the issue of membership of the EC came to play a central role.

The International Context

The rise in the price of oil of December 1973 plunged the world system into a degree of chaos. Not only did energy costs increase sharply; so did the price of food as a consequence of the high level of mechanization of agriculture, and the increase in the costs of chemical fertilizers derived from oil. The failure of the Soviet harvest in 1973 made matters worse, when the USSR in 1974 turned to the international market to make up the shortfall, pushing the price of grain up even further.

Most of the industrialized capitalist states found themselves having to cope with large balance of payments deficits and with inflation spiralling rapidly upwards, given a sharp twist by the increases in energy and food costs. A new phenomenon was the coexistence of these high rates of inflation with high levels of unemployment: the two had previously been considered by economists to be alternative evils. Now terms such as 'stagflation' were coined to describe this combination of stagnant growth and rising inflation.

The international monetary system, already under strain, was rendered even more unstable by the influx into the multinational commercial banks of large quantities of 'petro-dollars' (as the new-found wealth of the OPEC states came to be called). This had the effect of increasing the quantity of liquid assets in the system, which could be, and were, switched from one national currency to another in anticipation of changes in exchange rates. The management of exchange rates became exceedingly difficult, particularly for the currencies of the weaker national economies, including the dollar, which came under extreme downward pressure.

The United States had its own particular problems. In August 1974 Richard Nixon resigned the presidency in the wake of accusations that he had authorized the 'bugging' of the Democrats' Watergate campaign headquarters during the 1972 presidential election campaign. Gerald Ford, who as Nixon's Vice-President became President when Nixon resigned, found himself facing the worst US economic statistics for thirty years. Unemployment had risen by January 1975 to 7.5 million people, or 8.2 per cent of the labour force; and inflation had reached an annual rate of 14 per cent by the end of 1974. Starting as a conservative in fiscal matters, Ford felt obliged to introduce a mildly reflationary budget for 1975 in an attempt to reduce the unemployment level before the presidential election scheduled for the autumn of 1976, but the risk of feeding the high rate of inflation prevented him from going further.

In Europe, the West German economy did not come badly out of the crisis. The shock of the rise in oil prices hit the German economy when it was booming, and it withstood that shock better than any other OECD state except Switzerland. In the year from May 1974 to May 1975, the West German consumer price index rose by 6.1 per cent, compared to an EC average of 13.9 per cent (and 25 per cent in Britain). As a major producer of capital goods, the Federal Republic was in a strong position to boost its exports to the OPEC states, which wanted to use their income from oil to develop their industrial capacity, and as a result of this and of its underlying export strength the German economy did not run into deficit on its balance of payments.

Nevertheless, output was lost in Germany. Between the first quarter of 1974 and the first quarter of 1975 the Gross National Product (GNP) of the Federal Republic declined by 5 per cent; and unemployment quadrupled from the start of 1973 to the second quarter of 1975, to reach around one million, or 4.4 per cent of the labour force. As a result of declining tax revenues and increasing unemployment payments, the Federal budget ran into deficit during 1974, reviving traditional German fears of inflation. These in turn led to an announcement in 1975 of plans for cuts in virtually all sectors of public spending in 1976.

In these circumstances, the Federal German Government became cautious about agreeing to increases in the budget of the EC. A new assertiveness became apparent in its dealings with the Community, which was also a reflection of the change of leadership. Helmut Schmidt, the former Finance Minister, replaced Willy Brandt as Chancellor in May 1974; he was seen as a more forthright and strong-willed leader. He was also acutely aware that the continued health of the economy of the Federal Republic, whose exports amounted to 23 per cent of its GNP (compared to the 4 per cent share of the US GNP accounted for by US exports) was dependent on its customers being able to purchase its products. For that reason he authorized a substantial bilateral loan to Italy in September 1974. For that reason also he actively involved himself in attempting to organize the conditions for an international recovery from the recession.

The increasingly active role of the Federal Republic in international economic affairs was also encouraged by the position of the United States. Under Presidents Nixon and Ford, Henry Kissinger continued in his efforts to reassert US leadership, particularly in response to the challenge posed by OPEC. His proposal for an organization of oil-consuming nations caused division within the EC. France objected strongly to following a US lead, described Kissinger's approach as confrontational, and refused to join the International Energy Agency (IEA) that was set up following a conference of oil consumers in Washington in February 1974. However, eight of the EC member states were prepared to follow the United States, and it did seem as though the energy crisis had restored US leadership. But the Watergate affair and the crippling economic problems of the United States made it very difficult for Kissinger to sustain that position, and no effective initiatives were forthcoming from the United States in other economic areas.

The failure of the Ford Administration to organize an effective international response to the economic problems of the capitalist world encouraged the new European leaders to take the initiative. In this Schmidt came to work increasingly closely with Giscard d'Estaing, who was elected President of France in May 1974 following the death in office of Georges Pompidou in April. During 1974 and 1975 a new Franco–German axis emerged to replace the Franco–British axis that had seemed to exist for a while under Heath and Pompidou.

The start of what Kissinger would call 'one of the best periods of Atlantic co-operation in decades' coincided with the assumption of the presidency of the EC's Council of Ministers by France, in the second half of 1974. With Schmidt's support, Giscard was the undisputed prime mover in this phase of revival.[1]

Giscard met with Ford at Martinique, on French territory in the West Indies, in December 1974. Agreements were reached there that cleared some of the obstacles to co-operation between France and the United States. France agreed to co-operate with, although not formally to join, the IEA, and to abandon its demand for a return to fixed exchange rates, which cleared the way for co-operation on monetary matters. In return, Ford agreed to Giscard's plan for a conference of industrialized oil-consuming states, OPEC members, and developing countries, to discuss the problems of North–South relations in a wider framework than just the politics of oil.

Meanwhile, although the British Government kept itself informed of wider international developments, and participated in the first of the Western economic summits which took place in Rambouillet in November 1975, Britain temporarily took a back seat in the international arena, preoccupied with pressing domestic economic and political problems that were partly caused by the international crisis and were partly the legacy that Heath's failure to control the trade unions had bequeathed to Wilson.

The Domestic Context

Wilson had to deal with political problems at three levels. Within

[1] Guido Garavoglia, 'From Rambouillet to Williamsburg: A Historical Assessment', in Cesare Merlini (ed.), *Economic Summits and Western Decision-making* (London, 1984), 1–42.

his own party he had to face an offensive from the left, led by Tony Benn, who had decided that the failure of the 1964–70 Labour Governments had been due to their not having implemented what the Labour left described as socialist policies. At the parliamentary level he had to contend with the lack of a majority between February and October 1974, which meant that he had to ensure that he could win support from the minor parties for anything he attempted to do that required the approval of the legislature. And, perhaps most difficult of all, he had to deal with a country that was deeply divided.

The trade unions had mobilized against Heath's Government, and the National Union of Mineworkers had been instrumental in bringing about the downfall of that Government at the polls. In reaction, elements of other social classes were restive. Soaring inflation hit particularly those socio-economic groups that were unable to insulate themselves from its effects by demanding high increases in wages, as the larger trade unions were able to. There was talk of private armies being formed, and the army itself engaged in manœuvres at Heathrow airport that were described as anti-terrorist exercises, but which were seen in some quarters as a preparation for an increased military presence on the streets of Britain.

In these circumstances the primary task of the new Government had to be to restore some sort of domestic harmony; but this was not easy to effect in the face of a serious economic crisis. Inflation, which was 15 per cent when Labour came to office, was bound to rise in the aftermath of the rise in oil prices, especially since the Heath Government had index-linked wage increases to price increases through 'threshold agreements' in the third stage of its incomes policy. By December 1974 price inflation had reached 28 per cent, and was running at over 30 per cent by the summer of 1975. The balance of payments recorded a record deficit of £3,323 million in 1974; GNP fell by 2.5 per cent between the first quarter of 1974 and the first quarter of 1975; and by October 1975 unemployment had passed the one million mark.

Denis Healey, the Chancellor of the Exchequer, responded to the economic crisis by international borrowing to cover the balance of payments deficit, and the institution of price controls combined with voluntary wage restraint through the medium of the Labour Government's 'social contract' with the trade unions. The other side of this contract was a programme of social reforms that the country could ill afford in its straitened circumstances, but the great economic hope for Britain was the prospect of oil being produced from the North Sea in the near future. So the Wilson Government tried to buy time until the oil revenues came gushing to the rescue.

The European Community as a Domestic Political Issue

For the Government, membership of the EC was an issue on which it was useful to focus attention because it cut across the class lines along which the country was divided. It also allowed the Prime Minister to promote unity in pursuing the national interest. There is no surer way of uniting a divided nation than for its leaders to wrap themselves in the national flag and conduct a campaign against an external foe. It was just unfortunate that the foe in this case consisted of Britain's partners in the Community, and the battle damaged relationships that were already strained.

As Raphaella Bilski had pointed out, the EC was also an important issue for the left within the Labour Party.[2] The project of the left was to take control of the Party and ensure that policies were enacted which would move Britain towards a form of state-directed capitalism that was described as socialism by its advocates. Such a programme was unacceptable to the social democrats within the Party, who occupied many of the leading positions, and it would probably not have received backing from a majority within the Parliamentary Labour Party, although it was supported by a number of constituency parties, and by enough of the big trade union leaders to make its imposition feasible.

The attraction for the left of the issue of membership of the EC was that it offered them the prospect of building a majority coalition against the leadership, because there were serious doubts about the Community amongst members of the Party who did not support the more radical economic policies of the left. Thus there was the potential for a coalition that the left could lead and utilize to strengthen its position within the Party. It was also an issue that might be used to lever out of key positions leading social democrats such as Roy Jenkins, then deputy leader of the Party, because the

[2] Raphaella Bilski, 'The Common Market and the Growing Strength of Labour's Left Wing', *Government and Opposition*, 12 (1977), 306–31.

necessity of EC membership was something on which many of the social democrats felt extremely strongly.

From Wilson's viewpoint, the question of EC membership offered the prospect of outmanœuvring the left, because if it lost on this issue it would be at least temporarily weakened, allowing Wilson to consolidate his position. It was, though, a high-risk strategy. Opinion polls showed EC membership to be extremely unpopular in the country. To some extent this was the fault of Heath's Government, which had allowed the Community to be used as a scapegoat for economic problems that were really little to do with it. Also, membership had been indelibly associated in the public mind with Heath, and therefore the task of selling continued membership to the Labour Party, and to Labour voters, was going to be particularly difficult.

The idea of a renegotiation of the terms of entry was a tactical device. There is no reason to think that Wilson himself had changed his view of the necessity of British membership. His rejection of British membership on the terms negotiated by the Heath Government was a useful compromise which allowed him to placate both the anti- and pro-Community elements within his party while in opposition. He now presented himself to the British people as a firmer champion of the British national interest than had been his predecessor; as a leader who would ensure that acceptable terms were negotiated. Added to this was a democratic claim: the Labour Government would put the renegotiated terms to the British people for approval. Initially it was not clear whether this would be in the form of a referendum or of a general election: Wilson may have harboured the idea that an election fought on this issue would be a good way to establish a firm majority, and to wrong-foot the left within the Party. If so, he must have abandoned the idea because a second election was held before the renegotiation was complete, and the commitment to allow a democratic choice on membership became a commitment to hold a referendum, which was originally a proposal of the left, but which became a fundamental part of Wilson's strategy.

The Opening of Negotiations

Wilson did not himself play a leading role in the renegotiation of the terms of entry. The chief role was given to the Foreign

Secretary, James Callaghan. A traditional Labour Party man who had close links with the trade unions, Callaghan's natural instincts, perhaps even more than Wilson's, were Atlanticist, and sceptical towards European unity. However, like Wilson, he seems to have appreciated the necessity of continued British membership.

In contrast to the position under Heath, who retained a Minister of State for European Affairs within the Cabinet Office, Wilson chose to make this position a junior ministerial post within the Foreign Office, so Callaghan had every opportunity to take control of the negotiations without external interference. The person appointed to be Minister was Roy Hattersley, once thought of as pro-Community, but a man who was at that time careful not to depart from the official Labour Party line.

The one major exception to this picture of a renegotiation entirely in the hands of the Foreign Secretary was the appointment of Peter Shore as Secretary of State for Trade. This was obviously a key portfolio so far as the EC was concerned, but, going even beyond its obvious importance, it soon came to be recognized that Shore would accompany Callaghan and Hattersley to most important meetings concerned with the renegotiations, and would act as the voice of the anti-membership faction within the Party.

Shore was not a left-winger. He typifies those individuals on the right and centre of the Party whom Benn and others on the left were able to enrol as allies on this particular issue of principle. In fact, Shore had been close to Wilson in the 1964–6 Government, and during the 1970–4 period in opposition. There can be no doubt, though, that on this issue he felt strongly, which made his presence in the Labour delegation acceptable to the opponents of membership. He was also generally judged to be the most intellectually able of the anti-marketeers; and during the early exchanges within the Cabinet he ran rings round Callaghan with his detailed knowledge of the issues at stake. Shore had briefed himself on the Community far beyond his immediate remit as a spokesman on trade matters, and Callaghan, although intent on taking overall charge of the negotiations, had less appetite for the mastering of detailed briefings on complex issues.

There was a great deal to play for in marking out the extent of the renegotiation mandate. It soon became obvious that the statement contained in the Labour Party's election manifesto had not been backed by any deep thought on the question. Apparently a form of words had been chosen 'which the anti-marketeers were able to interpret according to their wishes whilst the pro-marketeers did not feel bound to reject the formula'.[3]

But when the first public statement was made on the renegotiation, by Callaghan in the House of Commons on 19 March, the tone was reassuring to the other member states of the Community. The statement amounted to little more than a reiteration of the manifesto commitment, but Callaghan stressed the more reassuring points: that the Government would 'not aim to conduct the negotiations as a confrontation', that it would 'embark on these fundamental talks in good faith not to destroy or to wreck but to adapt and reshape'.[4]

Perhaps the tone was too mild, and the relieved reactions from the rest of the Community too favourable, because at the first meeting of the Council of Ministers to consider the renegotiations, on 1 April 1974, the Foreign Secretary adopted a much harder tone. Again, the statement amounted to little more than a reiteration of the manifesto commitment, but this time the emphasis was on the negative aspects: that the British Government reserved the right to propose changes in the Treaties as an essential condition of continued British membership; that it reserved the right to withdraw from the Community if satisfactory terms could not be agreed.

The reaction of Commission officials and representatives of other member states was disappointment, although not despair. It was felt that Callaghan's tone had been determined by the reassertion of left-wing pressure following his mild statement in the Commons. There was also a recognition that to some extent the Foreign Secretary had to play to a domestic public audience: the Government had committed itself to taking a strong nationalist stance, and had to appear to do so. Nevertheless, the tone was seen in some quarters as having limited the scope for greater British flexibility in the forthcoming negotiations.

As it happened, the negotiations took longer than anticipated to get started, because, on the day following the Luxemburg meeting, President Pompidou of France died. The consequent disruption to the French governmental process contributed to a delay of six weeks from the opening statement to the actual commencement of

[3] Ernst Albert, 'Britain again at the European Crossroads', *Aussenpolitik*, 25 (1974), 150–1.   [4] *Hansard*, 5th ser. 870 (19 Mar. 1974), col. 865.

negotiations. The delay was fortunate from the point of view of the pro-market forces in Britain. It allowed Callaghan time to get on top of his subject, so, whereas there had been a feeling in April that the Foreign Secretary was less knowledgeable than the Trade Secretary, the imbalance was less obvious by the end of May.

The death of Pompidou also led to a change of French Foreign Secretary, which was probably also a positive factor in favour of the success of the renegotiation. Michel Jobert, Pompidou's Foreign Secretary, had been constructive and helpful during the original negotiations on British entry, but that was at a time when Pompidou had himself assumed much of the responsibility for the content and tone of French foreign policy. As Pompidou's illness weakened his grip on affairs, Jobert had become more and more 'Gaullist' in his foreign policy positions, and had reacted strongly and badly to Callaghan's initial statement of position on 1 April. The feeling in London was that 'by getting rid of M. Jobert, President Pompidou's death got rid of quite a problem'.[5]

A change of personnel in the West German Government also proved helpful to the renegotiation. Helmut Schmidt, although he seems to have had little respect for Wilson, or initially for Callaghan, proved to be a good ally of theirs in several ways. First, he threw his weight behind reform of the CAP, one of the British Government's key renegotiation demands; for Schmidt the reining-in of agricultural expenditures was a necessity if tight control were to be maintained over the Federal German budget, Germany being the largest contributor to the Community budget. Secondly, Schmidt was himself a pragmatic supporter of the EC, and showed an understanding of the impatience of the British with the rhetoric of European union, in which his predecessor had himself been inclined to engage. Thirdly, Schmidt was prepared to offer strong leadership both within Germany and within the Community, and when the renegotiation was completed he was prepared to put his own personal prestige at the service of the British Government in getting the renegotiated terms accepted by the Labour Party and the British public.

Renegotiating

Eventually, on 4 June, the renegotiations did get under way.

    [5] David E. Butler and Uwe W. Kitzinger, *The 1975 Referendum* (London, 1976), 31–2.

Callaghan's new opening statement was much more conciliatory than his original one in April, reflecting perhaps the extent to which the tide now seemed to be flowing in the direction of the pro-membership elements within the Government. The delay had allowed several Ministers who had originally been counted in the opposition camp to experience the flexibility of the Community's procedures, and already some movement of position had taken place.

Four issues now emerged as the key items in the renegotiation: access to the Community for the products of the Commonwealth states; the freedom of the British Government to give state aids to industry and to the regions without what Callaghan had earlier described as 'interference' from Brussels; reform of the CAP; and the size of British contributions to the Community's budget.

On the first of these some progress had already been made prior to the formal opening of the renegotiation. Judith Hart, the Minister of Overseas Development, was an opponent of continued British membership, but she was prepared to work hard on behalf of the developing Commonwealth states, and indeed for the developing states that were already associated with the EC, to obtain the best possible terms for them should Britain remain a member. Together with Claude Cheysson, the French Socialist who was Commissioner for Overseas Development, she made a major contribution to getting the Community to agree to increase its aid to poor states, and to offer the maximum access for the products of those states to the Community market, without an insistence that they give preference to Community products in return. These agreements were eventually formalized in the Lomé Convention, which was signed after the referendum. Such was the skill and ability of Hart, and the mutual respect that was built up between her and the members of the Commission with whom she worked, that there was genuine disappointment when she decided to campaign against continued membership, putting her loyalty to the left of her party before the new relationships she had built up in working for the good of the developing states.

Peter Shore also impressed Commission officials with his abilities in bargaining extensive concessions for access to the Community for the products of the states of the Indian subcontinent, which were excluded from the Lomé Convention. Although there were some jokes about the number of immigrants on the electoral register in Stepney, Shore's London constituency, and though Shore continued to be unpopular in Brussels, there was widespread recognition even by his opponents that he did a good job on behalf of the Asian Commonwealth countries. The fact that the concessions that Shore extracted from the Community actually weakened his own case for Britain leaving the EC is indicative of the integrity of the man, a rare quality in a politician, and one not shared by all his Cabinet colleagues.

Tony Benn, as Secretary of State for Industry, was not in the front line of the renegotiation, but he was able to make a significant contribution to hindering Callaghan's work. The issue of state aids to industry and the regions was one that was particularly sensitive within the Labour Party, as it had an interventionist domestic programme that opponents of EC membership maintained would be blocked by the Commission. Callaghan asked the Commission to set up a special working group to look at the question of how far what Labour was proposing might be incompatible with EC rules. But the working party was unable to work, apparently because Benn refused to allow his officials to send it internal Department of Industry documents on such matters as how the proposed regional employment premiums would be calculated. Eventually the dispute between Callaghan and Benn on this issue had to be resolved at full Cabinet level. Later Benn also dragged his heels on setting up academic regional studies that were to have been jointly financed by his Department and the Commission, until the point where the Commission had already committed the money to other projects. This effectively prevented Britain from benefiting from the ERDF in 1975, and thereby deprived the proponents of membership of an argument in favour of the Community in the referendum campaign.

Such behaviour naturally depressed those within the Commission and the other member states who were looking for renegotiations in good faith, as Callaghan had promised, and were intent on helping the Government to obtain acceptable terms that it would be able to recommend to the British people. However, it was not the pattern met with in most forums. As well as the positive attitude adopted by Hart and Shore in negotiations on access for the poorer Commonwealth countries, Fred Peart, the Minister of Agriculture, approached the question of reform of the CAP in a most diplomatic manner. His opening statement in June talked about seeking 'improvement' of the agricultural policy; and he showed himself quite prepared to play the Community's game of trading concessions in one area for concessions in others. His approach was quiet, low key, and achieved specific deals that were of benefit to the British consumer.

Peart also benefited from a development that was not of his own making when in September Helmut Schmidt publicly embarrassed the German Minister of Agriculture, Joseph Ertl, by refusing to ratify an agreement on high increases in farm prices that Ertl had accepted in Brussels, and insisting that a full stocktaking of the CAP be inaugurated. Although a move largely prompted by domestic German considerations, it achieved something that the British Government could present as a tangible sign of progress in bringing the CAP under control.

The most difficult issue, and the one that emerged as the key element in the whole renegotiation, was the question of Britain's contributions to the Community's budget. A paper prepared by the British Treasury and circulated in May 1974 calculated what British contributions might be in the future on the basis of median calculations of possible British growth rates, world food prices, and the scale of British imports from outside the Community. On this basis it concluded that gross contributions would increase from 11 per cent of the budget to around 21 per cent by 1979, and 24 per cent in 1980 once the transitional period of membership had been completed. This was compared to a 14 per cent British share of the Community's GNP.[6]

This calculation, and the estimated gap between percentage share of the budget and percentage share of average GNP, was taken as the basis for the renegotiation, although the anti-marketeers tried to insist that the more appropriate basis was the gap between contributions to and receipts from the budget.

In November 1974 the Commission produced its own paper on the British budgetary problem. Unlike the British Treasury, the Commission declined to project figures into the future; instead it calculated what British contributions would have been in 1973 and 1974 had they been based on the full own-resources system. For 1973 the Commission's estimate was that Britain would have paid 19.9 per cent of the total budget against a share of Community GNP of 16.4 per cent (and an actual contribution of 8.8 per cent).

[6] *The Economist*, 18 May 1974.

For 1974 the estimate was 22 per cent against a share of GNP of 15.9 per cent (and an actual contribution of 11 per cent).[7] The French Government's response to these calculations was to argue, as it had done before, that there could be no question of Britain counting the part of the contributions that came from import levies on agricultural produce and the application of the common external tariff on industrial goods as part of its contribution. These items were the Community's own resources. Only the contributions that came from a percentage of VAT revenues ought to be counted. The French also argued against any system of cash rebates.

The French position left the Commission with a difficult task: to find a formula that would satisfy the British demand for cash rebates based on the difference between gross contributions and average share of the Community's GNP; and which would satisfy the French demand that only VAT payments be counted as national contributions. It also had to meet the German demand that there should be strict limits on the size of rebates, and rigorous criteria to qualify.

In February 1975 the Commission came up with a complex formula. First, in order to qualify for a rebate a member state would have to be a *net* contributor to the budget: this immediately excluded Ireland and The Netherlands, which both benefited considerably from the CAP. Secondly, the state must have a rate of economic growth that was not more than 120 per cent of the Community's average; thirdly, the state must be experiencing a deficit on its balance of payments. The second and third of these criteria were designed to prevent prosperous states from claiming a rebate. If a state qualified under all these headings, its rebate would be calculated as the gap between its *total* payments to the budget and its percentage share of the Community's average GNP; but the refund could not exceed the country's VAT contributions, and would never be more than two-thirds of the total gap between its payments and its percentage of average GNP. Also, the gap between the state's percentage share of budgetary payments and its percentage share of the Community's average GNP would have to exceed 10 per cent of the share of GNP (e.g. a state that had a 14 per cent share of the average GNP of the Community would

[7] Ibid., 2 Nov. 1974.

have to pay more than 15.4 per cent of the total budget before it would qualify).[8]

The complexity of this formula was exceeded only by its ingeniousness as a means of squaring a circle. Nevertheless, it was not immediately acceptable to the British or the French. The British were unhappy about the requirement that a state have a balance of payments deficit in order to qualify for a rebate: the prospect of oil from the North Sea raised the possibility that Britain might escape from its perennial balance of payments deficits whilst retaining a comparatively weak manufacturing base. The French were not happy about conceding the principle that only VAT contributions were national contributions, even if the rebate formula did make an important concession in their direction.

So the question of budgetary contributions was one of two issues that Wilson took to the Dublin meeting of the European Council in March 1975. The other was the issue of access to the Community for New Zealand dairy produce.

The Dublin European Council

The institutionalization of summit meetings of the Heads of State and Government of the Community had been a proposal of President Giscard d'Estaing of France. He was a believer in informal meetings at the highest level, and hoped to use the new institution to give some direction and momentum to the Community. The idea was adopted, along with Giscard's proposal that direct elections to the European Parliament be scheduled, at the Paris summit in September 1974. Wilson accepted the proposals, although clearly far from happy with the second of them, in return for an understanding with the French President that agreement would be reached on renegotiated British terms of entry that could be sold to the British people. The architect of this agreement was Chancellor Schmidt of Germany, who pressed on Wilson the importance of gaining the agreement of the French during talks at Chequers in November 1974.

Given that Giscard wanted to present the first formal European Council as a success, and given that there was already an understanding that agreement would be reached on outstanding

[8] *Bulletin of the European Communities*, 1–1975, points 2506–10.

issues, Wilson's approach at Dublin was irritating to both Giscard and Schmidt. The British Prime Minister approached the meeting as being all about the finalization of British renegotiation demands, as indeed it turned out to be, because Wilson ensured that it was so. He made very strong statements about how he would accept no nonsense from the other member states on the two vital issues that remained to be agreed: the budgetary contributions and the access for New Zealand produce.

Of the two questions, the French and Germans failed entirely to understand how the latter could be termed an important issue, although there was a continuing disagreement. The British were insisting that the price paid by the Community for New Zealand butter be brought into line with the internal intervention price, in effect guaranteeing New Zealand farmers a return equal to that of EC farmers, and that the quantities that would be bought would continue at the same level after 1977 as had been originally agreed for the transitional period of British membership. The states that produced most of the Community's dairy produce naturally objected to this, as did the Germans, who would have to pay for any extra surpluses that resulted.

The suspicion amongst other member states was that Wilson was making this essentially minor issue into a major one for domestic political gain. The white Commonwealth countries were much more popular with the British people than was the EC, as opinion polls had repeatedly shown. In claiming to have forty-four relatives in New Zealand, Wilson was identifying himself with British people, particularly working-class people, many of whom had relatives who had emigrated to either New Zealand or Australia. It was a typical populist touch, and one made presumably with the forthcoming referendum campaign in mind.

The issue of budgetary contributions was also treated to a considerable amount of publicity. Wilson presented it as a battle in which a vital British national interest was at stake, and one which he meant to win. In fact, he settled for a formula that was almost identical to that proposed by the Commission in November, and knew in advance that he would win because the deal had already been set up before the Dublin summit. The point of the exercise was to present the Prime Minister as a 'St George' figure, who knew how to stand up to foreign dragons and would never sell his country short. This meant that when he recommended the renegotiated terms to the British people in the referendum campaign, and called for a 'yes' vote, he was not open to the charge from his opponents of having sold out British interests.

Although some of this was certainly understood by the other leaders, the extent to which Wilson insisted on the outstanding renegotiation issues dominating the agenda at Dublin, so that important international economic and political affairs could not be discussed, rankled, as did Wilson's attitude.

That same attitude had been evident in other interventions by the British Prime Minister in the renegotiations. For example, he told the Press after the Paris summit in September that he had informed his fellow statesmen that there was too much talk about harmonization, and that he had dismissed ideas for the creation of a 'Euroloaf' and 'Euro-beer', adding 'An imperial pint is good enough for me and for the British people, and we want it to stay that way.' In fact, as an anonymous official pointed out in a document that circulated in Community circles in November, the Commission's proposals for bread and beer were designed to set minimum European standards for exports and imports between member states, so as to prevent separate national standards being used as non-tariff barriers against trade. Britain stood to benefit from such measures, since one of the main offenders was West Germany, whose exacting purity standards for beer prevented British brewers from selling in the German market. There had never been any suggestion of forcing British pubs to sell beer in metric quantities rather than in the traditional pints and half-pints. That was a piece of anti-Community mischief dreamt up by the opponents of British membership, and relayed by the more gullible and ill-informed sections of the British Press. But instead of defending the Community against such a calumny, Wilson chose to treat the issue as if it were a serious one, and to present himself as having headed off an affront to national sensibilities.[9]

The Dublin meeting, then, added to the spirit of irritation and impatience with Britain that had been growing within the Community since soon after the arrival of the new member. Nevertheless, it did produce agreement on the two outstanding issues. New Zealand butter was to continue to be guaranteed access beyond 1977, something that Wilson was able to present as a major victory, and a study was to be made into the question of access for

[9] *The Economist*, 2 Nov. 1974.

New Zealand cheese. Also, a mechanism for calculating budgetary rebates was agreed, based closely on the Commission's proposals, but with the addition of a maximum limit to rebates of 250 million units of account, which met the West German demand for parsimony, and with an additional acknowledgement that an unacceptable situation could coexist with a balance of payments surplus, although in that case the rebate would be calculated solely on the basis of VAT payments. France made the biggest concession in arriving at the agreement, allowing contributions to be calculated to include customs duties and import levies, on condition that this would be only provisional, and that the system would be gradually amended to bring it into line with the French conviction that only VAT payments were properly national contributions.

Needless to say, Wilson did not dwell on the qualifications and exceptions when he outlined these agreements to the British Press. They were presented as an unequivocal acceptance of the British demands, a capitulation of the foreign dragons to the courage of the British champion. The next task was to gain the acceptance of the total package of renegotiated terms by the British people in the promised referendum.

The Referendum: The First Moves

The referendum campaign began before the renegotiated terms of entry were finalized. If this seems odd, it should be borne in mind that the issue was never really the terms. The opponents of membership were opposed whatever the terms; the advocates equally committed, including the pragmatists like Wilson and Callaghan. In a sense, the whole renegotiation exercise was part of the campaign to get the British people to accept membership of the Community in a manner that would be unequivocal, and decisive.

The idea of a referendum, a constitutional device that was alien to British practice, was first advocated by Tony Benn. It was initially supported by the left-wing opponents of membership, because they hoped to be able to appeal over the heads of the Party leaders to the nationalist prejudices of the British people. Some of the more conservative opponents of membership had doubts about the idea, because it was seen as a weakening of the authority of Parliament. Supporters of British membership, such as the social democrats within the Labour Cabinet, opposed the idea on ostensibly similar grounds, although in practice their main objection was that they feared the outcome would go against them. By November 1974 opinion polls were starting to run in favour of continued membership: a Harris poll showed 53 per cent of the population wanted Britain to remain in the Community 'on the right terms'.[10] Under these circumstances, most of the Labour supporters of membership began to forget their objections in principle to a referendum. In any case, the general election of October 1974 made it impractical to hold another election so soon afterwards.

Opponents of membership responded to the apparent change of mood in the country by attempting to take control of the Labour Party machine, in the hope of using it to mount an anti-membership campaign, and to force the supporters of continued membership to put themselves in opposition to the official line of the Party. Their first big push in this direction was at the annual Party Conference, which, because of the election, was held later than usual, at the end of November.

A fringe meeting at the Conference indicated how little the opponents cared about the precise terms of membership. Peter Shore stated that sovereignty was the heart of the matter, a theme that was to become increasingly prominent in the speeches of the anti-marketeers as it became obvious that they were unlikely to win the argument on the bread-and-butter issues that had been the subject of the renegotiation. Sovereignty, of course, was not negotiable. There was room for argument about how far membership meant a loss of sovereignty, and about whether sovereignty was a meaningful concept in the modern interdependent world; but whatever loss of sovereignty would occur, and even the supporters of membership were obliged to accept that there would be some such loss, the issue was no different under the Wilson/Callaghan terms that it had been under the Heath terms.

Clive Jenkins, the leader of the Association of Scientific, Technical, and Managerial Staffs (ASTMS), and a leading left-wing member of the Labour Party's National Executive Committee (NEC), baldly declared at this same meeting that 'the common market is politically, culturally and economically unacceptable' and promised that the trade unions would provide the 'muscle' (a favourite word in industrial relations at that time) to get Britain

[10] Ibid., 16 Nov. 1974.

out. He also argued that a special Party Conference should be held once the renegotiated terms were finalized, and that, if this Conference rejected the terms, 'every minister must be loyal to the Labour movement' and campaign against continued membership, or resign from the Cabinet.[11]

The November Conference went on to pass a hardline resolution opposing British membership. But on the final day there was a remarkable change of mood. Helmut Schmidt, the German Chancellor, addressed the Conference and pleaded with the Labour Party not to leave the Community in the interests of socialist solidarity. The speech was widely seen by the Press as a triumph. Schmidt flattered the British for their pragmatism, talked about the EC in hard-headed practical terms rather than employing the language of European union that was so disliked by most British politicians, and suggested to the Labour Party and the country that he was a friend who was asking them to stay in for his sake as much as their own.

Perhaps even more significant than Schmidt's address to the Labour Conference were his discussions with Wilson at Chequers over the remainder of that weekend. Butler and Kitzinger suggest that he here persuaded Wilson finally to come down from the fence on which he had been sitting for so long, and to declare, as he did on 7 December, that, were the renegotiation successful, he would recommend the British people to accept the terms.[12] However, the hard-faced attitude of the Labour left on the issue during the Conference, which had certainly upset the social democrats within the Government, may have contributed as much or more to Wilson's decision as Schmidt's blandishments.

Soon after Christmas the first public breaking of ranks by a Cabinet Minister occurred when Tony Benn, in a letter to his Bristol constituents, attacked continued British membership on the grounds that it removed sovereignty from the British Parliament. He was answered on 7 January by Roy Hattersley, speaking in Bristol, who poured scorn on the argument about sovereignty, and suggested that Britain's 'pursuit of total independence could well leave it with the right to have the lowest growth rate in western Europe'.[13]

---

[11] Ibid., 30 Nov. 1974.
[12] Butler and Kitzinger, *The 1975 Referendum*, p. 37.
[13] *The Economist*, 11 Jan. 1975.

Both Ministers were in breach of a Cabinet agreement not to campaign until the renegotiated terms were published, but it is difficult to believe that Hattersley acted on his own initiative. He was not a supporter of membership on principle, but one of what David Marquand had called the 'pragmatists';[14] and he was widely seen as a person who hesitated to stick his neck out lest he damage his ambitions. It seems most likely that the Prime Minister and the Foreign Secretary both knew of, and possibly prompted, the comments of the Minister for European Community Affairs.

Nevertheless, the incident showed clearly that there was little prospect of holding the Cabinet to the principle of collective responsibility, whatever the vote on the renegotiated terms. This view was reinforced a fortnight later, when Peter Shore made a weekend speech that painted a gloomy picture of Britain trapped inside an organization with which it had an expanding trade gap, and which condemned it to runaway food prices and an almost total loss of sovereignty. This speech so annoyed the supporters of membership that they threatened to break ranks also.

Recognizing, as he undoubtedly had for some time, that he was not going to be able to make collective Cabinet responsibility stick on the issue, Wilson announced in the Commons in January that there would indeed be a referendum, that it would be held no later than June, that the renegotiated terms would be published within the next few weeks, and that the Government would be making a recommendation to the British people on whether to accept the terms, but that individual members of the Government would be free to dissent from this view in public, and to campaign on the other side in the referendum debate.

The Referendum: The Parties' Positions

Once the terms were known, the parties had to take up their positions prior to the referendum. There was a vote in the Cabinet on 18 March 1975, followed by a vote in Parliament on 9 April, and a special Labour Party Conference on the issue on 26 April.

The vote in Cabinet was 16 to 7 in favour of acceptance of the renegotiated terms. Five Ministers who had been opposed to membership in 1971 had changed sides, notably Fred Peart, who at one time had been the leader of the Labour campaign to oppose

[14] David Marquand, *Parliament for Europe* (London, 1979), 7–10.

membership. The seven Cabinet Ministers against acceptance of the terms were Tony Benn, Barbara Castle, Michael Foot, Willie Ross, Peter Shore, John Silkin, and Eric Varley.[15]

When Parliament voted on the terms on 9 April, there was a clear majority of Labour MPs opposed to acceptance, 137 voting for, 145 against, and 33 abstaining. However, the vote went in favour of acceptance by 396 votes to 172, a larger majority than the Government was expecting, because of the support given by the opposition parties.[16] The Conservatives resisted the temptation to vote against in order to bring the Government down, and Margaret Thatcher, their new leader, 'took the opportunity of the debate to reiterate the Conservative commitment to the Community under her leadership, and gave as her three principal reasons peace for security, guaranteed food supplies and a future world role for Britain'.[17]

Only eight out of 275 Conservative MPs voted against acceptance of the new terms, with a further eighteen abstaining. The Liberals were even more unified, with twelve out of their thirteen MPs voting for the Government, the other not voting. The nationalist parties (Scottish Nationalist Party (SNP) and Plaid Cymru) were as solid in the opposite direction: thirteen out of fourteen voted against, one not voting. Only six of the ten Ulster Unionists voted, all against the Government.[18]

Despite the solidity of the Conservative vote in Parliament, the whole issue of Community membership continued to cause doubts in some quarters in the party, and Conservative MP Neil Marten was a leading figure in the campaign for a 'no' vote in the referendum. Former Conservative MP Enoch Powell, by 1975 an Ulster Unionist but still highly respected amongst Conservative Party members in mainland Britain, was also very prominent in the campaign against continued membership.

But Labour was undoubtedly the most divided of the political parties, as had been evident for some time. The point was underlined at the special Party Conference at the end of April when the opponents of membership, backed by the block votes of the big

[15] Harold Wilson, *Final Term: The Labour Government, 1974–6* (London, 1979), 103.

[16] Butler and Kitzinger, *The 1975 Referendum*, p. 52; Wilson, *Final Term*, p. 105.

[17] Ashford, 'The Conservative Party and European Integration', fo. 314.

[18] Butler and Kitzinger, *The 1975 Referendum*, p. 52.

trade unions, won a two-to-one victory for rejection of the terms. The country thus witnessed the spectacle of a Labour Government recommending to the people in a referendum a line of action that it was official Labour Party policy to oppose. Nor was it only because of the antiquated system of trade unions' block votes that the Conference came out against continued membership: the constituency party representatives voted three-to-one against.[19]

Having obtained the backing of the Conference for opposition to their own Government, the leading critics of membership then attempted to capture the Labour Party electoral machinery to campaign against membership, but this move was quashed by the General Secretary of the Party, Ron Hayward, who stated unequivocally that the Party had no money for a campaign.

In the event the campaign was conducted by two umbrella groups: Britain in Europe, and the rather less obviously named National Referendum Campaign.

The Referendum: The Official Campaign

When the referendum campaign proper began, the tone was scarcely elevated. As Michael Steed has observed:

On both sides, the committed would have liked a political debate about patriotism, sovereignty and federalism, which is what had moved them to work hard for many years to get Britain into Europe, or keep it from the clutches of Brussels. But, especially on the pro-Community side, practical politicians and campaigners moved in to steer a debate in which prices, income levels and economic security dominated. The ... federalist leadership of the European Movement was manœuvred out of the way ... The familiar bread and butter issues of a British general election took top place in the minds of the publicity men and in the answers pollsters obtained about what the referendum question meant.[20]

The media also played their part in trivializing the campaign. Although some sections of the Press endeavoured to discuss the issues, they focused primarily on those described by Steed as 'the familiar bread and butter issues'. This was partly because the issue of sovereignty was complex, and difficult to deal with in a manner deemed appropriate to the readership of the more popular newspapers. But there was also a suspicion amongst the opponents

[19] *The Economist*, 3 May 1975.
[20] Michael Steed, 'The Landmarks of the British Referendum', *Parliamentary Affairs*, 30 (1977), 130–1.

of continued membership that the low level of attention given to the issue reflected the generally pro-Community sentiments of the Press. It was the supporters of entry who wished to concentrate on the mundane issues, because here the renegotiated terms could be presented as having met many of the doubts expressed by the Labour leadership at the time of entry.

In fact, it is difficult to see that the renegotiation had achieved anything fundamental so far as matters such as the price of food were concerned. But the CAP, which the opponents of membership continued to attempt to present as a device for guaranteeing high prices, was no longer seen in such an unfavourable light because of the coincidence that world food prices had risen above the level of EC intervention prices, so that the defenders of membership could make the point that food would actually be more expensive outside the Community than inside it. The message presented was that 'the era of cheap food is over'.

Perhaps even more importantly, large sections of the media came inevitably to focus on the personalities involved rather than on the issues. Here the pro-membership forces had a distinct advantage. The opponents of membership were a motley collection, ranging from the extreme right to the extreme left of the political spectrum. Not only were Tony Benn and Enoch Powell odd allies; the campaign for a 'no' vote was supported by the British Communist Party, almost all of the Trotskyist and Maoist groups that were left over from the 1960s, and the National Front. Collectively they formed an easy target for satirists.

Against that, so did the most ardent proponents of entry. Philip Goodhart quotes 'an unkind *Daily Telegraph* columnist' as saying that 'the campaign managers of Britain in Europe looked as though they had lunched well at the Savoy'.[21] It was a theme that the opponents of membership tried to exploit: that it was the establishment which wanted Britain in the Community. But the Press was less inclined to stress that side of the 'personalities' argument than it was the eccentric nature of the leading figures in the National Referendum Campaign.

In the final analysis, a lot of British people appear to have cast their votes in the referendum on the strength of the support given to continued membership by figures with proven experience of

[21] Philip Goodhart, *Full-hearted Consent: The Story of the Referendum Campaign—and the Campaign for the Referendum* (London, 1976), 119.

government. Comparative analysis of the referendum results in Norway in 1972 and Britain in 1975 has suggested that in both cases voters tended to follow the guidance of the leading figures in their parties. The British voting showed Conservative and Liberal voters following their parties' lead and voting overwhelmingly 'yes'. The most divided voters were those who had voted Labour at the previous election, but even amongst them there was a small majority voting 'yes', indicating the impression made by the fact that the party leader himself favoured a vote in that direction.[22]

The impressive solidarity of the leading establishment figures behind membership reinforced the effect of the vote being for the status quo and therefore essentially conservative, a point emphasized by Butler and Kitzinger.

The referendum was not a vote cast for new departures or bold initiatives. It was a vote for the *status quo*. Those who had denounced referenda as instruments of conservatism may have been right. The public is usually slow to authorize change; the anti-Marketeers would have had a far better chance of winning a referendum on whether to go in than one on whether to stay in. Before entry, to vote for going in would have been to vote radically. But after entry, it was at least as radical and unsettling to vote for leaving . . . the verdict was not even necessarily a vote of confidence that things would be better in than out; it may have been no more than an expression of fear that things would be worse out than in.[23]

Whatever the reasons, the outcome of the campaign was an unexpectedly high 'yes' vote of 17,378,581 against a 'no' vote of 8,470,073; a division in percentage terms of 67.2 to 32.8, on a high turnout of 64.6 per cent. It was a landslide result, which produced, as the Prime Minister pointed out, a bigger majority than had ever been received by any government in any general election.[24] On the other hand, to quote Butler and Kitzinger again, 'the verdict of the referendum . . . was unequivocal but it was also unenthusiastic. Support for membership was wide but it did not run deep.'[25] Nor was it to mark a new era in British relations with the EC, as many people in other parts of the Community had hoped that it would.

[22] Roy Pierce, Henry Valen, and Ola Listhaug, 'Referendum Voting Behaviour: The Norwegian and British Referenda on Membership in the European Community', *American Journal of Political Science*, 27 (1983), 43–63.

[23] Butler and Kitzinger, *The 1975 Referendum*, p. 280.

[24] Wilson, *Final Term*, p. 108.

[25] Butler and Kitzinger, *The 1975 Referendum*, p. 280.

Post-Referendum

If there was an expectation that British behaviour would change dramatically after the referendum, it was soon disappointed. Wilson made it clear at the European Council meeting in Brussels in July that his Government would continue to stand up for national interests 'no more and no less than our EEC partners'.[26] This apparently reasonable statement was treated by the Brussels press corps as negative, although it was only so in the light of hopes for a new British crusade to unite Europe, that were hardly realistic on any objective review of the evidence.

Callaghan and Wilson had campaigned for the acceptance of the renegotiated terms on pragmatic grounds, not just because they believed that this was the best way to ensure their acceptance by the British electorate, but also because that was how they saw the Community themselves. Callaghan had shown his impatience with the rhetoric of European union, which came so easily to the lips of the representatives of many of the original member states, when he had refused to allow the term to be incorporated into the European declaration on NATO (one of the two declarations that eventually resulted from Kissinger's Year of Europe initiative) in June 1974. He had given the same message in October, when he had insisted that the Paris meeting of the European Council should have a predominantly economic agenda, and should not waste its time with discussion of European union. Leopards do not change their spots, whatever the outcome of referenda.

Nor had the political constraints facing Wilson and Callaghan changed much. Certainly the referendum result gave a boost to Wilson's authority, and enabled him to reshuffle his Cabinet so as to reduce the influence of the left. However, the moving of Tony Benn from Industry to Energy was hardly welcome within the EC, where the problem of energy was high on the agenda. As feared, Benn continued to act in an obstructionist manner in the Council of Ministers, despite the result, and to parade his hostility to the EC. On one occasion he publicly boasted that he had kept a Council of Energy Ministers waiting while he attended a local Labour Party meeting, a sense of priorities so bizarre as to suggest a calculated

---

[26] Gerald Segal, 'Unanswered Questions at Wilson's Summit', *Spectator*, 26 July 1975, p. 108.

insult to the Council. Peter Shore also appears to have acted in an obstructionist manner within the Council of Trade Ministers.[27]

That the opponents of membership were not prepared to accept a democratic decision against them even when it was overwhelming was indicated by the relaunching of the Labour Common Market Safeguards Committee in November 1975. It was sponsored by some fifty Labour MPs and trade unionists, including Benn, Shore, and Barbara Castle, and pledged itself to keep a vigilant watch on the ill-effects of Community membership on Britain. Later, in February 1976, Labour MPs were prominent in the launching of the Safeguard Britain Campaign, 'to combat European federalism and stop progress to direct elections to the European parliament'.[28]

Faced with such continued hostility to the EC within his own party, Wilson could not have been expected to change his spots even had he been capable of it and willing to do so. During the latter part of 1975 Britain found itself once more cast in the role of awkward partner in the Community on a range of issues, including measures to control pollution, the limitation of lorry drivers' hours, and the British approach to making claims from the ERDF.

The issue of pollution control concerned emissions of chemicals and other effluents into rivers. The Commission proposed maximum emission limits; the British maintained that these were inappropriate for Britain, which as an island had faster-flowing rivers that could clear pollution more quickly than could the rivers of the continental land mass, and could therefore take more effluent. There was some validity in this argument: because Britain and Ireland are islands they differ from their continental partners on a whole range of environmental and health issues. On the other hand, the suspicion in Brussels and other national capitals was that the British Government had been influenced by the chemical industry, which had balked at the cost of implementing the Commission's proposals. Yet it was precisely the cost which was the major issue for competitors of Britain's chemical industry, particularly West Germany. If British firms were allowed to get away with laxer emission standards, they would be given a price advantage over their continental competitors. Eventually the British case was accepted, but the incident left a bad taste.

The issue of limitations on lorry drivers' hours was a similarly minor matter which nevertheless helped to dissipate whatever fund

[27] *The Economist*, 27 Dec. 1975.   [28] Ibid., 7 Feb. 1976.

of goodwill Wilson might have managed to build up as a result of his success in swinging the referendum vote. The Commission had proposed, and the Transport Council had accepted, a reduction in the maximum number of hours that lorry drivers could drive in a day from ten to eight. This road-safety measure was due to be implemented on 1 January 1976. Britain was the only member state not to have passed the necessary domestic legislation by then. This was hardly unexpected, because nobody had done anything about drawing up the legislation pending the referendum result. But again the difference in national requirements appeared to give a competitive advantage to Britain for as long as it persisted, because the reduction in hours would inevitably increase domestic freight costs. British goods could be transported as far as the ports at lower cost than the products of industry in the other member states for as long as the British legislation remained out of line.

On the matter of claims from the ERDF, the accusation against Britain was that it was making claims for projects that would have been funded anyway from the available British funds for regional development. The guidelines for the ERDF indicated quite clearly that the projects put forward must be additional to any that were to be funded nationally. Other claimants had submitted a range of projects to the Fund Committee for consideration. But Britain submitted only enough projects to take up a proportion of its allocation of ERDF monies, and the suspicion was that most or all of these would have been nationally funded anyway. Here bureaucratic politics may have been at play: the Treasury had been trying to ensure for some time that the ERDF would save, not cost it money. New projects would cost the Treasury because the European funds were allocated only up to 50 per cent of the cost of projects, and the rest had to be found nationally. The Scottish, Welsh, and Northern Ireland Offices, and the Department of Industry, had opposed the Treasury's line. The dispute had delayed an application being made until the deadline of mid-August, and the application contained no indication that the projects were additional to national plans.

Again the issue was a relatively minor one, but again it indicated a lack of Community spirit to the other member states. The cumulative effect of such minor issues should not be underestimated. Nor should the intangible factor of the attitude of British representatives in the various meetings of the Council of Ministers.

With the exception of Fred Peart at Agriculture, who soon became adept at the peculiarities of EC diplomacy, the Ministerial representatives were either openly hostile to the Community or appeared to be unenthusiastic. This stricture applied right up to the highest levels, with Callaghan's attitude being described by one observer thus:

> the Foreign Secretary's hectoring manner in the Council of Ministers would conspire to lose even a cast-iron case. He's a man to whom rudeness comes naturally in formal negotiations, and is much resented for it. In presentational terms his arguments in the council are frequently disastrous.[29]

Another felt 'that folksiness which serves him so well in internal Labour Party disputes is hardly a subtle instrument of foreign policy—he conceals [by simplification] rather than clarifies the strategic importance of diplomatic issues'.[30]

Whether these criticisms were entirely fair or not, the other Foreign Ministers do seem to have had some difficulty in relating to Callaghan's direct and simple approach to complex questions. It also appears to have been the Foreign Secretary who led his Government and Prime Minister into the single major episode that did more to sour relations between Britain and the rest of the Community than all the others during the latter part of 1975: the dispute over representation at the North–South Conference in Paris.

The Energy Problem

Energy policy had been a problem for British relations with the rest of the Community under Heath's Government, and the first signs of some movement in the position of Lord Carrington, the Tory Secretary of State for Energy, were just becoming apparent when the change of Government came in 1974.

The arrival of Labour in office also coincided with a split within the Community over how to respond to US proposals for dealing with the world's energy crisis. At the Washington Energy Conference in February 1974 the United States proposed a package of measures including co-operation on energy conservation and

---

[29] David Haworth, 'The Odd Man Out of Europe', *New Statesman*, 24 Oct. 1975, p. 494.

[30] Patrick Cosgrave, 'Where is our European Policy?', *Spectator*, 15 Nov. 1975, p. 622.

restraint of demand, the development of new sources of oil, accelerated research and development of alternative forms of energy supply, and agreement on the sharing of oil in a crisis. Eight of the nine member states of the Community were prepared to go along with these proposals, but the French objected that the stance was confrontational towards the producers of oil, and prior to the conference Jobert, still French Foreign Minister at that time, pressed for the Community to have nothing to do with US attempts to assume leadership of the oil consumers and to concentrate instead on the Euro–Arab dialogue as the way forward. Jobert's wrecking tactics at Washington led him into sharp public exchanges with the German Finance Minister, Helmut Schmidt. On this issue of Atlantic solidarity the British and Germans found themselves on the same side despite the recent history of coolness in their bilateral relations.

At the conference, agreement was reached to set up the IEA, which France refused to join. Yet the approach adopted by the member states of the EC in general was much closer to that preferred by France than to that advocated by the United States. Joan Spero described the responses thus:

After the Washington conference, the United States, the Europeans, and the Japanese went their own ways. The United States tried to destroy producer unity and to divide the rest of the Third World from OPEC ... The Europeans sought special bilateral political and economic arrangements with the oil producers and resisted consumer bloc strategies. France, the strongest opponent of the American approach, refused to join the IEA and urged instead a producer–consumer dialogue.[31]

The French approach survived the change of Government in Paris, and it was this long-advocated dialogue that was to commence with the Paris conference in December 1975. At the insistence of the producers, the remit had been enlarged to cover more generally the relations of the industrial states of the northern hemisphere with the predominantly underdeveloped states of the southern hemisphere. The whole process therefore came to be known as the North–South dialogue.

But the EC approached the conference without a coherent energy policy of its own. The split over membership of the IEA had led the Commission to redouble its efforts to gain acceptance of some

[31] Spero, *The Politics of International Economic Relations*, pp. 305–6.

policy, but in this it had been singularly unsuccessful. A request to the British Government for a paper outlining its position on the forging of a common policy produced, in May 1974, a document that echoed strongly the sentiments repeatedly expressed during Heath's premiership on this vexed question. Although the Ministry of Energy was now presided over by Eric Varley and Lord Balogh, two figures thought to be left of centre, even if not in the Benn camp, the paper argued that there was no need for a Community policy on energy supply because the oil companies could be trusted to smooth out local supply difficulties, and to plough back profits into research and development of alternative resources. Thanks to the actions of the oil companies, the market for oil was asserted to have 'historically been far more orderly than other commodity markets';[32] and the companies were seen to have done a good job of distributing available supplies during the partial boycott in 1973.

The reason for left-leaning Ministers allowing such a paean of praise to be forwarded in the name of their Ministry may not have been entirely the influence of their officials, who had shown themselves to be closely aligned with the oil companies in the past in resisting all attempts at regulation, but may have been an expression of the Labour Party's determination to keep Brussels' nose out of the matter, especially because of the imminence of North Sea oil production.

Although the Commission leant over backwards to accommodate British objections to any effective controls being put on the production and distribution of oil, in order to get agreement on at least an outline energy policy, its efforts received a further upset at a meeting of the Council of Foreign Ministers in July 1974, when Peter Shore, in the absence of Callaghan and Hattersley who were tied up in dealing with the crisis caused by the Turkish invasion of Cyprus, blocked a declaration committing the Nine to a common stance on energy. Shore's statement that more time was needed for the British Government to consider the implications annoyed even the Dutch, who had been Britain's closest allies on the question of oil. The British were accused of going back on undertakings already given, and more of their scarce renegotiation capital was dissipated. Commission officials told themselves that this was merely an act of sabotage by Shore, but it seems more likely that Shore was making a point on behalf of the Labour Government—although eventually

[32] *The Economist*, 11 May 1975.

the statement was accepted, by Callaghan at a meeting in September.

Nevertheless, little progress had been made on agreeing the policy to which the declaration committed the Nine by the time that the Paris conference appeared on the immediate horizon in early 1975. It was in February that Callaghan first made the statement that was later to harden into a doggedly held principle, that Britain as an oil producer could not accept that it would not have separate representation at the conference.

The French had agreed with the oil producers that the number of the participants in the conference would be limited, and that only three of these would represent the rich oil-consuming nations. France was proposing that the three seats be occupied by Japan, the United States, and the EC. Callaghan declared that Britain was not prepared to be represented by the Community. At the time the incident caused annoyance, but it was assumed that the statement was an initial bargaining position from which Britain would shift once it had got certain concessions on the nature of the Community's delegation and the position that it would adopt.

But by October 1975 the British position had not shifted. By that time the number of seats allocated to industrial states had increased to nine, against eighteen for the non-industrial states, but France was still proposing a single seat for the EC. Callaghan's repetition of his point that Britain was about to become an oil producer, and could not therefore be expected to allow itself to be represented by a group of states which were oil consumers, only led again to a split with the Dutch, who pointed out that their production of natural gas made them currently the leading exporter of energy within the Community, so they could claim a separate seat too, with more justification, but they were not doing so. What made the restatement of Callaghan's original position particularly galling was that the other states had understood that he had dropped the demand in the summer, which Callaghan denied having done.

Soon after this, Helmut Schmidt circulated a letter to all the other Heads of Government of the EC in which he stated that Germany was not prepared to go on indefinitely subsidizing the rest of the Community if others could not exercise restraint, and act in a manner that was *communautaire*. He especially singled out Wilson for displeasure, and asked him to think again about the separate seat at the Paris conference. The British, Schmidt asserted, could not expect Germany to go on paying for EC policies that helped Britain if they carried on with their defiant stand on this issue.

In fact, as Ian Davidson pointed out at the time, Britain's position was out of line with its general attitude of enthusiastic support for a joint European approach to world problems, especially economic problems. The argument that Britain had different interests from the other member states because of North Sea oil seemed spurious. The strongest British interest was in seeing a stable price established which would be accepted by consumers and producers alike. Also, the conference was not just a conference on energy: its title was 'Conference on International Economic Co-operation' (CIEC), and it covered, in addition to energy, raw materials, development aid, finance, and investment. On none of these issues did Britain have any real differences from the other EC member states. All of which left a number of questions unanswered:

why did the government embark on this ludicrous crusade in the first place? To try and woo Scottish voters away from the SNP? A knee-jerk of nationalism? Or simply that the government is so overwhelmed by the press of economic and political events at home over which it appears to have lost any effective control, that decisions on foreign policy questions are adopted without forethought and clung to without purpose?[33]

It seems that Callaghan's revival of the demand for a separate seat in October 1975 may have been an example of the last circumstance suggested by Davidson, and it was suggested that Wilson did not realize how far his Foreign Secretary was boxing him into a corner on the issue. At the European Council meeting in Rome in December, Wilson came under heavy fire from Schmidt, who is reported to have shouted at the British Prime Minister at one stage, and to have pointed out quite ruthlessly that Britain, with one of the weakest economies in the Community, was hardly in a position to negotiate on such issues without heed to the consequences.

In the face of such a determined assault, Wilson gave way and accepted that Britain would be represented by the EC delegation, in return for an assurance that the Community would argue in favour of a minimum floor-price for oil, which was the main British demand that some of the other member states were unhappy about.

[33] Ian Davidson, 'The Ludicrous Oil Crusade', *Spectator*, 1 Nov. 1975, p. 564.

It was also agreed that Callaghan would be allowed to make a brief statement as part of the EC's introductory remarks. And that appeared to be that. Britain had obtained what it mainly wanted, although later in the day than it could have, and at the cost of more of its scarce goodwill with other member states. The whole episode had been handled badly, and it is difficult to see any good reason for this other than stubbornness on the part of the Foreign Secretary. But that stubbornness extended further, because when Callaghan came to make his promised contribution to the opening remarks of the Community's delegation at the Paris conference he went on for twelve minutes, rather than the two minutes allocated, and emphasized in his comments the failure of the Community to arrive at a common policy on energy, without mentioning that this owed more than a little to the attitude of the British Government.

Naturally, the intervention enraged other members of the Community; yet in a way it was a fitting conclusion to what had been a very bad year for Britain's reputation within the EC.

Conclusion

In March 1976 Harold Wilson resigned as Prime Minister, stating that he had never intended to serve for more than two years when he assumed office in February 1974, and that he felt it was time for him to give somebody else a chance as leader of the Labour Party. The somebody else who was elected by the Parliamentary Labour Party was James Callaghan, who was actually older than Wilson.

It was as good a time as any for Wilson to step down. He had led the country through the renegotiation and referendum, and, although there were formidable problems ahead, at least one stage had been achieved in the process of bringing Britain back from the low point that it had reached in the winter of 1973–4. There was no longer any room for doubt about whether the country would remain a member of the EC, and with North Sea oil on the immediate horizon the prospects for his successor were rather better than those that had faced Wilson when he assumed office two years earlier.

Most of those two years had been spent in pursuing a policy towards the Community that was driven by the imperatives of domestic politics. The need to hold the Labour Party and the country together had dictated the sometimes aggressive tone of the renegotiation. Some further damage had been done to the reputation of Britain with its Community partners, but there had been general relief within the EC when the referendum result went in favour of continued membership.

The continued awkwardness of Britain after the referendum was something of a disappointment to the other member states of the Community, but it was no more than a continuation of the same attitude and approach that had been dominant during 1973, under Heath. Despite the inclination of the Press to attribute these attitudes to the political leaders, their persistence under different Governments suggests that at least in part they were also a reflection of the attitudes of permanent officials, although the complexities of bureaucratic politics, the interplay of attitudes between officials and politicians, and between different Departments of State, is something that we cannot investigate properly until thirty years after the events, when official records are opened to public scrutiny, and perhaps not even then given the inherent incompleteness of the written record.

The circumstantial evidence suggests that the renegotiation was perhaps conducted in a more sympathetic manner than some of the routine negotiations between Britain and the rest of the Community, precisely because it was a highly visible and politicized process, which had to reach a favourable outcome. Although the tone was at times deliberately confrontational, the outcome was never seriously in doubt. In the disagreements that came after the renegotiation, there was no certainty that the British representatives were prepared to accept any compromise agreement if they felt that they were in the right, nor that politicians would intervene to ensure that agreement was reached.

This underlying reluctance to agree on steps forward for the Community was perhaps more damaging to Britain's relations with the EC than the very special circumstances of the renegotiation. The other member states could at least understand the reasons for the renegotiation in a way that they could not understand British attitudes on pollution levels or energy.

The association of Callaghan with the tiresome dispute over the separate seat for Britain at the Paris conference, combined with memories of his dogged approach during the renegotiation, did not make him a particularly popular choice within the EC as Wilson's successor. Nevertheless, Callaghan was to prove a more active premier than Wilson in Community affairs, and especially in the wider international arena, where Britain emerged under his leadership from beneath the shadow of the Franco–German axis and began to play a more central role in efforts to co-ordinate the recovery of the capitalist world from recession.

4. The Callaghan Government, 1976–1979

ALTHOUGH when Callaghan became Prime Minister in March 1976 conditions were better than they had been in 1974, the British and world economies were still experiencing difficulties in recovering fully from the recession that the 1973 rise in the price of oil had precipitated. Callaghan had to tackle his domestic economic problems with a fragile majority in the House of Commons, which continued to diminish until early 1977, when it disappeared altogether, leaving him with a minority Government that was only able to survive because of support from the Liberals. He also had to contend with growing disaffection with his economic policies from the left of the Party, and at the international level to deal with a growing split between the United States and the Franco–German alliance on how to handle the world economy. Domestic political constraints and international economic objectives came together to mould the positions taken up by the British Government on each of the European issues which arose during the period of Callaghan's premiership.

The International Context

During the period of Callaghan's Government the differences grew wider between the United States on the one hand, and France and Germany on the other, on how to manage the international system. The economic summits that had been initiated by Giscard in 1975 continued to operate as a forum for co-ordinating policy responses, but Helmut Schmidt in particular found it increasingly difficult to accept that the United States was exercising responsible leadership. In these circumstances, the Franco–German inclination was to move ahead to adopt European solutions, particularly to monetary problems, whereas Callaghan emerged as an advocate of continued Atlantic co-operation and as a mediator between the EC and the United States.

The Ford Administration in the United States was marked by a degree of confusion in its foreign policy: 'it was often unclear by whom—and in the light of which guiding principles—United States foreign policy was being made in the years 1974–76.'[1] It was in response to this confusion that Giscard proposed the Rambouillet summit. Ford was reluctant to participate, but allowed himself to be persuaded by Schmidt. He subsequently, in May 1976, proposed a second summit himself, to be held in June 1976 in Puerto Rico. There was considerable scepticism in Europe about the need for another summit so soon after Rambouillet, and particularly about the inadequate time allowed for preparation between the proposal and the holding of the meeting. The move was seen as related to the US presidential election which was due in the autumn of 1976, and the West Germans, with elections themselves in the same year, were prepared to play along with this.

Although the summit produced the sort of press coverage that President Ford obviously wanted—'Summit Leaders Endorse Ford's Economic Policy' read one US newspaper headline[2]—it did not enable him to win the election. The arrival in office of the Democrat Jimmy Carter caused even more problems and tensions with the French and Germans.

Carter himself, and several of his closest officials, including his National Security Advisor Zbigniew Brzezinski, had been members of a private organization known as the 'Trilateral Commission', which was committed to the view that the international system had to be managed by co-operation between the United States, Japan, and Western Europe. Carter declared that co-ordination of policy with his country's allies would be a basic principle of his presidency. But the new Administration also had definite ideas about the basis on which co-ordination would occur. In economic policy, for example, the United States advocated a 'locomotive' theory of the way in which the world could be pulled out of recession. It involved the economies with balance of payments surpluses, primarily Japan and Germany, doing the pulling, by expanding demand so as to allow economies with trade deficits to

---

[1] M. H. Smith and R. Carey, 'The Nixon Legacy and American Foreign Policy', *Yearbook of World Affairs*, 32 (1978), 41.

[2] Robert Putnam, 'The Western Economic Summits: A Political Interpretation', in Merlini (ed.), *Economic Summits and Western Decision-making*, ch. 2; p. 76.

boost their exports to them. The Germans and Japanese were less than enthusiastic about this approach. For the Germans in particular it seemed to imply taking risks with the rate of inflation in order to stimulate demand, the reversal of a long-held policy preference.

Another US policy initiative helped relations to get off to a bad start. Carter, in an attempt to stop the proliferation of nuclear materials, suggested that Germany and France should cancel contracts that they had signed to supply nuclear power stations to Brazil and Pakistan. This issue caused friction in the run-up to the London economic summit of May 1977, and, although a compromise was reached whereby the existing contracts would be honoured but France and Germany undertook not to seek any further such contracts, the ill-will generated by the episode helped ensure that Carter's 'locomotive' would make little headway. All that emerged from the London summit in the way of a co-ordination of policy was a statement of targets for national rates of growth for 1977: for the United States the target was 5.8 per cent of GNP, for Japan 6.7 per cent, and for West Germany 5 per cent. In the event only the United States came anywhere near fulfilling this target, and Germany and Japan took no steps to make up the shortfall, which in Germany's case (with an actual rate of 2.6 per cent) was considerable.

Schmidt and Carter also clashed at the London summit over the US policy of allowing the dollar to depreciate in value on the international exchanges. This was having adverse effects on Germany because a lot of the liquid assets that were leaving the dollar were moving into the Deutschmark, forcing up its value. This was making German exports less competitive in comparison with US exports.

The decline in the value of the dollar continued, and indeed accelerated during the rest of 1977, as the US economy expanded more rapidly than the rest of the industrialized capitalist world, sucking in imports without a corresponding expansion of exports, and pushing the balance of payments into serious deficit. Although some corrective measures were taken at the start of 1978, these were largely ineffective. The main European leaders were becoming more and more worried by the deteriorating prospects for economic growth in the face of persistently high rates of unemployment, and Schmidt in particular was 'exasperated that the

United States Government seemed preoccupied with viewing economic policy through domestic eyes only'.[3]

This growing impatience with the US Administration's approach to international economic matters was compounded by political differences. Carter's introduction of the defence of human rights as a basic principle of US foreign policy was one issue that caused unease. Although the French and Germans were in favour of human rights being respected, they felt that adoption of the ideal as a policy commitment threatened to damage the progress that had been made in relations with the Soviet Union. In this respect they had been much happier with Henry Kissinger's *Realpolitik*, which had stressed the need to achieve a balance of power in international affairs, and had been content to treat such matters as human rights as being the internal affairs of other states. This approach had been strongly criticized within the United States, and the Congress had forced on to Kissinger a number of deviations from the line, through such means as the Jackson–Vanik Amendment, which linked US trade credits for the USSR to Soviet concessions on human rights. Carter was responding to this sentiment in US public opinion, but the Germans were worried about the uncertainty that it brought into East–West relations. 'The SPD-led Government, which had risked so much to achieve a relaxation of tension within Europe and concrete gains for ethnic Germans, was not prepared to have these achievements threatened by an American President, whose primary motive appeared to be public opinion at home'.[4]

That it was not just the Germans who were concerned was clear when Giscard d'Estaing told *Newsweek* magazine, in an interview in July 1977, that he felt the United States had unilaterally changed the rules of *détente* by linking improved East–West relations with Soviet respect for human rights.[5]

By the end of 1977 Carter had retreated from this emphasis on human rights in relations with the Soviet Union in the face of criticism from the United States' European allies. Policy did not, however, become more predictable. In April 1978 the President announced his decision not to produce the enhanced radiation warhead ('neutron bomb') for deployment in Western Europe as a

[3] James Callaghan, *Time and Chance* (London, 1987), 488.
[4] Gebhard Schweigler, 'Carter's *détente* Policy: Change or Continuity?' *World Today*, 34 (1978), 87.
[5] J. L. S. Girling, 'Carter's Foreign Policy: Realism or Ideology?' *World Today*, 33 (1977), 423.

counter to the increased mechanized strength of the Warsaw Pact's forces. This led to accusations that the United States was unmindful of the needs of its allies, whom the President had failed to consult, and that Carter had capitulated to a Soviet propaganda campaign.[6] Just before this incident, on 23 March 1978, Callaghan had visited Carter in Washington with new proposals for economic co-ordination. He had outlined his ideas to a domestic audience at a Finance Houses Association dinner on 14 March, when he had elaborated a five-point plan for economic regeneration including joint commitments on policies to promote economic growth, energy policies to conserve supplies, trade expansion to help guard against protectionism, increased capital flows to developing countries, and promotion of currency stability through the agency of the IMF. These were the ideas which he now took with him to Washington, in the hope of bridging the growing gap between Carter and Schmidt.

His view was that since the international economic system was now integrated to a high degree, a successful approach to its problems required the participation of all its leading members. He used the analogy of a 'convoy' moving together to describe this approach, as opposed to the earlier suggestion . . . that the strong economies, by increasing their growth, should act as 'locomotives' to drag forward the weaker ones.[7]

Callaghan was encouraged by Carter's response to his plan, and when he returned he immediately reported to Schmidt, who, however, remained 'pessimistic that anything would result'.[8] It subsequently appeared that Schmidt had already hatched a scheme for a European initiative to restore monetary stability, and was about to discuss it with Giscard. This emerged as the proposal for a European Monetary System (EMS), which is discussed later in this chapter.

Callaghan persisted with his attempts to formulate a response to international economic problems that would fully involve the United States, and his five-point plan was closely examined within the OECD. It was also taken on to the agenda of the officials who were preparing for the next economic summit in Bonn in July 1978. Schmidt was quite prepared to support this effort, although he

[6] Robert McGeehan, 'American Policies and the US–Soviet Relationship', *World Today*, 34 (1978), 349–50.

[7] Jocelyn Statler, 'British Foreign Policy to 1985: The European Monetary System: From Conception to Birth', *International Affairs*, 55 (1979), 207–8.

[8] Callaghan, *Time and Chance*, p. 492.

remained sceptical of the prospects for Carter turning over a new leaf in his economic policies, especially as US commitments that were made in the IMF in April to reduce imports of oil and to increase short-term interest rates produced no effective action before the summit. Because of his scepticism, Schmidt continued to press the EMS scheme strongly as a complementary approach, although most observers saw it as an alternative.

The Bonn summit was in fact surprisingly successful. A whole series of commitments was entered into in line with Callaghan's 'convoy' approach. In return for US promises on anti-inflation measures, efforts to reduce its imports of oil, and action to bring its domestic price for oil up to world levels by 1980, Schmidt agreed to submit to the Bundestag within six weeks expansionist measures equivalent to 1 per cent of GNP. All the other participant states also committed themselves to specific action as part of the overall programme, with the most far-reaching measures being required of Japan.

Not only were commitments made: they were honoured. The programme was the most successful effort at international co-ordination to date, and it could have had mutually beneficial effects had a second oil crisis not broken out within a few months of the summit. The events that provoked the crisis began in Iran at the end of 1978, and, after causing what at first appeared to be temporary disruptions in the supply of oil, culminated in the announcement by OPEC of a sharp increase in the price of oil in March 1979, just at the time that the Callaghan Government was losing office at the polls.

The Domestic Context

When Callaghan took over, British economic indicators were looking optimistic:

There had been no known breaches of the pay policy, and average earnings had risen by 7.5 per cent in the first six months of its operation, compared with over 12 per cent in the previous six months. Over the same period to February, prices (excluding seasonal food) had risen by 6.7 per cent, which was under half the increase in the previous six months. World trade had picked up as expected, and the economy was experiencing an export-led recovery. Output was rising at a rate of about 2.5 per cent a year, which was expected to lead before long to an end to the fall in employment, which by then was some 400,000 below its 1974 peak. Unemployment was over

1.2 million and still rising—but by around 10,000 a month compared with 30,000 a month a year earlier. The exchange rate had remained stable since November, and interest rates fell about 2 per cent in the first quarter.[9]

Yet within weeks of taking over Callaghan faced a sterling crisis. It began before Wilson's resignation, when on 4 March the Bank of England sold sterling to counteract a temporary increase in the exchange rate. This coincided with some free-market selling to precipitate a small fall in the value of the pound, which was misinterpreted by the markets. The Treasury was widely believed to favour a controlled devaluation as a means of boosting the competitiveness of exports, and the events of 4 March were seen as the beginning of that process. Anxious not to suffer a loss in the value of their assets, holders of sterling began to move into other currencies, bringing about the 5 per cent devaluation which the Treasury was believed to favour in the space of just one week, despite support-buying by the Bank of England. The fall did not stop there, however. Labour problems in the motor industry, statements by some Trades Union Congress (TUC) leaders opposing a further round of pay restraint, and the uncertainty surrounding Wilson's resignation all added momentum to the avalanche of selling and precipitated a 26 per cent fall in the six months to September, despite the successful conclusion of a stage two of pay policy and continued support-buying.

With its reserves of foreign currency severely depleted by the abortive support operation, the Bank of England in June negotiated a standby facility of $5.3 billion with other Central Banks. This was followed in July by an announcement by the Chancellor of the Exchequer of reductions in public expenditure and an increase in employers' national insurance contributions, as a means of reducing the budget deficit: but the downward pressure continued, and over $1 billion of the standby had been used by September.

At the insistence of the United States, the standby facility had only been extended until the end of the year, when any sums taken up in the meantime would have to be repaid. This was a deliberate move to force Britain to apply to the IMF for a loan, which would only be given with conditions attached. The application for a loan of £3.9 billion was made in September. The terms were negotiated in the period up to December, and involved a reduction in public-spending plans of £1 billion in 1977–8, and £1.5 billion in 1978–9,

[9] Gardner, *Decade of Discontent*, p. 60.

plus the sale of £500 million of the Government's shares in British Petroleum to reduce the Public Sector Borrowing Requirement even further. The agreement immediately ended the run on the pound, but it caused considerable disaffection within the Labour Party. The IMF conditions meant a final retreat from the extensive programme of social welfare measures that had formed the basis of the Labour manifesto in 1974. This led some back-benchers on the left of the Party to feel that the claim of the leadership on their loyalty had been forfeited, which made the task of the Whips in ensuring solidity of support for the Government very difficult. The 1977 budget plans were disrupted when Labour back-benchers voted with the opposition on the index-linking of tax allowances to inflation, and the threat of rebellion, especially on unpopular issues such as direct elections to the European Parliament, remained a constant pressure on the Government.

The capacity for mischief of back-benchers was increased by the fact that the Government by March 1977 did not have an overall majority in Parliament. Even in October 1974 the Labour majority over all other parties had been only four. This had been eroded by the defection of two Scottish MPs to form the Scottish Labour Party and by defeats in by-elections, so that in March 1977 Callaghan was facing a vote of confidence with no certainty of survival. It was in these circumstances that a pact was formed with the Liberal Party, which also had no wish to see a general election at a time when opinion polls indicated a possible landslide Conservative victory. David Steel, the new Liberal leader, agreed to support the Government in return for a regular input into discussions of future business, and commitments from Callaghan to introduce legislation to facilitate direct elections to the European Parliament and to try to make progress on the devolution of powers to a Scottish Assembly. Unfortunately, both of these were issues that were opposed by Labour back-benchers. So Callaghan found himself facing a solution that is common in continental European politics (where coalition governments are normal), but rare in British politics, of having to reconcile the conflicting demands of maintaining intra-party and inter-party support.

The 'Lib.–Lab. pact' allowed the Government to survive into the 1977–8 parliamentary session, by which time the economic indicators had improved again.

By the autumn of 1977, barely nine months after the IMF trauma, the Labour Government had not only survived but now appeared to be witnessing a remarkable economic revival. The problem of sterling being too weak had so evaporated during 1977 that by October the Treasury announced the pound was free to float upward, which it did ... The balance of payments, which had been in deficit in the second quarter of 1977, showed a £483 million surplus in the third quarter and a £351 million surplus in the fourth quarter. Boosted by the much anticipated North Sea oil revenues, the Chancellor's headache of financing the external balance had been transformed into a prospect for genuine economic recovery. Foreign currency reserves rose from $7.196 million to $20,557 million during 1977 ... From the 30 per cent levels of 1975, inflation was down to under 10 per cent by 1978.[10]

Unemployment had also levelled off, and all this good news, combined with an expansionary budget in April, led to speculation that Callaghan would call an autumn election. The speculation was fuelled by the announcement of the Liberals in May that they would not continue the Lib.–Lab. pact after the end of that session of Parliament.

During the summer the expectation of an autumn election built up to the point where the Conservative Party had even begun its preparations. But on 7 September, in a surprise announcement to the first Cabinet meeting after the summer holiday, Callaghan declared that the Government would continue in office. In retrospect this has been seen as a great mistake. However, it has to be borne in mind that there was no certainty of Labour winning an overall majority in the autumn of 1978, and there was no reason to think that the economy would not continue to improve, and with it the prospects for Labour in a spring election.

Callaghan's real mistake, and again it is a judgement that can only be made in retrospect, was to try to achieve a phase four of pay policy with a 5 per cent norm for wage and salary increases. The trade unions had co-operated with phases one and two of Labour's pay policy, which had been successful, but the TUC had not felt able to agree on a third phase. The Government had unilaterally declared a 10 per cent target for 1977–8, which had held in theory, even if in practice increased overtime earnings, bonuses, and 'self-financing productivity deals' had pushed the increase in earnings up to 15 per cent. Trade union leaders advised the Prime Minister that the mood of their members was hostile to a continuation of pay

[10] Martin Holmes, *The Labour Government, 1974–79: Political Aims and Economic Reality* (London, 1985), 111–2.

restraint, especially as the economy appeared to be picking up, but Callaghan was determined not to allow the gains which had been made in the fight against inflation to slip away, and he clearly attributed these to the success of the pay policy.[11]

On New Year's Day 1978, in a radio broadcast, Callaghan suggested that 5 per cent might be a suitable target figure for the next round of pay policy. Treasury officials maintain that this was the first time they had heard the figure, and one suggested that it resulted from Callaghan's recent visit to Helmut Schmidt.[12] Certainly international co-ordination of policy was a cause that Callaghan had taken up enthusiastically, and his well-known suspicion of the Treasury may have made him more inclined to discuss such matters with Schmidt, to whom he now felt quite close, than with his own Treasury officials. Whatever the source of the figure, it was a mistake. The reaction of trade unionists was hostile: many of them appear to have felt that their living standards had been eroded by pay restraint, and that this would erode them even further. The figure may only have got through Cabinet because it was assumed that it would never be tested, as there would be an election before the autumn pay-round got under way, after which policy could be revised.

The weapon that the Government intended to use to enforce its pay policy was to refuse to award state contracts to companies that breached it. The first breach of the 5 per cent came in November 1978, when, after a short strike, Ford conceded a 15 per cent rise to its workers. The capacity of disaffected back-benchers to damage their own Government was demonstrated when, by abstaining on a Conservative motion to abandon any attempt to impose sanctions on companies that breached the 5 per cent limit, members of the left-wing Tribune Group caused the Government to lose the one means that it had to enforce its policy.

That result opened the floodgates for massive claims from several groups of workers, including petrol tanker drivers and road haulage workers, whose strikes in support of their claims caused shortages of heating fuel and of food in the shops. They were followed by strikes in the public sector that produced the closure of hospitals, the appearance of piles of rubbish in the streets, and the

---

[11] Other observers have attributed the decline in inflation to the cuts in public expenditure that were enforced by the IMF, see for example, Holmes, *The Labour Government*.   [12] Ibid., 126.

contamination of water supplies. These bitter industrial battles were the cause of the defeat of the Callaghan Government in May 1979, when, in the aftermath of the referenda on devolution, which they lost, the Scottish and Welsh Nationalists withdrew the support that had kept the beleagured Government alive throughout the winter. The Conservatives under Margaret Thatcher were elected on a platform that included a commitment to abandon pay policy and to weaken the power of trade unions.

The European Agenda

During his premiership Callaghan had to handle several questions at the Community level that had important implications for Britain's relationship with the EC. The issue of direct elections to the European Parliament was already firmly on the agenda when he became Prime Minister; the Heads of Government agreed at the September 1976 meeting of the European Council in Brussels to hold elections in 1978. In January 1977 Britain assumed the presidency of the Council of Ministers of the Community for the first time, and had to tackle the increasingly urgent problem of finding agreement on a common policy on fisheries, an issue that was particularly sensitive for the British. In 1978 the EMS proposal, jointly sponsored by the German Chancellor and the French President, caused more difficulties for Britain. And towards the end of his premiership Callaghan found himself having to respond to a delicate situation in which Britain was rapidly emerging as one of only two net contributors to the Community's budget.

Direct Elections to the European Parliament

Direct elections to the European Parliament were a commitment in the Treaty of Rome, but pending their introduction the European Parliament had consisted of nominated representatives of the national parliaments. The question of direct elections was one of a number of institutional reforms put on to the Community's agenda by Giscard d'Estaing when he became President of France, and which had been agreed to by the Governments of the other member states.

Ironically, given the domestic political problems that it was to cause for Callaghan, Giscard's motive for promoting a measure that ran counter to the previous policy of his own party was largely a consideration of domestic politics. Although dependent on the Gaullists for his majority in the National Assembly, Giscard aspired to construct a new majority that would allow him to dispense with the more conservative Gaullists. To do this he actively courted the remnants of the centre parties of the Fourth Republic, for whom a commitment to European integration was an item of faith. It was as part of his attempt to incorporate these previously independent parties into his parliamentary majority that Giscard pressed for the direct elections.[13]

Wilson's agreement in principle to the measure was probably part of the price that he was prepared to pay in order to get French agreement to the formula for budgetary rebates that he had made into such an important test of the acceptability of the renegotiated terms of entry. Callaghan perhaps felt bound by the same understanding when he agreed to the commitment made by the Heads of Government in September 1976 to hold elections in the course of 1978, which would require the passage of domestic enabling legislation. A British parliamentary committee that was asked to investigate the question concluded that a Bill would need to be introduced into the House of Commons by the start of 1977 for it to be sure to pass through all the necessary legislative procedure in time for elections to be held in the spring of 1978.

Callaghan's first Party Conference as Prime Minister, at which he was formally elected leader of the Labour Party, took place in October 1976. It had before it a resolution from the NEC of the Party, which at this time was dominated by the left, that rejected the idea of holding direct elections to the European Parliament. The arguments echoed the claims about loss of sovereignty that had been made at the time of the referendum campaign. Instead of seeing a directly elected European Parliament as a potential ally in the task of ensuring democratic control over the business of the Community, the NEC argued that the new chamber would engage in a power struggle with national parliaments in an attempt to wrest power from them. Into the ensuing vacuum would step the Commission, increasing the power of the 'Brussels bureaucrats' (a favourite bogyman of the anti-Community forces).

[13] Jean-Louis Burban, 'La Dialectique des élections européennes', *Revue française de science politique*, 27 (1977), 377–406.

The resolution was passed by Conference, but Anthony Crosland, the new Foreign Secretary, warned that the Government felt obliged to fulfil its commitments in this respect under Article 118 of the Treaty of Rome. Nevertheless, the Government took no steps to draft legislation in implementation of the commitment prior to the deadline suggested by the parliamentary committee. The explanation of this paradox is presumably that the Government was in no hurry to plunge itself into an internal party dispute. The Foreign Secretary had been careful to refer to the Treaty commitment, which was unspecific with respect to the date for the introduction of elections, and not to the agreement at the Brussels European Council, which had been more specific. Callaghan was still intent on settling himself into office, trying to consolidate his authority as leader and as Prime Minister, and particularly seeking as a priority to keep his Cabinet united behind his domestic economic programme. It was also felt, even by some pro-Europeans within the Party, that elections if held too soon might prove extremely embarrassing for the Government. It was not riding a wave of popularity in the context of an economic policy that imposed sacrifices on a large part of the electorate, and a resounding rebuff in European elections would make its position even more difficult.

It was not until the late June of 1977 that a Bill to implement direct elections was introduced. By this time the only way in which it might have been possible to get the draft through the legislative timetable to meet the spring 1978 target for elections was to dispense with the idea of using a modified version of the British constituency system for electing the British Members of the European Parliament (MEPs), and to adopt a form of proportional representation based on national party lists. It was this option that was supported by Callaghan when he presented the Bill to Parliament, a major reversal of his own previous position, which had been totally opposed to any form of proportional representation.

The arguments against proportional representation were spelt out in the NEC paper that accompanied the resolution to Conference. The use of proportional representation in European elections was deemed to be the thin end of the wedge for introducing it for national elections. This was a curious argument, because it seemed to assume that once the electorate was allowed to use proportional representation in an election it would come to like the system, whereas the arguments against the use of proportional representation in national elections had always included an assertion that it was not a system that the British people wanted, together with a related assertion that it was too complicated a system for the British electorate to handle. Perhaps the NEC was admitting that, once the electorate had access to proportional representation, it would discover that it was not as incompetent as the Labour Party insisted on viewing it. Whatever the logic of the position, what it amounted to in practical terms was a fear that the introduction of proportional representation might prevent the Labour Party from alternating in government with the Conservatives and force it into coalitions if it were to form part of the government at all.

This was not just a position taken up by the left of the Party: it was a common sentiment throughout the Labour movement, and had previously been defended strongly by Callaghan. It was the Prime Minister who had insisted at the Brussels meeting that the proposed elections should not initially be held under common rules throughout the Community, which would certainly have implied the use of some form of proportional representation, but that each member state should be allowed to choose its own method of electing its MEPs.

Callaghan's change of heart on the matter had everything to do with the Labour pact with the Liberals, which became necessary in early 1977 to keep the Government in office, as by-elections whittled its majority away altogether. The Liberal leader, David Steel, recalls in his account that one of the conditions for Liberal support was that a Bill be introduced as soon as possible to facilitate the holding of the elections on schedule in 1978.[14] Given the parliamentary timetable for the passage of Bills, it was clear that there would be no time for a boundary commission to draw up European constituencies: proportional representation was the only way of getting the legislation through in time. Callaghan apparently told Steel that he could not guarantee to deliver proportional representation, but that he would do his best, and that he would personally support the system.[15]

When Callaghan put the matter to his Cabinet he was faced with the threat of resignations from Tony Benn, Stan Orme, Albert

[14] David Steel, *A House Divided: The Lib–Lab Pact and the Future of British Politics* (London, 1980), 39.   [15] Ibid., 39.

Booth, and Bruce Millan; so, although Callaghan told the NEC on 28 November that he would personally support proportional representation, the Parliamentary Labour Party was given a free vote on the issue when the legislation came before the House of Commons. Because the Conservatives were generally as opposed to proportional representation as were most Labour MPs, the measure was lost by 87 votes; the Parliamentary Labour Party divided 146 for and 115 against proportional representation.

The consequence of all this was that Callaghan had to tell the rest of the EC that Britain alone would not be in a position to hold the first direct elections as scheduled in the spring of 1978. Because of the priority given to domestic political considerations, Britain appeared again to be in breach of the spirit of the Community, an impression reinforced by the way in which the British Government handled its tenure of the presidency of the Council of Ministers in the first half of 1977.

The British Presidency

There were hopes that perhaps the British Government would use the opportunity provided by its first spell in the presidency of the Council of Ministers, which lasted from January to June 1977, to 'convince the other eight governments and the Commission that Britain could and would play a full part in the Community irrespective of particular issues' and to 'achieve public awareness that Community membership provides simply a different framework for grappling with unavoidable national problems'.[16]

Callaghan's Foreign Secretary, Anthony Crosland, told the European Parliament in his inaugural address on 12 January that Her Majesty's Government would attempt to achieve the feasible during the presidency. He singled out progress on enlargment of the Community as a priority issue, and also stressed the importance which Britain attached to the development of procedures for co-ordinating the foreign policies of the member states, under the process called European Political Co-operation (EPC).[17]

There were other issues on the agenda, though, which threatened to be more controversial. Chief amongst these was the framing of a common policy on fisheries, although it was actually the more

---

[16] Geoffrey Edwards and Helen Wallace, 'EEC: The British Presidency in Retrospect', *World Today*, 33 (1977), 286.   [17] Ibid., 284.

routine annual business of settling the support prices for agricultural produce which caused the most ill-will between Britain and the rest of the Community.

Both issues fell under the remit of John Silkin, the Minister for Agriculture. Whereas his predecessor, Fred Peart, had been the most adept of British Ministers at playing the Community game, and was the best-liked member of the Cabinet with his European colleagues, Silkin courted no popularity within the EC. He had ambitions to assume the leadership of the Labour Party, and consequently used the Community forum to play to a domestic audience. Given the anti-market majority within the Labour Party, Silkin was inclined to play the role of a national champion.

Fisheries was an issue that had been catapulted to the top of the Community's agenda by international developments. Following the conclusion of a United Nations Conference on the Law of the Sea, several states had unilaterally declared the extension of their territorial waters to two hundred miles from their coast. This was largely prompted by a desire to claim rights over minerals that might be extracted from the sea-bed, something that had become economically viable in an era of rapidly rising prices for basic commodities. But the most immediate effect was on the traditional pattern of activity of the fishing industry. Iceland declared a two-hundred-mile economic zone in October 1975, and attempted to exclude the fishing boats of other states from their waters, despite the fact that these were traditional fishing grounds for most European nations.

The Community response to this was to declare its own two-hundred-mile zone, but agreement on how fishing quotas should be divided between the member states proved more difficult to achieve. A temporary agreement was reached early in 1976, but when the British Government assumed the EC presidency in early 1977 this agreement was due to expire. The problem for Britain was that it was one of the chief protagonists in the dispute, together with Ireland taking the view that a predominant share of the fishing quota should be allocated to the states whose territorial boundaries accounted for a majority of the zone, which meant Britain and Ireland.

The matter was not settled during the British presidency, largely because of what the other member states saw as the biased chairing of the Council of Ministers by the British. Despite the urgency of reaching agreement, Silkin was not prepared to make concessions, and appeared to some representatives to be trying to block rather than further agreement. The reason for this was perhaps not just Silkin's determination to appear a strongman: many constituencies in which fishing was a major employer were also marginal. Given the precarious majority of the Labour Government, it presumably did not feel able to make concessions that would be seen as damaging to the interests of the electorate in those constituencies.

Electoral considerations were also believed in some quarters to have been at least partially responsible for the failure of the Council of Agricultural Ministers to reach agreement on the level of support prices for 1977 by the normal deadline of the end of March. When the last scheduled meeting of the Council was held on 29 March there was a by-election pending in the Birmingham constituency of Stechford. The breakdown of the agricultural talks was presented by the Government as an example of Labour Ministers getting tough with the EC over the unpopular (in Britain) CAP. Yet a month later it proved possible to reach an agreement.

The failure to agree price levels was traumatic for most member states: the agricultural lobby is extremely influential throughout most of the Community. Silkin was congratulated in some quarters in Britain for his refusal to adopt the normal 'knee-jerk reaction to the farming lobby',[18] but what really offended the other member states was the narrow nationalistic line adopted by Silkin from the Chair. He insisted that there could be no question of Britain revaluing the 'green pound', the artificial rate of exchange that was used to translate common food prices from units of account into national currencies, even though its gross overvaluation was costing the Community a vast amount in subsidies to the British consumer. At the same time, he insisted that what were relatively modest price increases by EC standards, averaging 1.5 per cent, were unacceptable not because they would increase food surpluses within the Community, but because they would add to the British rate of inflation.

It was true that, because Britain was due to come to the end of its transitional period at the end of 1978, the 1.5 per cent rise would mean an effective 3 per cent rise in Britain, and that this would add about 0.7 per cent to the cost of living index at a time when the Labour Government was struggling to keep down the rate of

[18] David Haworth, 'Six Wasted Months', *New Statesman*, 8 July 1977, p. 42.

inflation.[19] What caused resentment was the blatant statement of narrow national interests from the Chair as a reason for not reaching agreement.

Against this, the modest progress that was made on other issues, such as the harmonization of transport regulations, the Sixth VAT directive, and the position of the EC in the continuing CIEC, did little to enhance the reputation of Britain. Indeed, on the preparations for the final Ministerial conference of the CIEC, Stephen Taylor reported that the British insisted on duplicating much of the work of the Council Secretariat, and so, despite doing an extremely effective job, 'once again gave the impression of being anti-*communautaire*'.[20]

To David Haworth, Ministers seemed to have a total misconception of what the presidency meant, and generally treated it as though it 'represented a *carte blanche* for Britain to get her own way for six months'. Despite all the preparation in Whitehall, officials were not exempt from this criticism. There were some successes: Judith Hart once again impressed her colleagues within the EC, and at official level Haworth singled out Sir Donald Maitland, the British Permanent Representative in Brussels, and his deputy Bob Goldsmith for praise, observing that they 'bore the brunt of Whitehall's constant misunderstanding of what the presidency meant'. But overall the judgement was that these had been 'six wasted months'.[21]

Wallace and Edwards placed the blame on the Government's retreat in the face of a resurgence of anti-Community feeling in its own party. The result was to leave Britain's relations with its Community partners as troubled as before the presidency.[22] Following the 1977 Labour Party Conference they became even more troubled.

The 1977 Labour Party Conference

In some ways the 1977 Conference represented a compromise between those who supported and those who opposed membership of the EC. The NEC resolution on the Community, although

---

[19] Trevor Parfitt, 'Bad Blood in Brussels', *World Today*, 33 (1977), 203–6.

[20] Stephen Taylor, 'EEC Co-ordination for the North–South Conference', *World Today*, 33 (1977), 440.

[21] Haworth, 'Six Wasted Months'.

[22] Edwards and Wallace, 'EEC: the British Presidency', p. 286.

critical, contained no mention of the threat of withdrawal: and Conference declined to support a hardline constituency resolution calling for another referendum. But this appearance of compromise was based on a letter from Callaghan to the Labour General Secretary, Ron Hayward, which defined the Government's policy to the EC in a way that caused offence to its partners in the Community.

The letter started positively, by defending the record of membership on the grounds that the apparent adverse effects should be at least partially blamed on the rise in the price of oil and the subsequent recession. But it went on to accept that 'there are aspects of present Community policies which do not work in our interests or may work counter to our concepts of how Britain and Europe should develop'. Although Callaghan firmly rejected withdrawal as a solution to these difficulties, he did so not because it would be against the treaty commitments entered into by Her Majesty's Government, against the interests of Britain, and against the verdict of the referendum, but because it would 'cause a profound upheaval in our relations with Europe but also more widely, particularly in our relations with the United States'. That last phrase would not help Britain's reputation with other member states that already suspected the British Government of giving undue attention to its relationship with the United States.

Callaghan went on to outline a six-point plan for British policy towards the EC, starting with the maintenance of the authority of national governments and parliaments, which involved the clear rejection of any increase in the powers of the European Parliament. Although in his second point he talked of the need to make the EC more democratically accountable, it was not the European Parliament that he envisaged performing this function; instead he talked of the need to improve the effectiveness of the British Parliament's scrutiny procedures, and took up an idea that had been aired by Tony Benn during the British presidency, that some meetings of the Council of Ministers should be open to the public.

The third point of the plan asserted the necessity for national governments to be able to achieve their economic, regional, and industrial policy objectives, and admitted that Britain had stretched EC rules 'in the matter of British Leyland, Chrysler, Meriden and Alfred Herbert'.

Reform of the CAP was predictably on the list; but so,

surprisingly, was the need for the EC to develop a common energy policy, a point that must have particularly upset those member states of the Community that had been trying for some years to get Britain to agree to just such a policy.

Enlargement of the Community to bring in Greece, Spain, and Portugal to membership was presented as a policy that was meritorious in its own right, but also as one that would dilute the degree of integration in the EC. 'The dangers of an over-centralized, over-bureaucratized and over-harmonized Community will be far less with twelve than with nine'.[23]

Although clearly intended for domestic consumption, the letter gave offence in other Community capitals, and the new Foreign Secretary, David Owen, who took over following the death of Crosland in February 1977, found himself facing close questioning from the West German Foreign Minister, Hans Dietrich Genscher, at the meeting of the Council of Ministers that took place just a week later.

The European Monetary System

Although Schmidt and Giscard first broached the subject of the EMS with the other Heads of Government in a private meeting at the Copenhagen European Council of 7–8 April 1978,[24] the details of the scheme were not at that stage worked out, and it did not become public knowledge until July 1978, when it was unveiled at the Bremen meeting of the European Council.

The idea for a zone of monetary stability in the EC was not original to Helmut Schmidt. Roy Jenkins, who in January 1977 had become President of the Commission, had endeavoured to revive the idea of European economic and monetary union in a lecture given in Florence in October 1977.[25] But it was Schmidt who put political momentum behind the project. It appealed to him because he was increasingly tired of the adverse effects on the German economy of the decline in the value of the US dollar.

[23] *The Times*, 1 Oct. 1977. The whole text of the letter is reproduced here.

[24] Peter Ludlow, *The Making of the European Monetary System: A Case Study of the Politics of the European Community* (London, 1982), 88–122.

[25] Roy Jenkins, 'Europe's Present Challenge and Future Opportunity', The First Jean Monnet Lecture delivered at the European University Institute, Florence, 27 Oct. 1977, *Bulletin of the European Communities, Supplement 10–1977*, pp. 6–14.

The damaging effects of this decline on the German economy were twofold. First, West Germany was a major competitor of the United States, particularly in the capital goods sector. Consequently German exports were damaged by the undervaluation of the dollar, which made US goods comparatively cheaper. Secondly, the speculative funds that flowed out of the dollar tended to flow into either the Japanese Yen or the Deutschmark, because these were the strongest currencies. This put upward pressure on the Deutschmark, which if it had not been constantly resisted would have led to a further decline in the competitiveness of German exports. There was also a move for the Deutschmark to be used as an international reserve currency, a development that the Germans resisted by controls on currency inflows and foreign ownership of financial assets; but these measures could not prevent the Deutschmark displacing sterling as the second most widely held currency in foreign exchange reserves between 1970 and 1977. The last thing that the Germans wanted was the increased difficulty of economic management imposed on a country when its currency had the status of an international reserve.

These problems would be considerably eased by the creation of a system that tied together the values of the currencies of the EC. First, the removal of uncertainty about currency values would help to offset the competitive advance of the United States over West Germany in trade with the other members of the EC. Importers would weigh the advantages of a lower price against the possibility that, by the time they had to pay for the goods, the value of the dollar would have shifted back upwards, so leaving them with a bigger than expected bill; if their own currency had a fixed parity with the Deutschmark, the price to be paid would be more calculable. Secondly, and more importantly, the guarantee that the values of the Deutschmark and of other EC currencies would remain fixed would take the speculative pressure off the Deutschmark. It would make other currencies look a better bet for speculators to move their funds into; and it would mean that the currencies of weaker EC economies would not lose the confidence of investors, so leading to the removal of more funds that would flow into the Deutschmark.

More altruistically, Schmidt was convinced that the United States had no policies to offer that might pull the capitalist world out of the combination of recession and inflation that it was then experiencing. He determined that Germany would have to take a lead if the United States could or would not. In his view, which was the consensus view in Germany, the major enemy was inflation. So Schmidt's phrase 'zone of monetary stability' had a double meaning: not only would fluctuations in exchange rates be stabilized; so would fluctuations in the values of currencies resulting from high inflation rates.

The French President was prepared to agree to this proposal because:

His aim and that of Raymond Barre, the Prime Minister responsible for the 'Plan Barre', was to restructure the French economy so that by the late 1980s France would be able to compete with Germany and Japan in the top industrial league, rather than with countries producing less sophisticated goods. A period of relative exchange rate stability would be needed to build confidence in the commercial and industrial sectors, and for this purpose the French President preferred a system of fixed to one of floating exchange rates.[26]

When the scheme was put to Callaghan he responded favourably to the idea of monetary stability, but expressed technical doubts about the working of the system. Behind these doubts, though, lay a more fundamental lack of sympathy with the plan. Callaghan had already made public his own five-point plan for the recovery of the world economy, putting the emphasis on action through existing international institutions such as the IMF. Nevertheless, at the Copenhagen meeting of the European Council, in return for an agreement to conduct concurrent studies of the action needed to strengthen the economies of the less prosperous member states, he agreed to appoint one of the three 'wise men' who were charged to consider and develop the plan. But the person whom he appointed, Ken Couzens, was a senior official in the Treasury, which, according to Statler, 'had played an active part in developing Mr Callaghan's five-point plan',[27] and which had traditionally been suspicious of regional as opposed to wider globalist approaches to issues of international economic management.

Although Denis Healey responded more constructively to the proposals during discussions in the Council of Economic and Finance Ministers in May and June, the impression left on the other member states by Callaghan's reaction at Copenhagen was of a

---

[26] Statler, 'British Foreign Policy', p. 215.   [27] Ibid., 216.

distinct lack of British enthusiasm. This was almost certainly accurate. Not only did the German plan conflict with Callaghan's plan, it also conflicted with the Atlantic orientation of British policy, and with the British emphasis on the stimulation of economic growth as the answer to the recession, because the implications of the German plan were deflationary.

At a bilateral meeting at Chequers in April 1978, Schmidt endeavoured to overcome Callaghan's objections. At the press conference which followed he insisted that there was no fundamental incompatibility between his plan and Callaghan's: the two approaches were complementary, not contradictory. He had no wish to organize a European monetary zone hostile to the United States. On the contrary, he believed that a unified European currency bloc would help the dollar by curtailing speculative flows between currencies. Callaghan for his part supported the objective of monetary stability, but emphasized the priority that he attached to growth through economic expansion.

It became clear, at an IMF interim committee meeting at the end of April, that the IMF, the OECD, and the United States supported the British view that international economic problems should be tackled through existing international institutions. This was hardly surprising. But at the Bonn economic summit in July it appeared that the German view, shared by the Japanese, that the artificial stimulation of demand was not desirable, was gaining ground. Nevertheless, a package of measures that combined fighting inflation in those national economies with the highest rates of inflation and stimulation of demand in those with low rates of inflation was agreed. The German Government played its part by reaching agreement on 28 July on a package of tax cuts and increased government spending to fulfil its commitment to boost demand by 1 per cent of GNP.

The good faith and willingness to compromise shown by Schmidt seems to have inclined Callaghan towards participation in the EMS when it was considered again at the Bremen meeting of the European Council in July 1978. But before the system could come into operation, the 1978 Labour Party Conference intervened. According to Peter Jenkins, writing in the *Guardian*, Callaghan changed his mind about participation in the EMS during the weekend of 8 October, following the spectacle of speaker after speaker at the Conference coming to the podium to condemn the idea.[28] Again considerations of party unity seem to have been instrumental in swaying a Labour Prime Minister in a direction that would put Britain out of step with the rest of the Community. This explanation for Callaghan's refusal to take sterling into the EMS is accepted by Peter Ludlow, although he adds: 'but critics and sceptics were already in the ascendant before then'.[29] Jocelyn Statler similarly does not dismiss the influence of party political considerations, but emphasizes that considerations of economic strategy must have also weighed heavily with Callaghan.[30] The risk of subjecting the British economy to the deflationary effects of the EMS before inflation levels had been brought down to something like German rates may have been more influential in the Prime Minister's thinking than the reaction of the Labour Conference delegates.

Initially the Italians and Irish also refused to join the system as it was finalized at Bremen. But soon afterwards they were bought into the scheme by the offer of funds from Germany to assist them in the adjustments to their economies that would be necessary, and the concession that, instead of having to tie their currencies to the others within a 2.25 per cent margin of fluctuation, they would be able to operate within a less restrictive 6 per cent band.

Surprisingly, the British announced that, although they would not be entering the joint float of currencies, they would endeavour to maintain the value of sterling as though it were in the float, and within the narrower band of fluctuation. They also decided to participate in the partial pooling of gold and foreign currency reserves to create the new European currency unit (Ecu). So although Britain was not formally a member of the system, it acted as though it were actually a fuller member than Italy, which was formally a full member. This may indicate that political considerations, both domestic and international, were uppermost in the decision; by not joining formally the Government quietened the protests from within the Labour Party and demonstrated its continued determination not to be drawn into an institution that was regarded with suspicion by the United States; by adapting its policy voluntarily, and also declaring an intention to join eventually, it kept on the right side of the Germans. The compromise did,

---

[28] Quoted in Ludlow, *The Making of the European Monetary System*, p. 217.
[29] Ibid. 218.   [30] Statler, 'British Foreign Policy', p. 223.

though, increase Britain's reputation with less pragmatic members of the EC than Helmut Schmidt for being an awkward partner. The episode contributed to that reputation in another way too. Italy and Ireland, as mentioned above, also had doubts about the effect of the EMS on their economies; but they tried to use the issue as a bargaining counter to increase the size of the Community's redistributive funds, particularly the ERDF. The British, who had formed the third leg of the alliance in favour of an ERDF during Heath's premiership, declined to join this coalition. Instead of requesting increased redistributive funds, Britain asked for side-payments in terms of a reduction of its contributions to the Community's budget, to be achieved by a combination of rebates and reductions in the overall size of the budget. In particular, there was a renewed British attack on the CAP, which the Irish were particularly concerned to defend.

This approach was in line with the attitude of the Labour Party ever since it had returned to office. It had shown itself unwilling to solve any imbalance in its budgetary payments by a balancing increase in its receipts, which had been the strategy of Heath's Government, but had instead insisted on reducing the receipts of others by reducing the size of the budget as a whole. The issue became of renewed salience as the end of the transitional period of British membership approached, and it became increasingly obvious that Britain's payments would be disproportionate to its relative economic strength despite the rebate mechanism that had been negotiated by Wilson in 1975.

The Budgetary Imbalance

Already by 1976, while transitional arrangements still limited the extent of its contributions, Britain was the third biggest net contributor to the Community's budget, behind West Germany and Belgium. In 1977, still under transitional arrangements, the British net contribution was the second largest to that of West Germany, and the deficit was estimated at £423 million, well in excess of the maximum refund permitted under the 1975 formula, which in 1978 would have converted into sterling as about £160 million.[31] By mid-1978 it was becoming apparent that, once the full

[31] Malcolm Crawford, 'The Billion Pound Drain: What it Costs us to be in Europe', *Sunday Times*, 23 July 1978, p. 62.

transitional period of membership came to an end in 1980, Britain would become the largest net contributor to the budget. It was confidentially estimated by the Economic Policy Committee of the EC that by 1980 the 1977 deficit would have nearly doubled to around £800 million.

The size of Britain's payments into the budget arose from the nature of the system of financing, which it will be recalled consisted of the revenue from tariffs on industrial goods entering the Community, and the levies on imported agricultural products, together with up to a 1 per cent share of national VAT revenues, calculated on a notional common base.

There were difficulties in respect to both these elements. First, Britain imported more goods, especially foodstuffs, from outside the EC than did the other member states. Although the percentage of British imports coming from other Community states had increased from 25 per cent prior to entry to 43 per cent in 1979, it was still well below the average of 50.8 per cent recorded by the original Six.[32] This was the legacy of pre-existing trading relationships, especially with the Commonwealth. The result was that British consumers had to pay extra for their non-Community produce, because of the CAP levy, and the money had to be surrendered entirely to Brussels.

The second problem was that Britain was consuming more than its relative economic strength justified. The system of VAT contributions would result in a rough parity between the wealth of a member state and the size of its contribution if the country was living within its means, since consumers would be able to buy more when the country was doing well, and would therefore pay more VAT, which would result in higher payments to the Community budget. Conversely, when the country was doing less well economically, consumers would buy less, and VAT payments would be correspondingly less. However, if a state with a weak economy continued to experience a high level of consumer expenditure, VAT revenues would remain proportionately higher than they ought to be according to the strength of the economy, and contributions to the Community budget would similarly be higher than economic strength would indicate.

This was the position of Britain in 1979, and it arose because of

[32] Françoise de la Serre, *La Grande-Bretagne et la Communauté européenne* (Paris, 1987) p. 155.

the existence of North Sea oil. The tax revenues from the oil provided a windfall subsidy to the British Treasury, which was used to keep levels of personal direct taxation lower than they would otherwise have been; and the fact that Britain was a producer of oil kept confidence in the currency high, so that the pound was overvalued on international financial markets, resulting in cheaper imports.[33]

Britain's *net* contributions (that is, the difference between what it payed into the budget and what it received from it) were also particularly high because, not only were its payments to the budget higher than those of wealthier member states, but also its receipts from the budget were lower. The source of this problem was the dominance of the CAP within the EC budget. It was the only major common policy that the Community had, and it accounted for two-thirds of the payments from the budget in 1979. Although British farmers received their share of the disbursements under the CAP, there were far fewer farmers in Britain than in several of the other member states, which meant lower benefits to Britain than, say, to France. Also, because Britain was not an exporter of food to the rest of the world, it did not receive the export subsidies that were paid out of the Community budget to compensate farmers for the difference between world prices and the guaranteed price under the CAP.

From Britain's viewpoint the result of all this was a situation that was clearly unacceptable, a point made strongly by Callaghan in a speech at the annual Lord Mayor's banquet in the Guildhall in London on 13 November 1978. He said that Britain could not agree to become the largest contributor to the budget when it was seventh in the economic league table of Community members.[34] The following day the Foreign Secretary, David Owen, told the House of Commons that the situation whereby 'the United Kingdom has the third lowest per capita gross domestic product in the Community' and yet was already the second highest net contributor to the budget 'cannot be good for the Community any more than it is for the United Kingdom', and promised the House that the Government would 'be working to achieve a better balance, especially in relation to agricultural expenditure, to curb the excessive United Kingdom net contribution'.[35]

[33] Michael Shanks, 'The EEC Budget Crisis: Is our Oil the Answer?', *The Times*, 29 Nov. 1979, p. 16.   [34] *The Times*, 14 Nov. 1978.
[35] *Hansard*. 5th ser. 958 (14 Nov. 1978), col. 214.

But the position did not look so clear from the side of the original six member states, who on this issue were joined by Ireland. First, they argued that the arrangements which produced this anomaly were a painfully negotiated achievement, and to unravel them would be a retrograde step. Britain had not been a party to the original agreement on funding the budget, but had accepted it as part of the *acquis communautaire* when joining. Since then the terms of entry had been irritatingly renegotiated, and accepted by the British people in a referendum. Now it appeared as though the British Government was turning round and saying, 'No, we still do not like the rules, you must change them to suit us yet again.' This was certainly the outraged reaction of most of the French Press following Owen's comment to the Brussels' press corps in August 1978 that: 'Everyone knows we did not get a good deal in 1972, and we must continue our efforts to change that.'[36]

Secondly, it was argued that, if Britain's payments into the budget were too high, this was largely the fault of Britain. Nobody was forcing the British to consume Commonwealth produce in preference to French, Irish, or Danish foodstuffs. To do so was a wilful anti-Communitarian gesture, and if the British wished to reduce that element of their contribution to the Community budget, all they had to do was exercise Community preference.

Similarly, the high level of VAT payments was an indication of poor financial control, a major folly in the eyes of the West German Government in particular, for whom monetary probity was the ultimate economic virtue. If the British wished to reduce this item of their contributions, they only had to start living within their means.

Discussion of the problem was never likely to be easy, therefore, especially as the British insisted that the solution to the problem lay in cutting back on the CAP, a sacred cow of the Six, and their single greatest achievement. Little progress had been made in resolving the problem when the Labour Party was beaten by the Conservatives in the June 1979 general election. The new Government inherited the budgetary problem as its first item of Community business.

Conclusion

The Callaghan premiership illustrates well the inadequacy of

[36] Michael Hornsby, 'How Britain Loses out when they Balance the Books in Brussels', *The Times*, 11 Aug. 1978, p. 12.

explanations of the relationship between Britain and the EC which put excessive emphasis on the personal prejudices of the Prime Minister of the day. Although initially sceptical about the merits of British membership of the EC, and unsympathetic to the idea of European unity, Callaghan, once he became Prime Minister, appears to have become less hostile than he sometimes seemed whilst Foreign Secretary. He had already become aware of the advantages of EPC, and he steadily became aware of the advantages of co-operating with Britain's European partners on economic matters in the face of their common problems. In this process he was almost certainly helped by the increasingly close working relationship that he developed with Helmut Schmidt. So, although he never became a convert to the ideal of European unity, Callaghan did not remain oblivious to the advantages of Britain becoming a more co-operative partner.

That Britain continued to appear the awkward partner within the EC despite the move of Callaghan to a more sympathetic stance is best explained by reference to the two factors that have been repeatedly stressed in this book: the influence of domestic political considerations, and the response to developments in the wider international system.

The domestic political constraints were not perhaps as tight for Callaghan as they had been for Wilson. Nevertheless, with a precarious and dwindling parliamentary majority, and in the face of continued blind hostility to the EC on the part of a significant section of the Labour Party, it was difficult for Callaghan to adopt too co-operative a position. However much he might have undergone a rapid learning process himself on the advantages of closer European co-operation, he had to guard his back against a hostile domestic reaction. This almost certainly explains the dragging of feet on direct elections, and the more nationalistic aspects of some of the British chairing of meetings of the Council of Ministers during the first part of 1977. It was also clearly behind Callaghan's letter to Hayward that caused several of Britain's EC partners a good deal of disappointment by its negative tone.

Although domestic political considerations also played a role in holding Britain back from full participation in the EMS, international considerations were perhaps even more significant here. The traditional British reluctance to see regional, as opposed to wider global solutions to international economic problems came to the fore on this issue, and was reinforced by Callaghan's own deeply ingrained Atlanticism. The stance was not just based on a traditional prejudice, though. It reflected also Britain's international trading position, which remained more diversified than that of many of its EC partners.

That same trading position also lay at the root of the problem of Britain's budgetary contributions, the legacy that the Callaghan Government passed to its Conservative successor, and which came to dominate the relations of Britain and the EC in the first phase of the Thatcher Governments.

5. The Thatcher Governments, 1979–1984: Settling the Budgetary Dispute

WHEN a Conservative Government under Margaret Thatcher was elected in Britain in 1979, there may have been hopes in some quarters that it would adopt a more co-operative attitude towards the Community than its Labour predecessors. There were reasons for such hopes. The party while in opposition had been very critical of Labour's handling of Community affairs. But hopes of a more co-operative approach did not last long. The new Government soon took up the theme of the unacceptable size of Britain's net contributions to the Community's budget. Shortly after coming into office Sir Geoffrey Howe, the Chancellor of the Exchequer, announced that the size of the problem was far greater than the Conservatives had realized whilst in opposition, and something would have to be done about it urgently. The issue was to dominate Community affairs for the next five years, during which time Britain became more isolated than ever within the EC, and other member states began making plans to further European unity, if necessary without British participation.

The International Context

A second oil crisis was sparked off by developments in Iran, where a popular mass movement against the Shah led to strikes in the oilfields in October 1978, which by December had resulted in the complete cutting off of Iranian oil to the world market. Although much of the shortfall was made up by increased production by other OPEC states, especially Saudi Arabia, the revolution in Iran, which deposed the Shah in January 1979, led to panic buying of oil on the spot markets as stocks were laid in against the possibility of shortages. The spot markets deal in oil that has not been committed for sale by contract between the producer states and the oil companies. When spot prices soared above the contracted price, OPEC moved to raise its contracted price, and this produced the first rise in price in real terms since December 1973.

This oil crisis found the Western states little more unified than had the first. Although there was an agreement within the IEA in March 1979 to cut consumption of oil by 5 per cent in 1979 and 1980, it was left to each individual state to decide how it would achieve this, and a few days after confirming the commitment in Paris in May the US Administration put a $5.00 a barrel subsidy on imported oil.

Faced with a lack of US leadership in responding to the crisis, the EC took the initiative by agreeing in June to hold overall imports of crude oil to their 1978 level in each year from 1980 to 1985, and to institute a register of dealings on the spot markets. The next week the Tokyo summit of the seven major capitalist states followed the lead of the EC, despite doubts expressed by the non-European participants (the United States, Japan, and Canada).

Iran continued to be a source of concern to the West, since the revolution that unseated the Shah put the government of that strategically important country into the hands of Islamic fundamentalists who showed themselves to be no friends of the West in general, and of the United States in particular. When staff of the US embassy in Tehran were taken hostage by revolutionary guards in November 1979, Carter responded by imposing economic sanctions, and then in April 1980 by attempting a military rescue, which failed. This approach was considered unhelpful by most of the European allies of the United States, who thought that it only served to exacerbate the situation. But Carter was by this time being driven along by a rising tide of aggressive nationalism in the US electorate, in an election year.

That same sentiment contributed to a worsening of East–West relations. Carter was facing accusations from his right-wing opponents of being soft on the USSR, and allowing it to gain a superiority in armaments over the United States. When the Soviet Union moved troops into Afghanistan in December 1979 it said that it was responding to a request from the Afghan government for assistance in suppressing right-wing insurgents. This explanation was not, however, accepted by the newly bellicose Carter Administration, which accused the Soviet Union of blatant expansionism in an area already rendered unstable by the Iranian revolution. Carter announced immediate economic sanctions, including an embargo on exports of high-technology goods to the Eastern bloc and an embargo on sales of grain to the USSR in excess of those contracted under a 1975 agreement. He also announced that US athletes would not compete in the 1980 Olympic games, which were to be held in Moscow.

The response of the French and West German Governments was more measured. Both Giscard and Schmidt said that they would go ahead with planned visits to Moscow in the hope of being able to negotiate some settlement to the dispute. In the event the West Germans kept their athletes away from the Olympics also, but the other European states did not. Only Britain, now under Margaret Thatcher's leadership, gave enthusiastic public support to the US measures, even though British athletes did compete in the Moscow Olympics. Other European leaders appear to have resented the way in which the United States used the issue to bring about a deterioration in relations with the East.

The bellicose tendencies of the United States were reinforced considerably with the election of Ronald Reagan to the presidency. His Administration, which took office in January 1981, returned to the rhetoric of the Cold War as a justification for a massive increase in spending on armaments. It also endeavoured to enforce on the West Europeans the embargo on the sale of high-technology goods to the Eastern bloc, although the grain embargo, which had damaged US farmers, was lifted. The policy on high-technology exports reached its height in 1982 over the question of the Siberian gas pipeline.

The Reagan Administration was unhappy about a joint project between several West European states and the Soviet Union to pipe natural gas from Siberia to Western Europe. The pipeline was being built by the USSR using materials and equipment that it was buying from the West Europeans on the basis of extended credits at low rates of interest. The scheme was mutually beneficial: it provided orders for private engineering firms in the West, it offered the West Europeans an opportunity to diversify their energy supplies away from the Middle East, it opened up the prospect to the Soviet Union of selling gas as a source of hard-currency income in the future, and it gave the USSR immediate access to gas extraction and supply equipment that could be used for other internal projects after the pipeline was finished.

The Reagan Administration, however, argued that the pipeline would lead to a dangerous dependence of Western Europe on energy supplies from the USSR; that the granting of export credits at advantageous rates of interest was 'bailing out' the economy of the Soviet Union, which was in serious trouble; and that the future export earnings from the sale of gas would supply the USSR with the means to increase its stock of weapons. The assumption behind these arguments was that the USSR was an enemy to be destroyed, by economic means if possible, whereas the West Europeans, with the exception of Margaret Thatcher, worked on the assumption that the best way of dealing with the Soviet Union was to enmesh it in a web of interdependence.

The issue produced a serious conflict between the United States and the West Europeans. On 13 December 1981 the Government of Poland, in the face of widespread strikes and protests organized around the Solidarity trade union, declared martial law. The United States decided that the Soviet Union had to be punished for its 'complicity' in this act, and on 29 December announced a series of economic sanctions, including a ban on the supply of US oil- and gas-technology to the Soviet Union. When US firms protested that this put them at a commercial disadvantage, the Administration extended the ban to all subsidiaries of US companies operating abroad, and to all foreign companies producing US products under licence. This action, which had no basis in international law, caused outrage in the EC. Most of the equipment for the Siberian pipeline was of US origin. Some of the companies most affected by the ban were suffering severely from the recession and were dependent on the pipeline contracts for survival: this was the case with John Brown Engineering in Britain, and AEG–Kanis in West Germany.

Eventually, faced with united opposition from the EC, including Britain, which had emerged under Margaret Thatcher as the strongest supporter of the Reagan Administration on most other issues, the United States backed down and rescinded the ban in return for a commitment from the Europeans not to enter into any new agreements of a similar nature with the USSR, and agreement to extend the number of products that could not be sold to the Eastern bloc without prior vetting by the COCOM agency which was set up by NATO to monitor trade with the Soviet Union involving technology that has a potential significance for defence.

European discontent with the high-handed approach of the Reagan Administration to foreign policy did not end there, though.

In the autumn of 1983 US troops invaded the Caribbean island of Grenada, to unseat the socialist government which the United States accused of being a Soviet puppet. A civil airfield that was being constructed by Cuban workers was identified by the United States as a military airfield, and was the ostensible occasion for the invasion. The action was taken without the French or West Germans being informed in advance; since the action had implications for relations between the developed capitalist world and the Third World in general, this was resented. Britain was informed in advance of the US plans, and invited to join the invasion, but declined to do so, and urged the United States not to invade. Since Grenada was a former British colony, and a member of the Commonwealth, the action of the United States was particularly embarrassing to the British Government, which felt obliged to dissociate itself from the invasion. This response was prudent in view of the widespread condemnation of the invasion by Third World states with which the EC was attempting to form closer relations.

Thus, by its high-handed actions, the United States helped to push the EC states closer together on foreign policy issues. At the same time the way in which the Reagan Administration handled its domestic economic problems also had an effect on the Community. The attempt of the Carter Administration to promote international co-operation was abandoned, and the United States unilaterally embarked on a policy that had worrying implications for the other advanced capitalist states.

Reagan inherited an emphasis by the Federal Reserve Board on control of the money supply as a means of controlling inflation, which continued, but he combined this with cutting taxes to stimulate investment, on the theory, expounded by the so-called 'supply-side' economists, that the effect would be to increase tax revenue by raising the level of economic activity. Reagan also made cuts in domestic social welfare programmes, but this was matched by the increase in expenditure on armaments, to increase rather than lessen the large budget deficit that Reagan had also inherited from Carter. The deficit was financed by borrowing, which meant raising US interest rates to unprecedentedly high levels. The influx of liquid assets into US Treasury bonds was such that the dollar was rapidly converted from being an undervalued currency to being overvalued. European states found themselves facing a net outflow of capital across the Atlantic. To stem that tide they had no choice but to raise their own interest rates, but this had a depressive effect on investment, and choked off the incipient recovery that had appeared in 1980, so that the international economy entered a new phase of recession in 1981.

The US economy, however, began to show every sign of riding out this new downturn. Whereas high interest rates in Western Europe were discouraging businesses from borrowing in order to invest, in the United States the federal spending programme on armaments was having the opposite effect, and producing recovery despite the high interest rates. The Europeans strongly suspected the United States of using the rhetoric of Cold War as an excuse for spending money in ways that would restore the technological lead of the United States over the Europeans and Japanese.

The concern was not just that the US economy was recovering whilst the EC economy was stagnating. The recovery that was taking place in the United States was not simply a recovery of the old industries. It was based on one of those periodical technological breakthroughs that have revived capitalism throughout its history just when the laws of entropy that Marx identified appeared to be overtaking it. The industries that formed the basis of the US recovery were the new technology industries of computers, robotics, telecommunications, and lasers. These were precisely the defence-related industries that were given such a boost by the Reagan spending programme. Their application was not only to defence, though. Nor did they result simply in a new range of consumer goods, although they did have that effect. They also provided the basis for a new generation of capital goods, which facilitated the automation of production lines in the older industries of the 'second industrial revolution', such as automobiles.

These developments caused tremendous concern in Europe, and in France and West Germany in particular. The West German economy had been moving more and more into specialization on capital goods for some time. This was the basis of its spectacular export success.[1] The French economy, under the Barre plan,

[1] On the structure of the Federal German economy, see Michael Kreile, 'West Germany: The Dynamics of Expansion', *International Organization*, 33 (1977), 775–808; Frieder Schlupp, 'Federal Republic of Germany', in Dudley Seers and

formulated by Giscard's last Prime Minister, was attempting to restructure its economy so as to move away from older industries into the high value-added industries and the new technological areas, in an attempt to catch up with and perhaps overtake West Germany as the core economy of the European economic zone, which extended beyond the boundaries of the EC to encompass the European Free Trade Association (EFTA) states, the Mediterranean periphery, the associated states of Africa, the Pacific and Caribbean, and increasingly also the states of Eastern Europe.[2] This approach was equally favoured by the new French president, François Mitterrand, who succeeded Giscard in May 1981.

Apprehension that Western Europe might get left behind by the United States, and by Japan, which was keeping up with the Americans in technological advance through a programme of research and development that also received considerable state support, inspired German and French leaders to float proposals for a revival of the stalled project of European integration at the beginning of the 1980s. These included a proposal that was discussed at the November 1981 European Council meeting in London, from the West German Foreign Minister, Hans Dietrich Genscher, and his Italian counterpart, Emilio Colombo, for a new European Act to replace the Treaty of Rome; and a 'very ambitious project' proposed by Mitterrand in April 1985, with West German support, for a programme of European research in high technology, which was seen as a counter to the Strategic Defense Initiative (SDI) that the US President had announced shortly before. The SDI appeared to the French to be the most blatant example of the United States using defence expenditure to promote technological advance.

British responses to such initiatives were complicated by three factors: the renewal of the special relationship with the United States that was promoted by the British Prime Minister as soon as she came into office, and developed even more on the election of Ronald Reagan, who was an ideological soul-mate; the economic

Constantine Vaitsos (eds.), *Integration and Unequal Development: The Experience of the EEC* (London, 1980), ch. 10; Frieder Schlupp, 'Modell Deutschland and the International Division of Labour', in Krippendorf and Rittberger (eds.), *The Foreign Policy of West Germany*, ch. 2.

[2] This point is made specifically by Statler, 'British Foreign Policy', p. 215; see also Udo Rehfeldt, 'France', in Seers and Vaitsos (eds.), *Integration and Unequal Development*, ch. 9.

programme and strong nationalism of the new Conservative Government; and the continuation of the dispute that had begun under Callaghan over the size of British contributions to the Community's budget.

The Domestic Context

The new Conservative leader, Margaret Thatcher, was elected in 1975 as a more right-wing candidate than Edward Heath, although her success almost certainly owed more to Heath's unpopularity in the parliamentary party, combined with the loyalty of more obvious contenders, who declined to stand against him on the first ballot, than it did to her credentials as an ideologue of the free market, credentials which at that time were no means clear-cut. Initially Thatcher moved cautiously in changing the direction of the Conservative Party. Her Shadow Cabinet, although it excluded Heath, included several who supported similar positions, and there was no sudden repudiation of the recent past. Gradually, though, a Thatcherite programme began to be developed in speeches and in attacks on the Labour Government.

The main lines of the Thatcherite economic programme were a rejection of incomes policies, and commitments to reduce the power of trade unions, to combat inflation through tight control of the money supply, to lower taxes, and to end subsidies for inefficient nationalized industries. In international affairs, Thatcher earned herself the soubriquet 'the Iron Lady' from the Soviet Union when she adopted the rhetoric of Cold War, suggesting that social democratic governments were putting at risk the freedom of the West by their soft line towards the USSR, expressed in the policy of *détente*. She recommitted the Conservatives firmly to the Atlantic Alliance, and to support for the United States in its recent harder line towards the USSR. One of her first foreign policy acts on becoming Prime Minister in 1979 was to visit Washington and publicly pledge total support for Carter in his argument with the rest of Western Europe over *détente*. Although there was no question of repudiating British membership of the EC, it was also clear that the new leader was reversing the priority that Heath had given to Europe over America. That orientation was strengthened when Ronald Reagan succeeded to the White House: he and

Thatcher struck up a strong personal rapport that reinforced their ideological like-mindedness.

For the first three years of its term of office the new Government faced a renewed world recession sparked off by the 1979 rise in the price of oil. Unlike 1974, when the Labour Government took no steps to tackle the inflationary effects of the December 1973 rise in oil prices, the Thatcher Government introduced a number of deflationary measures in 1979, including a budget that fulfilled the manifesto pledge to reduce income tax, but almost doubled VAT from 8 to 15 per cent; and an increase in interest rates from 12 to 14 per cent in June, and to 17 per cent in November. These measures, the recession in the rest of the world, and the persistently high value of sterling that was a result of its status as the currency of an oil-producing state, combined to produce a serious downturn in economic activity in Britain in 1980. Bankruptcies and unemployment both soared to unprecedented heights, and the Government's popularity fell to correspondingly low levels in opinion polls.

In this context Thatcher's declared aim of reducing public expenditure proved difficult to achieve. The higher levels of unemployment increased social security payments, and attempts to make nationalized industries more efficient imposed short-term costs. In an attempt to prevent public expenditure from actually rising, the Government began to look for savings in every possible direction. Prescription charges were increased, regional aid was cut, the fees of overseas students were increased by several hundred per cent, the price of school meals and council house rents were raised. It is in this context that the battle over British contributions to the Community's budget has to be viewed.

The turning-point for Thatcher came in 1982. Its most dramatic manifestation was the war with Argentina over the Falkland Islands. The invasion of this small remnant of the British Empire by the Argentinian armed forces seems to have been an attempt by the military government of Argentina to divert attention from a rapidly deteriorating domestic economic and political situation by a popular victory in foreign affairs. The claim of Argentina to the islands, which lay some 250 miles off its coast, was long-standing, and unquestioned by any section of political opinion in the country. The Foreign Office had been engaged in talks with Argentina about the status of the islands, as part of the same policy of completing disengagement from expensive old imperial entanglements that had produced agreement on independence for Zimbabwe in 1980. The withdrawal of the one British naval protection vessel seemed to signal the indifference of Britain to the fate of the islands, and must have encourage General Galtieri, the Argentinian leader, to believe that he could pull off a successful operation without meeting more than token resistance. He seriously miscalculated.

The invasion plunged the British Government into difficulty because it was open to the charge of having facilitated it. But it also provided Thatcher with an opportunity to demonstrate her resolve and patriotism, which she was quick to seize. The dispatch of a naval task force to the islands followed quickly amidst a revival of popular jingoism that scarcely seemed credible to much of the British establishment, and may even have surprised the Prime Minister. Urged on by the popular Press, which treated the whole conflict as though it were a soccer international, Thatcher refused to allow mediation efforts to stand between her and a complete military victory, which predictably was achieved by the professional British forces against the conscript, and less well-equipped Argentinians.

One effect of the Falklands conflict was to transform the popularity of Thatcher, whom opinion polls had at one stage shown to be the most unpopular Prime Minister of the post-war period. It dispelled attempts to portray her as less concerned about the national interest than her opponents in the opposition parties and within her own party, a claim that had been given some credence by decisions such as the scrapping of exchange controls on the movement of capital out of the country. It may also have contributed to the 1983 general election victory, although the economic upturn probably had more responsibility.[3]

The recovery of the world economy was fragile and uneven, based as it was on the US budget and trade deficits, but the benefits to Britain were greater than to other European states because Britain was an oil producer. The price of oil is demarcated in dollars, so, although the real price of oil fell by 10 per cent between 1979 and 1983, the cost to other European states of the high dollar was greater than it was to Britain, and offset the benefits of their higher exports to the United States. The strength of the dollar also

[3] David Sanders, Hugh Ward, and David Marsh (with Tony Fletcher), 'Government Popularity and the Falklands War: A Reassessment', *British Journal of Political Science*, 17 (1987), 281–313.

took some of the pressure off the pound, which came down in value to levels that gave British exporters a more reasonable basis from which to compete for markets.

By 1983 unemployment, although still high, was no longer increasing; inflation had been brought back down from the high levels that it attained in the first two years of the Government; and industrial output had begun a slow recovery. The economy had been through a painful restructuring, which had destroyed much of the old industrial base. Prosperity had come first to the south-east of the country, partly as a spin-off from the tremendous success of the City of London which was quick to take advantage of the deregulation of capital movements to confirm its position as one of the three leading financial centres of the world, alongside New York and Tokyo. Microelectronics companies, mainly Japanese or American, moved into the Thames valley and parts of the Scottish Highlands to take advantage of labour that was cheap by European standards. Investment by Japanese manufacturers of cars and electrical goods increased in the face of hostility from the EC to the volume of Japanese exports: production in Britain allowed them to circumvent export quotas throughout the Community, and for a variety of reasons, including lower wages, Britain was favoured over other member states.

By 1983 enough people were feeling better off than they had been previously to ensure the Government of re-election, especially in the light of the division within the opposition. The Labour Party had split in the autumn of 1980, with several of its more prominent members leaving to form the Social Democratic Party (SDP). An alliance between the SDP and the Liberals proved a popular home in by-elections for voters who disliked Thatcherism but also were not attracted by the leftward drift of the Labour Party in opposition. But although the Alliance attracted 25.4 per cent of the votes cast in 1983, the effect of the electoral system was that it won only 23 seats in Parliament (Liberals 17, SDP 6), whereas the Labour Party, with only 2.3 per cent more of the votes, won 209 seats. The main effect of the Alliance challenge was to allow the Conservatives to win a large majority of seats, 397 of the 650, on just 42.4 per cent of the vote.

The election cleared the way for a number of new developments that the Government had been hesistant to pursue beforehand. These included a renewed offensive against the power of the trade unions, culminating in the miners' strike from March 1984 to February 1985, which ended in the defeat of the union that had long been in the vanguard of working-class militancy, showing quite clearly who was now to govern the country. They also included a change of direction in the Government's policy within the EC, although it took until June 1984 to clear the outstanding business of the budgetary dispute.

From Strasburg to Dublin

Thatcher initially presented her case reasonably enough at her first meeting of the European Council, in Strasburg in June 1979. Her approach here was even described as *'communautaire'*.[4] It was backed up by an announcement on the first day of the meeting that Britain would deposit its share of gold and foreign currency reserves with the European Monetary Co-operation Fund that had been set up to administer the EMS. This meant that sterling would form part of the basket of currencies on the basis of which the value of the Ecu would be determined, and the move was widely interpreted as a sign that sterling would soon be taken into the exchange-rate mechanism of the EMS.

Discussion of the issue of budgetary contributions at Strasburg was brief and limited to agreeing the procedure for analysing the problem. It was agreed that the Commission would prepare a report by September, which would be discussed by the Finance Ministers, after which member states would be asked to submit their own suggestions for a solution, in time for the Commission to prepare its proposals for presentation to the next European Council in Dublin in late November.

At that November 1979 European Council Thatcher adopted an entirely different tone. The Commission proposed to revise the 1975 rebate mechanism so as to give Britain a cash rebate of £350 million, plus increased spending in Britain. In contrast to her later attitude to plans that involved increased expenditure, as opposed to straight rebates, Thatcher indicated her willingness to accept this approach, but insisted from the outset that the total return to Britain should amount to £1 billion. The French indicated that they were not prepared to agree to any more than the £350 million, which Britain would have to accept as full and final settlement of its

[4] *The Economist*, 30 June 1979.

claim. This provoked an argument that lasted ten hours, in the course of which Thatcher upset her partners by her uncompromising demands for what she insensitively described as her 'own money back'; and she in turn was apparently offended by the attitude of the German Chancellor, Helmut Schmidt, and the French President, Valéry Giscard d'Estaing, who appear to have intimated that they were not about to be browbeaten by a mere woman with no experience of international affairs.[5] Such an approach would clearly act like a red rag to a bull so far as the British Prime Minister was concerned.

The 'May Mandate'

After various formulas for calculating rebates on their contributions were rejected by the British at the Luxemburg European Council in April 1980, mainly on the grounds that they contained no guarantees of what would happen after 1980, a meeting of Foreign Ministers in May 1980 agreed a formula for reductions in the British contributions in 1980 and 1981, and asked the Commission to put forward proposals by the end of June 1981 for restructuring the budget in such a way as 'to prevent the recurrence of unacceptable situations' for any member state, but 'without calling into question the common financial responsibility for these policies which are financed from the Community's own resources, or the basic principles of the common agricultural policy'.[6]

By this time the need to settle the dispute had become more urgent because the Community was threatened with bankruptcy. An explosive rise in the cost of the CAP meant that the need for a more permanent solution to the problem was acute. The Community was in danger of running out of money entirely unless the 1 per cent ceiling on VAT revenues was raised, and was facing the imminent arrival of Spain and Portugal as full members, which would put new demands on the financial structure. The raising of the VAT ceiling would require approval in each of the national parliaments, and the British were not prepared to agree to any such increase until a permanent settlement to the budgetary imbalance, acceptable to

[5] Christopher Tugendhat, 'Out of Step to a United Europe', *The Times*, 21 Jan. 1986.
[6] *Bulletin of the European Communities*, 6–1981, point 1.2.1.

Britain, was found. The financial crisis presented Britain with an opportunity to force such a permanent settlement.

The response of the Commission to what came to be known as the 'May mandate' was set out in three main chapters, covering adaptation of the CAP, the development of other Community policies, and the problem of adjustments to the Community budget,[7] which Britain insisted must be discussed and agreed upon together, not separately. But the document served only to focus disagreements rather than to resolve them.

Relations between Britain and the other member states became increasingly strained during the negotiations on the budgetary contributions, and reached their nadir in May 1982. Britain was holding up agreement on agricultural prices for 1982–3, linking agreement here to agreement on a permanent settlement of the dispute over budgetary contributions. The irritation of the other member states with this behaviour was heightened by the refusal of Britain to give any ground on this front in reciprocation for the promptness with which its partners had supported it over the Falklands, despite serious reservations amongst some of them about the British response to the invasion.

On 18 May the Belgian presidency called a majority vote in the Council of Agricultural Ministers on the price levels. Britain protested that this breached the right of any member state to exercise a veto, but the French in particular rejected such an interpretation of the 1966 agreement, known as 'the Luxemburg compromise', on the grounds that it was only applicable to issues that were a vital national interest of a member state, and agricultural price levels for one year clearly were not a vital national interest for Britain.

The Need to Revive the Community

Shortly after the incident of the majority vote in the Agricultural Council, both the new French President, François Mitterrand, and his Foreign Minister, Claude Cheysson, suggested publicly that it might be better for all concerned if Britain ceased to be a full member of the Community and instead negotiated some 'special status'. Although Thatcher rejected this solution in the House of Commons on 20 May, asserting 'we are full members of the

[7] *Bulletin of the European Communities*, Supplement 1–1981.

Community, and we intend to remain full members',[8] the resolution of the French Government, and the signs of frustration amongst other member states evidenced by the majority vote on agricultural prices, may well have given the British Government cause for thought about the need to agree a settlement of the budgetary dispute, especially when seen in the light of earlier developments. Talk of the need to get the Community moving once again had increased in the aftermath of the arrival in office of the Reagan Administration in the United States. The economic policy of the Administration presented the risk of the EC being left behind in economic terms, and there was also considerable concern about the foreign and defence policies of confrontation with the Soviet Union, which particularly worried the West Germans, who benefited from *détente* economically, and were in the front line should any military confrontation take place.

It was in response to this concern that the Genscher–Colombo plan was formulated. In a speech presenting his ideas to the European Parliament in November 1981, Genscher argued that:

The economic problems now confronting us to go to the roots of our democracies and of the European Community. Nevertheless, we cannot focus our efforts solely on the economic issues. We must, instead, set our sights on the grand design of the political unification of Europe, for it is from that design that we shall draw the strength to act as one and take decisions, on economic matters and others, which will not simply paper over the cracks but provide forward-looking solutions.[9]

The momentum generated by that initiative led to the adoption of a 'Solemn Declaration' on European Union by the Heads of Government at the meeting of the European Council in Stuttgart on 19 June 1983, together with a plan to 'relaunch' the Community through 'a major negotiation' over the next six months 'to tackle the most pressing problems facing the Community so as to provide a solid basis for the further dynamic development of the Community over the rest of the decade'.[10] The negotiation took the form of special meetings of the Foreign Ministers, Finance Ministers, and Agricultural Ministers.

Britain welcomed the inclusion on the agenda of the question of budgetary contributions, the need for future budgetary discipline,

[8] *Hansard*, 6th ser. 24 (20 May 1982), col. 468.
[9] *Bulletin of the European Communities*, 11–1981, point 1.2.2.
[10] *Bulletin of the European Communities*, 6–1983, point 1.6.1. *et seq.*

the re-examination of the CAP, and the difficulties surrounding the accession of Spain and Portugal to membership. What worried the British were references to European union, to strengthening the powers of the European Parliament. All of these themes were present in a Draft Treaty on European Union, promoted by the veteran Italian federalist Altiero Spinelli, and adopted by the European Parliament in February 1984.[11]

From the British perspective the enthusiasm for such ideas of some of the other member states, particularly Italy and the Benelux countries, was something of a mystery. For Britain there were certain practical steps that needed to be taken, and strengthening the central institutions of the Community was irrelevant to these. One such step was improving the EPC procedure. Another was removing the barriers that still existed to the free working of the internal Community market, a high priority for Britain, particularly so far as it affected free trade in financial services.

Most of the other member states at least paid lip-service to the idea of progress in these areas. But some of the original members, Italy in particular, argued that constitutional reform was a necessary prerequisite to such progress. As Quentin Peel reflected at a later stage in the negotiations, there was 'a very real divide in European psychology: between those for whom the political symbols come first . . . and the practical steps are assured to follow; and those like Britain who would take it the opposite way round'.[12]

Perhaps not just philosophical principles were at stake; there may also have been more practical reasons for the political leaders of some states to support the strengthening of the central institutions. Nevertheless, the idea of weakening national sovereignty through majority voting in the Council of Ministers, and through strengthening the powers of the European Parliament, remained anathema to Britain, as it did indeed to Denmark and Greece. What the British Government wanted to avoid was the Community moving in a federalist direction. What it appeared to want was to move the Community in the direction that British policy had long favoured: towards becoming a genuine economic common market, with the addition of co-operation on foreign policy.

The question was whether Britain could play a leading role in the

[11] *Bulletin of the European Communities*, 2–1984, points 1.1.1, 1.1.2.
[12] Quentin Peel, 'After the EEC Summit: Why it all went wrong', *Financial Times*, 1 July 1985.

movement for reform, and guide it in the British direction. In doing so it was severely hampered by the ill-will generated by the dispute over its budgetary contributions. So long as that dispute ran on there was an increasing risk of the lead being taken by other states, particularly the original six members states, and of Britain being left behind as the Community moved in another direction.

The Search for a Settlement

In their statement following the Stuttgart meeting of the European Council, the Heads of State and Government committed their Ministers to completing the special negotiations within six months. The results were to be presented to the European Council meeting in Athens in December 1983. There was an expectation that a final decision would be taken there on the budgetary issue, and perhaps on other issues; but the meeting failed totally to reach any agreements, and was dubbed 'the most disastrous since these formal thrice-yearly meetings of heads of government started in 1974'.[13]

Much of the blame for the failure was laid at the door of President Mitterrand. He did not throw his weight behind attempts to agree limits to the CAP, although this was perhaps understandable given the importance of the agricultural vote in French electoral politics. But he also sank hopes of a settlement on the British budgetary contributions with a declaration that the aim of the meeting should be to agree another *ad hoc* payment rather than to agree a permanent formula.

This intervention was either a terrible error, or an indication of more Machiavellian thinking. If it was an error, it was of considerable proportions; Mitterrand's statement ignored the fact that France had been participating for the previous six months in negotiations aimed at finding a permanent formula, and it ignored the clear statement by the European Parliament that it would approve no further *ad hoc* payments. If it was Machiavellian, it was one way of ensuring that the discussions carried over into the French presidency of the Council of Ministers, and that the French Government would therefore be able to claim the credit for reaching an agreement.

[13] John Wyles, 'EEC Summit—President Mitterrand's Exocet', *Financial Times*, 7 Dec. 1983.

France took over the presidency from Greece at the beginning of 1984. Mitterrand immediately announced his intention to reach an agreement on the British problem and all the related budgetary issues, which included restraint of agricultural expenditure, and the increase in VAT contributions, by the March European Council in Brussels. He then embarked on a tour of national capitals, to meet other Heads of Government, starting and ending with Thatcher in London.

By the time of the Brussels European Council on 19–20 March, provisional agreement had been reached by Ministers of Agriculture on curbing milk production and on reducing the level of monetary compensatory amounts, which acted as a major factor distorting Community agricultural trade.[14] Finalization of these agreements was, however, left to the European Council, and was dependent on agreement being reached on the other issues. Even then, Ireland was threatening to veto the curbs on dairy production unless it was exempted at least temporarily, arguing that the effect on its national economy would be catastrophic, since milk production accounted for 9 per cent of its GNP.

The summit got off to a bad start, with Thatcher lecturing the other member states on the need for prudence in financial matters. But by the second day, thanks to the skill and patience of Mitterrand in the Chair, and the hard work of the French officials in producing successive draft formulae, hard negotiations were taking place.

Agreement was reached on the size of the increase in the VAT revenues: they would rise from 1 per cent to 1.4 per cent immediately, then to 1.6 per cent in 1986, subject to the agreement of all the member states, who by that time would include Spain and Portugal. But this was still dependent on the British rebate agreement being reached, and on the agricultural cut-backs being ratified.

One of the fundamental problems in the negotiations on the size of the British rebate was that Britain persisted in calculating its gross contributions to the budget in terms of both its VAT contributions *and* the tariffs and agricultural import levies that it paid over to the Community. This latter element was held in Community circles not to be part of national contributions because

[14] The origins and nature of monetary compensatory amounts are explained in George, *Politics and Policy in the European Community*, pp. 127–8.

the tariffs and levies were common Community instruments which national officials were merely collecting on behalf of the Community; consequently the other member states refused to consider it part of the British contribution.

The French devised a formula that attempted to cut through this problem. It referred only to VAT contributions for a member state that in the previous year had paid an amount into the budget through VAT contributions that exceeded its receipts from the budget by an agreed amount. The amounts were left to be negotiated at a level that would be acceptable to the British and to the other member states.

In a major concession, Thatcher agreed to negotiate on this basis, and progress was being made. Britain's initial demand for a 1984 rebate of 1.5 billion Ecu had been reduced to 1.35 billion. This was still more than the one billion that had been the initial French offer, but the gap was narrowing, and the next move was about to be made on the French side, when Chancellor Kohl of West Germany ineptly proposed a flat-rate of one billion Ecu in each of the three years 1984, 1985, and 1986. This was inept because it undermined the concept of an automatic mechanism which the French had been hoping to have accepted in order to prevent future wrangles, and it broke the momentum of the bargaining that had been in train around the formula.

The British delegation rejected the West German suggestion, and came back with a counter-proposal, but it was now too late in the meeting for serious bargaining to begin anew. Indeed, one of the Prime Ministers, Ireland's Garret FitzGerald, had already walked out after clashing with Thatcher over his insistence that Ireland be exempted from the proposed 5 per cent cut in milk production.

The final act in this tragi-comedy came after the formal end of the European Council, ten hours later than scheduled, when the Italians and French refused to lift a veto on the payment of Britain's 1983 rebate, that they had imposed following the failure in Athens, and the British Prime Minister responded to the news by threatening to withhold Britain's contributions to the 1984 budget.

The Fontainebleau Agreement

Just three months after rejecting the most favourable budget settlement yet offered, the British Government accepted a deal that was described by Thatcher as 'far better than the offer of the other nine member states at the last European Council',[15] but which conceded more to the position of the other member states than it did to the British position.

At the Fontainebleau meeting of the European Council, Thatcher accepted a rebate of one billion Ecu for 1984, and then 66 per cent of the difference between Britain's VAT contributions to the budget and its receipts from the budget in 1985 and future years, the arrangement to be reconsidered at the point when the next increase in VAT revenues, from 1.4 per cent to 1.6 per cent, came to be discussed.

This agreement represented two further concessions on the part of the British, to add to their acceptance at Brussels that only VAT payments would be calculated on the contributions side of the equation. First, they abandoned their insistence that an automatic and permanent formula be found for calculating the rebates, a demand that had been present in the British position throughout the five years of the dispute, and that after the Brussels summit had been converted into a demand that any settlement be based on the 'Brussels formula'. This was an important retreat, because following Brussels other member states, and Italy in particular, had become concerned that the formula that had nearly been agreed could in fact involve West Germany also receiving a rebate under certain circumstances. Since West Germany was easily the richest member state, this was felt to be totally unacceptable.

The second concession was in pure cash terms. The 66 per cent rebate for 1985 and 1986, to which Thatcher agreed, represented, on the best calculations available at the time, approximately 1,070 million Ecu in each year. That was more than the one billion on offer at the end of the Brussels summit, but it was much nearer to the offer of the other member states than to the demand of the British. Also *Le Monde* calculated that, if the formula had been applied to the period 1980–3, it would have produced a rebate of around 915 million Ecu, less than the 1,017 million Ecu that Britain had received in *ad hoc* rebates between 1980 and 1983.[16]

There is even room for argument over whether the Fontainebleau formula was more beneficial than that offered and rejected in March. *Le Monde* argued that the March formula would have

---

[15] *Hansard*, 6th ser. 62 (27 June 1984), col. 993.
[16] *Le Monde*, 28 June 1984.

given Britain bigger future rebates if Community expenditure were not brought under control, and so strengthened the British bargaining position when it came to negotiating budgetary restraint.[17] Even if this argument is not accepted, it is difficult to see that the settlement was more than a marginal improvement on the offer tabled in March, and it seems more than likely that such a deal could have been secured in Brussels had Britain shown the same willingness to compromise as was evident at Fontainebleau. So what had changed in the meantime?

One thing that had changed was that on 31 March the Ministers of Agriculture had agreed on a small overall reduction in farm prices, and cuts in dairy quotas; Ireland had been given a special dispensation. This certainly cleared one of the minor complicating factors out of the way for the Fontainebleau meeting, but perhaps more importantly it allowed the British Government to maintain that it was not agreeing to an increase in the rate of VAT contributions to 1.4 per cent without some indication that the Community was in earnest about reining in CAP expenditure.

Secondly, the elections to the European Parliament had happened, on 14 and 17 June. Although the European Parliament is not important in its own right, the elections are always turned into a measure of the popularity of the Government by national media. As *The Economist* explained, 'There seems to be a tacit agreement not to talk about the British problem again before the European parliamentary elections (on June 14 and 17) are out of the way. It would be too risky for member governments to make further concessions before the votes are counted.'[18]

The most likely explanation of the failure at Brussels, though, is that Thatcher overplayed her hand. It is quite possible that she wanted a settlement at Brussels, but, not temperamentally inclined to compromise in negotiations, she may simply have proved incapable of negotiating it. It is possible that she expected the other member states to capitulate to her, and was wrong.

Having failed to win the confrontation, she responded in typically aggressive fashion by threatening to withhold Britain's 1984 contributions to the Community budget when the Foreign Ministers (predictably) refused to allow the release of the 1983 rebate. But here again the Prime Minister appears to have miscalculated, and this time to have misjudged the mood amongst

[17] Ibid.   [18] *The Economist*, 19 May 1984.

her own supporters. She seems to have been genuinely surprised when her Chief Whip reported to her that there was a back-bench rebellion against such an act of illegality. Whether she bowed to this pressure, or to the patient blandishments of President Mitterrand, she agreed a few days later not to carry out the threat. The reason given in Parliament was that President Mitterrand had called a special meeting of Foreign Ministers, that this had changed the situation, and that 'the Government will take no action which might damage the prospects of decisive progress'.[19]

Mitterrand kept the pressure on Britain when he addressed the European Parliament on 24 May. He pledged his Government's support for a new treaty of European union, supported the increased use of majority voting in the Council of Ministers, and spoke of the possibility of a 'two-speed Europe' if not all the member states wished to move quickly along this route.[20] All of this alarmed the Foreign Office, because it was precisely the threat that they had hoped to avoid. Instead of Britain taking the lead in the EC and moving it in the direction long desired by Britain, there re-emerged the prospect of a lead being given in a direction not in line with British preferences, and of Britain again becoming an outsider.

Sir Geoffrey Howe, now Foreign Secretary, in Paris for discussions a few days later, was vigorous in his assertion of Britain's pro-Community credentials. Britain, he maintained, was in the forefront of the Community on many issues. He rejected the concept of a two-speed Community, but said that, if any such thing did happen, he would expect to see Britain in the front rank, not in the slower stream as most observers seemed to think President Mitterrand had implied. What Britain wanted, said Howe, was not a two-speed Europe but a high-speed Europe.

It was against this background that the British Prime Minister went to Fontainebleau, taking with her not just an apparent determination to remove the budgetary dispute as an obstacle to closer Anglo–French collaboration, but also a discussion paper entitled 'Europe—The Future',[21] which was submitted as a contribution to the discussion. The paper outlined the British view on where the Community ought to be going. Its very existence was an

---

[19] *Hansard*, 6th ser. 56 (22 Mar. 1984), cols. 1173–4.
[20] *Bulletin of the European Communities*, 5–1984, point 3.4.1.
[21] H. M. Government, 'Europe—The Future', *Journal of Common Market Studies*, 23 (1984), 74–81.

indication that Britain no longer intended to allow others to make all the running, although its contents were rather controversial. Clearly Britain's vision of the future differed somewhat from that put forward by the European Parliament and supported by President Mitterrand. Nevertheless, Britain was apparently ready to move beyond the sterile negativism that had marked its position in the Community for the first decade of its membership and engage in constructive dialogue about the future. That could only take place once the budgetary dispute was settled, as it was at Fontainebleau.

The settlement did not quite mark the end, though, of British awkwardness on budgetary issues. Between July and December 1984 Her Majesty's Government was again standing out from the rest of the Community on a matter connected with the budget.

The Battle for Budgetary Discipline

Press reaction to Fontainebleau indicated an expectation that the settlement of the dispute over budgetary contributions and the presentation of the British discussion document did mean a new era in Britain's relations with the EC. Yet shortly afterwards new doubts were raised when Sir Geoffrey Howe blocked a supplementary budget for the Community for 1984.

With the EC's money due to run out in November, the Commission proposed that a supplementary budget of two billion Ecu be voted to carry them through to the end of the year (which is also the Community's financial year). The British Government argued that such a supplementary budget would be illegal and would set a bad precedent. The other member states were treated to a typical British homily on the need for the Community to learn to live within its means, and not to keep pouring good money away maintaining bad policies.

Instead of a supplementary budget, Britain proposed that the shortfall should be covered by cuts in expenditure and by deferring as many payments as possible to 1985. In order to avoid an even worse crisis in 1985 as a result of the deferred payments, Britain proposed that the increase in VAT revenues from 1 per cent to 1.4 per cent should be brought forward from 1986 to 1985.

The other member states and the Commission were not prepared to accept the British argument that the supplementary budget would be illegal, nor that a 'whip-round' would set a bad precedent. And they suspected Britain of baser motives than Howe admitted. If the extra payments were deferred and added to the 1985 budget, Britain would receive a 66 per cent rebate on its contribution, whereas its total rebate for 1984 had been fixed at a cash sum of 1 billion Ecu. As *The Economist* put it, 'the British have a respectable case . . . But so unpopular has Mrs Thatcher become during her budget battle that British arguments often prove counter-productive.'[22]

Ian Murray, writing in *The Times*, expressed his personal disappointment that Britain was still being awkward about money. Although this time it was Sir Geoffrey Howe who was insisting on sticking to Community rules, it still appeared to the other member states as a case of Britain being miserly, refusing to allow the Community more money to bail it out of its financial crisis. The British argument that the Community must learn to live within its means was correct, but Britain was building up a legacy of more ill-will, when it ought to be trying to move the Community 'to develop more along the lines it wanted when it joined. That means achieving objectives like tearing down internal frontiers, clearing the way to cheaper air fares and opening up the insurance market throughout the Community to British companies.'[23]

Murray's outline of British governmental objectives was an accurate reflection of what the Government wanted to achieve. The difference lay in the tactics to achieve it. Murray, being a journalist, had to react to the immediate impression created by British parsimony on this issue. But, taking a longer view, it could be argued that this was a necessary stance, and part of the process of clearing the ground prior to taking new initiatives. Britain had insisted ever since Thatcher came to office that Community expenditure must be brought under control. If the other member states thought that the question of rebates was the end of Britain's interest in the budget, they had mistaken their woman. Thatcher has frequently been described as a conviction-politician, and her conviction that high public expenditure is wrong has been the guiding light of all her governmental efforts. For Britain a change of attitude towards the Community did indeed mean trying to get it 'to develop more along the lines it wanted when it joined'; but an

---

[22] *The Economist*, 4 Aug. 1984.
[23] Ian Murray, 'How Sir Geoffrey Reversed Roles', *The Times*, 23 July 1984.

essential part of that course involved instilling a new thinking into the other member states and into the Commission.

In September Britain accepted that there should be a supplementary budget for 1984, although only amounting to one billion Ecu, rather than the two billion originally requested by the Commission. In return for this concession, Britain extracted a commitment that agreement would be reached quickly on strict financial guidelines to control future growth of the budget, especially the CAP.

The details of this commitment were worked out for subsequent approval by the Heads of Government at a meeting of Finance Ministers on 15–16 September at Dromoland Castle, County Clare, in Ireland. What was agreed there was not the fully codified system of budgetary constraints desired by Nigel Lawson, the British Chancellor of the Exchequer, but it did mark a considerable advance on the previous system, which had effectively allowed the Ministers of Agriculture to hijack the largest part of the budget by agreeing on agricultural prices for the following year before the budgetary procedure itself was carried out. Under the new system, a maximum limit would be set on budgetary commitments for the following year on 1 March, before the Agriculture Ministers negotiated the level of farm prices. Any overshoot on one year's budget would be clawed back over the next two years.

This arrangement was agreed at the Dublin meeting of the European Council in December 1984. It represented quite an achievement for the British. Of course, other member states were in favour of budgetary discipline, especially West Germany, which was the major contributor, and France, which was due to become a net contributor following the Fontainebleau settlement, and an even bigger net contributor as a consequence of the accession of Spain and Portugal (agreement on which was also finalized at Dublin). But neither of these states was in a position to make an issue of something that inevitably involved placing further restrictions on the CAP. Both countries' politicians had to watch the agricultural vote very carefully. So it was almost certainly necessary for Britain to make budgetary restraint an issue, since other major member states would not. On the other hand, it is doubtful whether there was quite such opposition to Britain's resistance to the supplementary budget and insistence on future budgetary restraint as publicly appeared.

Conclusion

Fontainebleau marked an end to one phase of Britain's relationship with the EC and the start of another. The phase of the budgetary dispute had several facets. One obviously was the determination of the British Government not only to limit the size of its own contributions to the Community's budget, but also to ensure that the budget as a whole was brought under control, which meant effectively bringing under control expenditure on the CAP. This was why Britain was still being awkward after Fontainebleau: budgetary discipline was a genuine matter of principle for the Thatcher Government.

There was also a strong domestic political aspect to the whole argument. When Thatcher launched her campaign for an effective and permanent rebate mechanism, Britain was going through a major recession, to which the Government's response was to tighten public expenditure, which in turn had the effect of making the recession deeper. As Thatcher herself said, in the course of the 1979 Winston Churchill Memorial Lecture, 'I cannot play Sister Bountiful to the Community while my own electorate are being asked to forego improvements in the field of health, education, welfare and the rest'.[24]

Although the condition of the British economy began to improve after 1981, and the need for the Government to find savings in public expenditure wherever possible consequently declined, there was no let-up in the campaign. The principle of reducing public expenditure remained at the heart of the Government's programme, and by that time a considerable amount of political capital had been invested in getting a settlement that could be presented as a victory.

Thatcher's resolute approach to domestic and international problems was an image that she cultivated during her first term of office. Her image as a leader who would not compromise on principles, nor effect a 'U-turn', was important both to her chances of re-election and to carrying through her radical economic programme against considerable opposition from a variety of vested interests. The budgetary battle with the rest of the Community became one piece of evidence that this was not a Prime Minister who would succumb to the temptation to compromise.

[24] *Guardian*, 19 Oct. 1979.

It also helped to establish her credentials as a national leader. In the face of criticism from within as well as outside her own party that she was dividing the nation, she attempted to unify it by wrapping herself in the Union flag and going into battle for the national interest. Of course, the Falklands conflict proved much more effective in this respect, but nobody could have foreseen such an opportunity falling into her lap. After the Falklands, it became much easier for Thatcher to make concessions to reach a budgetary deal because it was no longer necessary for her to prove her credentials as a national champion. On the other hand, the settlement clearly had to wait until after the general election so as to give no ammunition to the Labour Party, which went into the election campaign once more opposed to British membership. As Peter Riddell explains:

The vigorous approach of Mrs Thatcher was undoubtedly effective domestically in outmanœuvring Labour. The EEC issue was not rated as one of the two most important by most people at the 1983 election, but among those mentioning it the Conservative approach was preferred to Labour's by a margin of 50 per cent, according to the BBC/Gallup survey quoted in the *Guardian* of 14 June 1983, compared with an 8 per cent advantage for Labour on the EEC issue at the 1979 election. This turnround did not appear to reflect any upsurge in enthusiasm for the EEC. Instead the majority view could be characterized as favouring a strong assertion of British interests and accepting that British membership was now permanent after ten years . . .[25]

That it took so long after the election to reach a settlement owed something to the clumsiness of other EC leaders: Mitterrand in Athens and Kohl in Brussels brought negotiations to a halt by suggesting solutions that Thatcher clearly could not accept without loss of face. It also probably owed something to the character of the British Prime Minister, whose tendency to become impatient with diplomatic restraint is notorious.

The delay in finalizing an agreement after the election probably helped the Government to present the eventual settlement to the British electorate as a victory, despite the concessions that were made on the British side, and the doubts over whether the Fountainebleau deal was in fact as good as the one that had been rejected in Brussels three months earlier. The effect of the failures in Athens and Brussels was to put the issue back on to the front pages

[25] Peter Riddell, *The Thatcher Government* (Oxford, 1983), 214–5.

of newspapers, and to bring it back to the attention of the public, setting the scene for a victory declaration. The details of the settlement were far too complex to be absorbed by a majority of the British people, even had the popular Press attempted to explain them. The opposition in Parliament tried to attack the settlement as a retreat from the position that Thatcher had defended for so long, but the message that came across was that the Government had obtained a far better deal than had the Labour Government in 1975, and far better than had been on offer five years earlier. Both these claims were correct: that concessions had been made was difficult to convey given the technical nature of matters such as how budgetary contributions are calculated; that the settlement could have been obtained earlier had the concessions been made earlier was difficult to prove.

If it is accepted that the British Government could have chosen to delay reaching a settlement even longer had it wished to continue with the same manner it had adopted between 1979 and 1983, the question arises of why it chose to settle at Fontainebleau. The answer almost certainly lies in the momentum that had been generated within the EC by the perception that the United States and Japan were outstripping Europe in technological development, and the related apprehension about the direction of US foreign policy under Reagan.

For Britain these developments were less directly threatening than they were for West Germany and France. Thatcher agreed with Reagan on foreign policy much of the time, even if the Siberian pipeline incident and Grenada did cause friction. So far as technological development was concerned, Britain had allowed its own capital-goods industry to decline, and had effectively relinquished its hopes of competing independently in the high-technology industries, being content to import technology developed elsewhere and to act as an assembly shop for US and Japanese companies. In other words, Britain had become a dependent economy, precisely what West Germany and France wished to avoid becoming, and its dependence was to a large extent on the United States and Japan. Thus, were the rest of Western Europe to become technologically dependent on the United States and Japan, Britain would be no worse off. On the other hand, were the rest of Western Europe to go ahead without Britain in an attempt to develop an independent technological capacity and a unified market that could sustain that attempt, Britain would be considerably worse off. The US and Japanese investment that was attracted to Britain was attracted by the access that production in Britain gave to the EC market. If that market became more closely integrated and Britain remained outside, the same thing would be likely to happen as had happened in the 1960s, when Britain remained outside the original common market: direct foreign investment would start to bypass Britain and be channelled into economies that were inside the wider market. Also, Britain needed to remain in the forefront of any EC developments to ensure that the City of London would consolidate its position as the financial centre of the European economic zone.

For these reasons Britain was very keen not to be left behind should any move be made to strengthen the common market. At the same time, the thought that the economic strengthening might be accompanied by large common spending programmes on technological research did not appeal to a British Government that had turned its back on public enterprise. Nor did the prospect of a strengthening of the central political institutions of the Community appeal to Britain, yet it was clear that some of the original member states were determined to link such institutional development to closer economic integration.

It was in this context that the British Government tabled its own document on the future of the Community at the Fontainebleau European Council.

6. The Thatcher Governments after 1984: New Directions for the Community

BY mid-1984 there was the prospect of Britain becoming a more normal member of the Community. The settlement of the budgetary dispute cleared the way for such a development, but underlying trends also seemed to point in the same direction. Although there were issues, particularly concerning reform of the institutions, that worried Britain, there were other developments that were in line with British thinking.

The stubbornness of the Greek Prime Minister, Andreas Papandreou, on a number of important issues on the agenda of the EC made Britain look less obviously the most difficult member state. With the imminent enlargement of the Community to incorporate two more Mediterranean states, Spain and Portugal, this effect might have been expected to increase. The enlargement was also expected to reinforce tendencies for the Community to become a much looser organization than Britain had at one time feared.

Other developments in the direction of a looser form of Europe were the EUREKA initiative and discussion of defence co-operation. Both of these were taking place in forums other than the EC: EUREKA had emerged as a programme of research embracing the whole of Western Europe; defence co-operation came to be discussed within the WEU rather than the EC.

Above all, there was the key issue of the freeing of the internal market, which had emerged as one part of the programme of reforms that the French, Germans, and Italians had promoted, and which was entirely acceptable to the British Government as a way forward. The idea of a wider free market fitted in with the Thatcherite ideology, and was only a logical extension of the vision of the Community that had prevailed in Britain since the start of the 1960s. As Helen Wallace put it:

The internal market is important not only for its own sake, but because it is the first core Community issue for over a decade (as distinct from EPC) which has caught the imagination of British policy-makers and which is echoed by their counterparts elsewhere. Among its other effects, an internal market policy would redress the balance against the all-engulfing claims of the CAP. The pursuit of a thoroughly liberalized domestic European market has several great advantages: it fits Community philosophy, it suits the doctrinal preferences of the current British Conservative government, and it would draw in its train a mass of interconnections with other fields of Community action.[1]

If this could be put at the centre of the programme for the future, alongside the other long-standing British interest in EC membership, greater political co-operation, then a Community might emerge that closely resembled what Britain wanted to see when it joined. In 1984 it looked as though all that stood in the way of this was the apparent desire of some member states to link such developments with what were for Britain unacceptable institutional reforms. The Fontainebleau paper was the first of a series of attempts by the British Government, not to take over directing the Community, but to get a hand on the steering wheel to guide the vehicle away from the institutional quagmire, which most British officials felt that their partners also really wished to avoid.

Unfortunately, the British appear to have severely underestimated the genuine commitment of some of their partners to such institutional reform; and even before that issue was sorted out, other differences of perception about the future route became apparent as those 'interconnections with other fields of Community action' that Wallace mentioned were brought into the discussion.

International Context

The broad parameters of the international context shifted only slowly in the 1980s. The economic upturn in the United States continued, but the movement of the rest of the developed world out of recession did allow Western Europe gradually to compete with the United States for investment capital, aided by the decisions on freeing the internal market of the EC, and by the rapid decline in oil prices from their 1979 peak. By the end of 1986 the price of oil had gone down by some 40 per cent, and other commodity prices had also fallen.

The exposed position of the US economy in the early 1980s

[1] Helen Wallace, 'The British Presidency of the European Community's Council of Ministers: The Opportunity to Persuade', *International Affairs*, 62 (1986), 590.

prompted the Reagan Administration to move away from its original position of requiring the other major capitalist states to bring their economic policies into line with those of the United States, and to return to the pursuit of international co-operation. The most tangible outcome was an agreement within the so-called Group of Five (the United States, Britain, West Germany, France, Japan) to take concerted action to bring down the value of the dollar to a level more nearly reflecting the underlying strength of the US economy. This was immediately successful, with the dollar declining rapidly in value for a short period after the announcement of the agreement, then levelling off into a more steady decline which took its value down from its March 1985 peak by between 25 and 40 per cent against different OECD currencies. Concerted action to bring down interest rates followed, and in September 1986 agreement was reached in Punta del Este in Uruguay on the terms for a new round of GATT negotiations.

Although the United States continued to run a large budget deficit, the rate of growth was cut back in the 1986 budget, mainly by a levelling off of expenditure on armaments. That this was possible owed a great deal to the change in leadership in the Kremlin that took place in March 1985. Mikhail Gorbachev represented a new type of Soviet leader: younger, and more reform-minded than any of his predecessors. He was described in some quarters as 'a kind of Russian equivalent of John F. Kennedy'.[2] Gorbachev immediately launched a diplomatic offensive designed to open up negotiations with the capitalist world on a range of issues, including reductions in armaments, something that he desperately needed to achieve in order to free resources for domestic economic development. Following a personal meeting with Gorbachev, Margaret Thatcher described him as 'a man with whom we can do business', and Ronald Reagan clearly concurred with this assessment, since he soon set about doing such good business with Gorbachev that the West Europeans became rather alarmed.

A particular focus for West European concern was the summit meeting between Gorbachev and Reagan in Reykjavik, Iceland, in October 1986, at which agreements on a comprehensive package of reductions in nuclear weapons, including long-range and inter-

[2] Roderic Lyne, 'Making Waves: Mr. Gorbachev's Public Diplomacy, 1985–6', *International Affairs*, 63 (1987), 205, quoting the *Financial Times*, 22 Nov. 1986.

mediate-range missiles, was apparently prevented only by the reluctance of the US President to give up his SDI 'Star Wars' project, which the USSR insisted was a precondition of the other agreements being accepted by them. The cause for West European concern was that the US President did not consult his allies in advance on the proposals, and had apparently been prepared to commit NATO there and then over the heads of the other members. This incident aggravated fears that the nuclear umbrella that the United States had held over Western Europe since 1945 might be removed one day, and so moved the issue of closer West European collaboration on defence up the agenda of bilateral and multilateral discussion within Europe.

Political co-operation and the formulation of a common foreign policy for the EC was also given a boost by Reykjavik, and by other actions of the Reagan Administration. Concern in Western Europe over the so-called Reagan Doctrine, that the United States would support forces fighting against communist governments in the Third World, meant that no EC member joined the United States in supporting the Contra guerillas in Nicaragua, or the Mujaheddin forces in Afghanistan, or Unita in Angola. As Evan Luard has pointed out, this was partly an issue of principle, and partly one of tactics. On principle, the Europeans were worried about the implications for world stability of flouting the international convention that had prevailed since 1945, that no overt support should be given to forces that were attempting to overthrow an internationally recognized government, whatever its politics. On tactics, it was the common view of the West Europeans that political problems could not be solved by military intervention; that such intervention only succeeded in pushing the threatened governments more firmly into the arms of the Soviet Union; and that military assistance to right-wing forces would undermine the image of the advanced capitalist states in the Third World generally.[3]

Over the Middle East too, US policy caused unease in Western Europe. The Reagan Administration condemned certain states in the region for promoting terrorism, but on the basis of evidence that was not made available to its European allies. Both Syria and Libya were accused of involvement in the explosion of a bomb in a

---

[3] Evan Luard, 'Western Europe and the Reagan Doctrine', *International Affairs*, 63 (1987), 563–74.

discotheque in West Berlin on 5 April 1986, which killed a US serviceman. The United States claimed specifically to have 'indisputable evidence' of the involvement of the Libyan Government, and used this as justification for air attacks on Tripoli and Benghazi on 15 April, in which the quarters of the Libyan leader Colonel Gaddafi appeared to have been a particular target of the bombs. Of the West European states, only Britain approved of this action. Although Thatcher gave permission for US aircraft to fly from NATO bases in Britain to take part in the raid, the French and Spanish Governments refused even to allow the US bombers to fly over their airspace, and the general reaction in Europe was one of deep unease.

Syria's turn to be specifically accused came shortly afterwards, following an attempt to plant a bomb on an Israeli El-Al airliner at Heathrow airport in London. The United States and Britain accused Syria of involvement, and, despite vigorous denials by President Assad and Vice-President Khaddam, the United States placed Syria on a blacklist of countries that were banned from receiving US assistance via international organizations. Britain eventually persuaded the EC to impose sanctions on Syria, although Greece refused to go along with this, and there was considerable unease amongst most of the other member states. That such unease may have been justified might be indicated by the lifting of the US restrictions in early June following reported clandestine contacts between Syrian and US officials.

West European concern over US action in support of anti-communist guerrillas and over US policy in the Middle East came together in the light of the Iran–Contra affair. From late 1985 onwards it gradually became apparent that members of the National Security Council within the White House had been pursuing an independent and covert foreign policy involving the sale of armaments to Iran, then engaged in a war with Iraq and condemned by the President as a 'terrorist state'. The sale of these armaments seems also to have been linked with attempts to gain the release of US citizens who were being held hostage in Lebanon by pro-Iranian forces, despite the President's frequent assertion that there would be no deals for the release of the hostages; and the money received from the armament sales was being used to provide aid to the Contra rebels in Nicaragua, which was illegal following Congressional refusal to approve such aid. The whole episode undermined further the confidence of politicians and public in Western Europe in the leadership of the United States, and gave further impetus to moves for the EC to develop its own independent foreign policy.

The Domestic Context

The 1983 election victory paved the way for the next phase of the Thatcher Government's radical restructuring of British society and the British economy. Following the election, the struggle to reduce the power and influence of the trade unions was pressed home through vigorous resistance to the miners' strike and through new legislation on strikes and picketing. The Government also accelerated its programme of denationalizing public sector concerns, a process that it christened 'privatization'. The first concerns were sold off during the 1979–83 Government: the largest was the sale in November 1982 of 51 per cent of the ordinary shares in Britoil, the oil-exploration company that had previously been 100 per cent state-owned. Bigger sales were to follow: British Telecom, Jaguar Cars, British Gas, and British Airways were all floated out of the state sector and shares sold to the public during the second Thatcher Government. The Prime Minister explained her programme in general, and her sale of state assets in particular, as being designed to banish socialism to the margins of British politics.

The Government's passage was not entirely smooth, however. In 1986 it was shaken by an affair that had clear implications for the question of Britain's commitment to a European future. The Westland affair was complex, and resulted in the resignation of two Cabinet Ministers. It concerned the financial rescue of Britain's only helicopter production company, Westland, which had been in difficulties due to a shortage of orders since the start of 1985. When a take-over bid by Bristow, another British company, was withdrawn in June, Westland opened negotiations with the United Technologies Corporation (UTC), the parent company of the US helicopter firm, Sikorski. There was also an approach from a European consortium, consisting initially of Messerschmitt–Bolkow–Blohm of West Germany, Aerospatiale of France, and Agusta of Italy. UTC was eventually joined by Fiat of Italy in offering to buy 29.9 per cent of Westland shares, while the rival

European consortium was joined by the recently privatized British Aerospace.

The British Secretary of State for Defence, Michael Heseltine, became increasingly associated with the European bid. He pointed out to Westland's financial advisers, in a letter that was subsequently made public, that US involvement in the ownership of the company would debar it from participation in two important joint European projects, in which Westland had been expected to collaborate with the firms that formed the European consortium. Westland, on the other hand, clearly preferred the US offer, and the Chairman sought an assurance from the Prime Minister that the company would still be treated as a 'European company', if the UTC offer were accepted. This assurance was given.

Throughout the events surrounding the issue, the Prime Minister and her Secretary of State for Trade and Industry, Leon Brittan, insisted that the decision on which rescue package to accept was a purely commercial one, in which the Government should remain neutral. Heseltine disagreed and, following an attempt by the Prime Minister to force him to clear all his further statements or correspondence on the matter with Downing Street, he resigned from the Cabinet. In a public statement on his resignation, Heseltine maintained that 'in practice throughout the attempt has been made to remove any obstacles to the offer by Sikorski/Fiat, even to the extent of changing existing government policy'.[4]

From the point of view of Britain's policy towards the EC, the affair was interesting for two reasons. First, it appeared to indicate a lack of Europeanism on the part of the Prime Minister and a majority of her Cabinet; and secondly, an unexpectedly high level of public support emerged for the argument in favour of the European option.

On the first point, it is important to recognize that the issue was not a simple case of the Prime Minister and Leon Brittan favouring a connection with the United States rather than with Europe. As Lawrence Freedman pointed out, 'It was not so much a question of whether the most valuable associations were to be formed with the United States or Western Europe, as whether government should steer industrial policy at all'.[5] Nevertheless, the failure of the Prime

---

[4] Keesing's Contemporary Archives, p. 34193.
[5] Lawrence Freedman, 'The Case of Westland and the Bias to Europe', International Affairs, 63 (1986), 2.

Minister to support the European option appeared to indicate a lack of pro-European commitment, particularly because it was supposed to be government policy to foster European collaboration in such areas as the defence-related industries. To quote Freedman again:

Mr Heseltine believed himself to be following established government policy on European cooperation, something for which a succession of official statements had stated a preference. But the ambiguity at the heart of this policy—was European cooperation merely to be preferred when other things were equal, or was it a high priority in all circumstances?— had not been resolved.[6]

The second interesting point is that Heseltine fought a very public battle in favour of the European option, presenting the issue as one of Europe versus the United States, and received considerable public support. Although this certainly owed a good deal to increasing anti-Americanism in Britain, it was nevertheless significant that, as Christopher Tugendhat put it, 'a European cause . . . for the first time acquired both a popular and a populist ring'.[7]

Public opinion was also generally hostile towards the US action against Libya, and especially towards the British involvement. Combined with this, and perhaps because of it, the March 1987 Eurobarometer survey found 28 per cent of the British public to be in favour of a common European defence. Interestingly, 52 per cent were also in favour of a referendum being held on a new European constitution drafted by the European Parliament.[8]

These figures seem to indicate that Thatcher was increasingly getting out of step with public opinion in external relations. But the economy remained the most important factor influencing people's voting intentions, and Britain's success in this respect continued. Despite a significant drop in the price of oil, which reduced revenues from the North Sea, economic activity continued at a high level, with only a minor setback in the second half of 1985. The decline in the price of oil contributed to a depreciation in the value of sterling from mid-1985, which in turn contributed to a sharp revival of export growth. Unemployment started to come down from the middle of 1986, and wage increases continued to run well ahead of inflation. By early in 1987 more people in Britain were feeling better off than at any previous time since 1979.

[6] Ibid., 2.   [7] Tugendhat, 'Out of Step'.
[8] *Eurobarometer*, Special 30th Anniversary Edn., Mar. 1987, p. 28.

The Government was therefore able to call a general election in the spring of 1987 with every prospect of a comfortable victory, which is precisely what it achieved, although not before receiving something of a scare from the opinion polls during the campaign itself. The new leader of the Labour party, Neil Kinnock, ran a much better campaign than had his predecessor Michael Foot in 1983, and, in the view of many people, a better campaign than the Conservatives. Nevertheless, the result was very similar to that of 1983, with the Alliance of the Liberal and Social Democrat Parties splitting the anti-Thatcher vote with Labour, and allowing a Conservative victory by an even larger percentage of seats than in the previous election.

Thatcher's personal position both domestically and internationally was already strong before the election: it was even stronger after it. Domestically the room for criticism within the Conservative Party was reduced by her very success, although the Government was to run into some opposition from its own backbenchers over some of its domestic legislative programme. Internationally, Thatcher's position as the longest-serving European Head of Government appeared to give her an opportunity to play a dominant role in the EC, while her political longevity also gave her the opportunity to play a leading role on the wider world stage.

It began to look in the late 1980s as though the Conservative Party would be in office for a long time to come, and the Prime Minister's goal of banishing socialism to the margins of British political life was capable of realization. This was an issue that interacted with developments at the Community level throughout the period that was inaugurated by the Fontainebleau meeting of the European Council in 1984.

'Europe—The Future'

The document that was submitted to the Fontainebleau summit by the British Government was skilfully drafted to take up many of the themes that had been in the air throughout the discussions of new directions for the Community, whilst turning them in the direction favoured by Britain. It stressed the importance of overcoming the growing technological gap with the United States and Japan, and of doing something to alleviate the high level of unemployment in the

Community.[9] It referred to the need 'to make actions undertaken within the Community relevant to the lives of our people'.[10] There was a paragraph on pollution, and in particular the importance of tackling the problem of acid rain.[11] There was also a section on the need for Europe to emerge as an independent actor on the world stage,[12] and a section on defence co-operation that supported the strengthening of the European arm of NATO.[13]

The document showed that the Thatcher Government was willing to engage with the problems that concerned the other states, although the solutions offered to most of the problems had a minimalist and free-market orientation that was distinctively British. The growing technological gap with the United States and Japan, and high levels of unemployment in the Community, were both genuine concerns of other member states: but the proposed solution to both problems was the predictable British one of opening the internal market. The only specific examples in the document of measures that would make the Community more of a reality to its citizens were moves 'to simplify and speed up customs and other formalities affecting the ease with which our citizens can travel across intra-Community borders' and 'increased competition and deregulation of air services'.[14] The first of these measures obviously fitted in with the British aim of removing barriers to internal trade, since customs formalities could be removed more easily if restrictions on what could be sold in which countries were lifted; the second was a long-standing British objective.

The paragraph on the need to tackle pollution, and in particular the problem of acid rain, was the clearest example of a British concession on an issue of substance, and one that was presumably designed to appeal to the West Germans, for whom this was a major domestic political issue. Here was a sign that perhaps the British, who had been hesitant to become involved in environmental issues, not least because it was Britain which would have the most expense in limiting noxious emissions from its coal-fired power stations, really were prepared to engage in some sacrifices in order to win support for their package of proposals.

However, the distinctively British angle emerged again when the

[9] H. M. Government, 'Europe—The Future', p. 73, para. 6.
[10] Ibid., 74, para. 7.   [11] Ibid., 75, para. 10.
[12] Ibid., 76–8, paras. 14–19.   [13] Ibid., 20–3, paras. 78–9.
[14] Ibid., 74.

question of common policies on weapons procurement was related once more to the issue of the need to free the internal market.[15] Although the minimalist and free-market orientation of the document was certainly contrary to what was being advocated by some other member states, there is little doubt that it was meant as a serious statement of intent by the British Government. Ronald Butt reported that Thatcher was believed to have 'paid the closest personal attention to its details', and to have attached particular importance to the passage calling for the EC to 'aim beyond the Common Commercial Policy through political cooperation towards a common approach to external affairs'.[16]

Overall the document appeared to offer a basis for discussion, by providing something to interest at least each of the major member states, and possibly a basis for future progress. That it was not received with more enthusiasm by the other Heads of Government at the time can be explained by two factors. One was the circumstances in which it was presented, with the disappointments of Athens and Brussels still fresh in memories; the other was the very weak set of proposals on institutional reform.

Here the difference in conception and approach between the British and some of the other Europeans is most marked. For Britain institutional questions are secondary and get in the way of practical achievements. Institutions and procedures should be modified pragmatically as they prove unequal to the tasks required of them. For the other member states, institutional reform was the central issue in giving new impetus to the Community, and the very modest changes proposed in the British paper, especially the reassertion of the importance of the national veto and the suggestion that all that was needed so far as the European Parliament was concerned was 'to work out ways of keeping the Parliament better informed, responding to its suggestions and bringing it to work in greater harmony with the main decision making institutions of the Community',[17] were a sign that the British were still not converted to being good Europeans.

At the Fontainebleau European Council it was agreed to set up a committee of personal representatives of the Heads of State and Government to look into the question of institutional reform. This

[15] Ibid., 79, para. 23.
[16] Ronald Butt, 'Mrs. Thatcher's Modern Europe', *The Times*, 5 July 1984.
[17] 'Europe—The Future', p. 80, para. 24.

came to be known as the Dooge Committee, after its Chairman James Dooge of Ireland, and it reported in March 1985. In the meantime the disagreements over the issue continued.

Practical Steps versus Institutional Reform

The problem for Britain was to turn the direction of discussion towards the practical achievement of a free internal market and away from discussion of institutional reform, which was the preferred path of progress of Italy and the Benelux states, and to which the French and West Germans paid intermittent lip-service.

It was this difference of perspective which underlay the continuing statements of the Foreign Secretary about the need for 'serious, practical attainable improvements'. In Bonn for talks with his German counterpart in December 1984, Sir Geoffrey Howe reasserted his claims that Britain was a good European, had played 'a full part' since joining the EC, and wanted now to see real progress. 'We want, not proclamations masquerading as achievements, but achievements we can all be proud to proclaim.'[18]

The coded message was that the emphasis on institutional reforms would amount to no practical achievement. Although not so baldly stated, the British principle remained as enunciated in September 1983 by Malcolm Rifkind, then a Minister of State at the Foreign Office: 'To us, institutions must be subservient to policies. Closer co-operation should not be forced but must grow out of practical ways in which as a Community we can work together for our common good. Substance and reality must come before form'.[19]

The institutional question came back to the surface of the debate shortly after Sir Geoffrey made his statement in Bonn. In February 1985 François Mitterrand was making noises about 'a surprising initiative' to 'transform European institutions',[20] and then in March came the report of the Dooge Committee.

It was well known that the Committee had tended to divide throughout its deliberations into a majority group of those who were either enthusiastic about major reforms, or were at least prepared to support them, and a minimalist group, led by Britain

[18] *The Times*, 11 Dec. 1984.
[19] Quoted in David Judge, 'The British Government, European Union and EC Institutional Reform', *Political Quarterly*, 57 (1986), 324.
[20] *The Economist*, 9 Mar. 1985.

and supported by Greece and Denmark (and sometimes by Ireland), which opposed many of the proposed changes. Although named after James Dooge, the recommendations of the Committee were largely inspired by the French representative, Maurice Faure, who was known to be close to President Mitterrand. The British representative was the same Malcolm Rifkind whose views on institutional reform were quoted above.

The majority on the Committee argued that institutional reform was essential to the future of the Community because the Ten could only achieve their goals if they could agree to more rapid procedures for making decisions. Consequently they proposed that the veto be abandoned in favour of majority voting, except for specific areas designated in advance as being too sensitive to allow national interests to be overruled. This was in accordance with the original Treaty of Rome, and implied the repudiation of the so-called Luxemburg Compromise of 1966, a step that the British, Danish, and Greek representatives were not happy to countenance. They argued that the existence of the veto was assumed as part of their terms of membership, and must be retained in general. Instead of abandoning it, the British proposed that its use should be constrained by requiring any member state wishing to exercise a veto to provide a written justification for its use.

There were two other issues on which Rifkind tabled counter-proposals to those of Faure. One was on the method of selecting Commissioners. The French proposed, and the majority accepted, that only the President should be named by agreement between the member states, and the President should then choose his own team for endorsement by the member states. Rifkind insisted that the proper application of the existing system as formally laid down should be all that was needed to ensure a more cohesive Commission: that is, that the member states should first nominate the President and then choose the rest of the Commissioners in consultation with the nominee.

More controversial was the other issue. The majority on the Committee wanted to see an increase in the decision-making powers of the European Parliament. The minority wanted to see only a continuation of its consultative role. For Italy and the Benelux states this was an issue of some importance, but equally for the British, Danes, and Greeks the implied erosion of national sovereignty in Community affairs was seen as unacceptable.

The debate around the Dooge Report was obviously going to be crucial to the British chances of moving the Community in the direction favoured by Britain. But at the end of March 1985 things did not seem to be going the British way. The leadership seemed to be coming from France, in alliance with West Germany, and supported by the majority of the other member states.

The Stresa Paper

On 8–9 June 1985 Sir Geoffrey Howe used a scheduled informal meeting of Foreign Ministers at Stresa, on Lake Maggiore in Italy, to launch the British counter-proposals to the idea of a rewriting of the Treaty of Rome. These were discussed at a formal meeting of the Council of Foreign Ministers on 18 June in Luxemburg. The document outlining the proposals was, like the paper that had circulated at Fontainebleau, well thought out, and 'was seen as a model of British pragmatism'.[21] Many of the same themes of the Fontainebleau paper were reintroduced, with the emphasis very much on practical achievements rather than institutional reform.

The Stresa paper suggested the creation of a secretariat for improving foreign policy co-ordination, but the main procedural issue dealt with was the problem of making progress within the Council of Ministers given the continuation of the veto system. It suggested that the use of majority voting should be increased by mutual agreement, that the use of the veto should require formal justification at Foreign Minister level, and that priority areas should be agreed at European Council meetings, after which there would be no use of the veto on those issues.

Although Britain had jealously guarded the right of veto in the past, it seems that the Government, and the Prime Minister in particular, had become concerned lest the Greeks should be placed in a position to hold the rest of the Community to ransom by vetoing the freeing of the internal market until they got agreement on the allocation of much larger sums of money to them to assist in their development. Here a second area of disagreement emerged between Britain and some of the other member states, over whether the freeing of the internal market had as an inescapable corollary higher spending on redistributive measures.

[21] John Pinder, 'Pragmatikos and Federalis: reflections on a Conference', *Government and Opposition*, 20 (1985), 473–4.

The British proposals were placed on the agenda of the forthcoming European Council meeting in Milan. Before the European Council, some momentum in the direction favoured by Britain was generated when, on 15 June, Lord Cockfield, a British nominee to the new Commission, produced a detailed timetable for the creation of a unified market.[22] The plan contained three hundred proposals, with a target date for each. Here was a specific schedule for the achievement of an agreed objective, in contrast with the still vague and contentious constitutional reforms advocated as the way forward by some of the other member states. The only difficulty was that Cockfield, to the evident surprise of the British Government, included in his plans proposals for the harmonization of VAT rates between member states.

Milan: June 1985

Britain and West Germany both felt obliged to express reservations about these latter proposals at the Milan European Council; nevertheless, the timetable was approved, for implementation by 1992. There was also agreement on the abandonment of the veto in respect of certain specified articles of the Treaty of Rome, those that President of the Commission Jacques Delors insisted were the minimum necessary if there was to be any hope of achieving the freeing of the market by the chosen date.[23] It was agreed that these minimum charges could be ratified by national parliaments at the same time as the agreements on the accession of Spain and Portugal, and the increase in the Community's own resources.

But this apparent victory for the British approach was followed by an agreement to set up an inter-governmental conference on revision of the Treaty of Rome, which caused considerable controversy.

The trouble for the British view began with the circulation, literally on the eve of the summit, of a Franco–German paper entitled 'Draft Treaty on European Union'. This initiative in itself showed that the Franco–German axis was still holding together, although it is difficult to see what else it was intended to achieve,

[22] EC Commission Documents, COM(85) 310; *Bulletin of the European Communities*, 6–1985, points 1.3.1–1.3.9.

[23] See Emile Noel, 'Reflections on the Community in the Aftermath of the Meeting of the European Council in Milan', *Government and Opposition*, 20 (1985), 444–52.

and its late circulation caused some offence, particularly to the Danes, whose copy did not arrive until after Prime Minister Schluter had left for the airport to fly to Milan. The British also were annoyed at the circulation of the document, although this was mingled with mild amusement, because the paper, despite its grand-sounding title, appeared to be no more than a rehash of the ideas put forward by Howe a fortnight earlier, and indeed in some respects it was less radical.

It is possible that the Franco–German document was intended to offer a compromise acceptable to both the maximalists and the minimalists in the debate on reform of the Community. On this interpretation, the mention of 'European Union' in the title would be designed to please the Italians in particular, although in fact the title was the only place where the phrase appeared. The proposals themselves were so similar to those tabled by the British that Thatcher could hardly be expected to take exception to them. The retreat from the British position was in the area of foreign policy co-operation (which occupied the bulk of the paper), where the British suggestion that member states be required to vote together in the United Nations was removed; and in the area of co-operation on security matters, which was de-emphasized. It could be argued that both these moves were designed to make it easier for the Irish to accept the document.

The other difference from Howe's Stresa proposals was that the Franco–German document called for the changes to be embodied in a treaty that would have to be ratified by national parliaments. Thatcher insisted that there was no need for this and, together with the Prime Ministers of Denmark and Greece, opposed throughout the European Council meeting suggestions for the creation of a special conference to draw up such a treaty. But the Italian Prime Minister, Bettino Craxi, who was in the Chair, called a vote on the issue, as a result of which the meeting ended in considerable acrimony. It was the first time that a vote had ever been called at a European Council, and it split the participants seven to three.

To understand this outcome it is necessary to understand the position of Italy. The Italian Government had taken over the presidency of the Council at the beginning of the year. In his inaugural address to the European Parliament on 16 January, the Foreign Minister, Giulio Andreotti, had pledged his presidency to pursue the summoning of an inter-governmental conference before the end of June to negotiate a treaty on European union.[24] Bettino Craxi, the Prime Minister, now honoured that pledge by calling the vote at the European Council.

For Italy the commitment to European union was a cross-party issue. Altiero Spinelli, the Italian who had sponsored the draft treaty on European union that had been passed by the European Parliament in February 1984, sat as a member of the Communist delegation. Andreotti was a Christian Democrat; Craxi a Socialist. The commitment to the ideal of a federated Europe had been sponsored after the war by the Christian Democrats as part of their attempt to define a new but distinctively Western identity for their country. It had received support from more left-wing parties because it had been one of the distinctive elements in the ideology of the anti-fascist resistance. Support amongst the Italian public for European union was high, and the parties were vying one with another to polish their pro-Community credentials. With the summit being held in Italy, and chaired by the Italian Government, it had a high level of visibility within the country.

There were perhaps other reasons for the Italian support for constitutional changes. Italy had always been just on the edge of the inner circle of large states. The signs of a revived Franco–German axis, together with suggestions that Mitterrand would like to bring Britain into a three-way directorate, threatened to leave Italy even more on the outside of the real decision-making processes. The accession of Spain suggested that Italy might soon find itself only the fifth most influential member of the Community. Just as the Benelux states had always supported strong central institutions out of a sense of self-protection against domination by larger member states, so the Italian view may have been influenced by similar considerations.

Whatever the reasons, Italy did insist on a vote, and the vote did go in favour of a conference. Matters were then made worse by the insistence of the Greek Prime Minister that he could not agree to the implementation of the agreements that had already been reached on the abandonment of the veto in matters related to the construction of the internal market if there was also to be an inter-governmental conference. It was either a limited agreement, or a

---

[24] *Official Journal of the European Communities, Annex, Debates of the European Parliament*, 1984–5, no. 2–321/106.

study of possibly more far-reaching agreements, but Greece would not accept both. So the limited agreement fell.

The outcome clearly angered Thatcher, who told the Press: 'We came here with high hopes. We were prepared to take decisions on practical steps forward on the internal market, and on how best to co-operate politically. We have not made the progress we sought.'[25]

The Inter-governmental Conference

Despite Thatcher's anger at the decision to set it up, Britain did participate in the work of the inter-governmental conference. It appears that the Prime Minister was persuaded by Sir Geoffrey Howe and her personal adviser on EC affairs, David Williamson, that the other member states were less committed in practice to institutional reform than they were in theory. If Britain adopted a low profile during the proceedings of the inter-governmental conference, it was their view that the French and Germans would have to stop blaming Britain for lack of progress, and show the real extent of their commitment. The expectation was that the outcome in practical terms would be much less far-reaching than the rhetoric.

This marked a real change in the British approach from that adopted in the Dooge Committee, where Rifkind had frequently clashed with the French, and had tabled counter-proposals. Williamson, who acted as British representative in the conference, took a back seat so as not to give room for criticism. The outcome vindicated the approach: the agreements that were eventually reached at the Luxemburg meeting of the European Council in December 1985 were rather nearer to the British position than to the Italian.

Luxemburg: December 1985

British Press reactions to the outcome of the Luxemburg meeting differed somewhat. The *Guardian* considered that Britain was the victor.[26] The *Financial Times* on the other hand considered that the outcome 'was a deliberate fudge, designed to keep a disparate crew of 12 Heads of State and Government on the same boat'.[27] The truth lies somewhere between, of course.

[25] Peel, 'After the EEC Summit'.   [26] *Guardian*, 5 Dec. 1985.
[27] *Financial Times*, 5 Dec. 1985.

The agreement represented certain concessions by the British, who appeared to have learned the lesson of Milan, that the other member states were not about to abandon their own concerns and simply accept the agenda preferred by Britain. There also seemed at last to be signs that Britain recognized the attachment of other member states to the rhetoric of European union. This appeared in British acceptance that there should be a revision of the Treaty, that the revision should incorporate a statement that European union was the ultimate aim of the Community, and that this 'Single European Act' should also include mention of the EMS, which both the British and the West Germans had originally opposed.

In return for these amendments, the British achieved real progress in areas that mattered to them. Majority voting was extended only in limited areas: a few more articles of the Treaty were affected than had originally been agreed at Milan, but only areas related to freeing of the internal market were covered. Specifically excluded from the rules on majority voting were the areas of taxation, free movement of persons, health controls, and employees' rights. All of these mattered to the British Government: they were wedded for electoral reasons to keeping certain items, such as children's clothing, exempt from VAT; they had an obsession with the threat of rabies spreading from the mainland of Europe; they did not trust their EC partners to control the movements of terrorists; and they were totally opposed to the imposition of any controls on the rights of managements to treat their employees as they would.

The other clear victory for the British view was that no major increase was proposed in the powers of the European Parliament. A new legislative procedure was agreed in which the European Parliament retained its consultative role, but also was given the opportunity to amend decisions of the Council of Ministers, although for the amendments to stand they would have to be accepted by the Commission, and even then they could be rejected by the Council of Ministers if it was unanimous on the issue.

The limited increase in the powers of the European Parliament was the main point that failed to satisfy the Italians, who otherwise seemed to believe that they had made their point in Milan, and were not inclined to hold up the Community any longer. The Italian Government said that its ratification of the so-called Single

European Act would be conditional on its acceptance by the European Parliament. No other state took a strong line.

So, although the agreement was 'a fudge', the judgement of the *Guardian* was not incorrect either. At the end of 1985 the Community seemed to be embarked on a course very similar to that desired by Britain. The British seemed to have learned the need for some compromise in EC negotiations, to allow their partners to save face. A Franco–German–British axis seemed to be possible, around an agenda of freeing the internal market, advancing technological co-operation through EUREKA and a Community technological policy that was being promoted by the Commission, and foreign policy co-operation. The prospects for the EC on the eve of the enlargement to incorporate Spain and Portugal seemed better than they had done just a few months earlier; and the prospect for Britain being able to move the Community in the direction that it favoured was also good, particularly as Britain was due to assume the presidency of the Council in the second half of 1986.

The British Presidency

On 21 May Sir Geoffrey Howe outlined the agenda for the British presidency. At the top of the agenda was what Howe described as an 'action programme', designed to 'mobilize and energize the community to realize its full potential for generating jobs and prosperity'.[28] This programme contained three key elements.

The first, unsurprisingly, was progress in freeing the internal market. Thatcher had already made it abundantly clear that she saw this as being the main task that lay ahead of the Community, and as being a major contribution both to easing unemployment and to tackling the problem of Europe's lack of competitiveness with Japan and the United States.

The second element was the liberalization of transport. The emphasis here was specifically on air transport. The deregulation of air fares and the opening of routes to competition was a long-standing objective of the British; and it is possible that the Government's plans to privatize British Airways made such deregulation an even higher priority, because British Airways, being an efficient and popular airline, might have been expected to

[28] *The Times*, 22 May 1986.

benefit from competition. The measures were urged on the Community, though, in terms of the advance which it represented for European unity. The Foreign Secretary expressed the view that it would make a major contribution to the average European citizen's identification with the Community if air fares between the member states were reduced. Like the emphasis on progress in freeing the internal market, this was no surprise to observers.

The final element of the package, though, was something new. The Foreign Secretary announced that attempts to lift burdens on businesses, especially small- and medium-sized businesses, and to introduce flexibility into the labour market, would be a high priority of the presidency. He went on to say that these measures would not be directed against the trade unions, but that they would be expected to benefit the consumer and to enable the EC to compete in international markets.

The record of the Government in realizing its action programme was very patchy. It did have some success in freeing the internal market: forty-seven measures were agreed, mainly in a late flurry of activity in December, more than double the figure achieved in any previous presidency. This may have owed something to the personal intervention of the Prime Minister, who sent a letter to all the other Heads of Government in November asking them to use their influence to clear a blockage that had built up. On air fares, though, no real progress was achieved, despite the Transport Secretary, John Moore, producing a compromise suggestion in November which fell far short of the 'open-skies' policy that Britain had previously been championing. The most important part of the programme, though, was the set of proposals for employment policy, which were spelt out in more detail at a meeting of the Council of Employment Ministers on 5 June by Kenneth Clarke, the Paymaster General and deputy to Lord Young, the Secretary of State for Employment.

For some time the British Conservative Government had opposed the existing direction of Community employment policy, which had concentrated on extending employees' rights. Britain had been primarily responsible for blocking progress on implementation of the Vredeling directive, which would have given the employees of multinational corporations rights to information about the activities and plans of the company for which they worked, and on various other minor pieces of legislation. For example, at the very meeting at which the new British proposals were first outlined in June 1986, Kenneth Clarke blocked a proposal for statutory paternity leave for the fathers of new children.

The ideas of the British Government were contained in a nineteen-page document entitled *Employment Growth in the 1990s: A Strategy for the Labour Market*.[29] The plan proposed concentrating the work of the Employment Council on job creation to combat the high level of unemployment in the Community, which at 12 per cent represented 16 million people, the equivalent of the fifth largest state in the EC. It presented a four-point plan which involved aid for small businesses and the self-employed, the encouragement of more flexible working practices, better training, and more help for the long-term unemployed to find jobs.

The approach was distinctly Thatcherite in its emphasis on freeing the market rather than trying to use macro-economic reflation to combat unemployment. Nevertheless, it was a well-conceived initiative. A consensus had been growing for some time that the emphasis of Community employment policy must be reoriented towards the short-term problem of relieving unemployment, and the Vredeling directive had been shelved. The Delors Commission had also made action on unemployment one of its objectives, and the proposals in the document to some extent overlapped with ideas that had already emerged from the Commission. In addition, the British Government had persuaded the Irish and Italian Governments to join it in sponsoring the new plan, which bore the names of Ruairi Quinn and Gianni de Michelis, both socialists, in addition to those of Kenneth Clarke and Lord Young. Thus the plan could not be rejected as being a purely British document: criticism became that much more difficult.

The groundwork was also done well. After the initial presentation of the document prior to the start of the British presidency, a special informal meeting of Employment Ministers was held in Edinburgh in September to discuss the plan. At the press conference that accompanied it, both Lord Young and Mr Clarke made much of the fact that the plan's co-authors were socialists; and neither of them attempted to hide his dislike for the previous agenda of the Employment Ministers, Clarke speaking of 'sterile debate on obscure bits of employment law'.[30]

---

[29] The account given here of the content of the paper is reconstructed from newspaper reports.   [30] *Guardian*, 23 Sept. 1986.

Whether their co-authors shared their dislike for the previous agenda is doubtful, but no public criticism emerged from this meeting. Soon afterwards, though, the plan ran into a whole barrage of criticism, from the European Parliament, from the European Trade Union Confederation, and even from the EC employers' association, UNICE. The weight of all the criticism was that the proposals did not go far enough, that helping small businesses and providing better training would not in themselves reduce unemployment if no stimulus was given to the depressed national economies of the Community.

By the time of the London meeting of the European Council in December, Thatcher was having to throw her weight behind the proposals in an attempt to get support for them from the other Heads of Government. But strong opposition emerged from some of the other member states, and the price that Thatcher had to pay for having a commitment to the proposals written into the communiqué was acceptance that mention should also be given to the importance of EC-level discussions between employers and trade unions ('the social partners') with an invitation to the Commission to continue its efforts to encourage this co-operation. On this issue Thatcher, who fought hard to avoid any mention of the dialogue or the social partners, was opposed even by other conservative leaders such as Chancellor Kohl of West Germany and the Italian Foreign Minister (and leader of the Christian Democrats), Giulio Andreotti. As Quentin Peel observed, 'The debate emphasised the divide between the British Government's economic approach and that of most of the rest of the Community.'[31]

When the Employment Ministers came to approve concrete proposals for forty points of action based on the plan, on 11 December, pressure from the poorer member states, and to a lesser extent from West Germany, led to the inclusion of references to cooperation in promoting economic growth and to aid for the poorer regions of the Community. Although Kenneth Clarke treated the decisions as a success for the British approach, the final package went beyond what the Government had originally wanted.

Another important difference had emerged here between the British view of the future of the Community and that of a majority of other member states. The issue of the social dimension to the

[31] Quentin Peel, 'Mrs. Thatcher Finds the Middle Ground', *Financial Times*, 4 Dec. 1986.

project to free the internal market was soon to take its place alongside the questions of institutional reform and the role of redistributive funds as a fundamental point of disagreement.

From February 1987 to February 1988

In February 1987 the Commission produced a package of proposed reforms that embodied what Jacques Delors described as a 'social common market' approach. The package contained four main elements. The first two dealt with the question of the funding of the Community's activities, and was necessary because the collapse in the value of the dollar had led to a rapid escalation of EC expenditure on agricultural support and had brought it once again near to the brink of insolvency. Delors now looked for a further substantial increase in the legal limit on the annual income of the Community, and linked this to the second proposal, for a new system of funding based on member states' relative shares of the Community's Gross Domestic Product, which would reflect more accurately their relative ability to pay than did the system based on shares of VAT.

The third proposal was for a thorough reform of the CAP to lower support prices and to replace them with direct subsidies as the means of preserving the 'family farm' which was so important to the French and Germans. The fourth was for a large increase in EC funding for research, transport, and the environment, and a doubling of regional aid and job training by 1992.[32]

Predictably Britain liked only the third proposal, but the Belgians, who held the presidency in the first half of 1987, backed by the Mediterranean states, insisted on the package being taken as a whole. There was obviously no prospect of agreement being reached until after the British general election, so the package came to the meeting of the European Council in June in Brussels.

Yet again a European Council meeting ended in disarray, with the Community divided eleven to one. Thatcher's refusal to accept a Belgian draft communiqué that in the opinion of many observers went much further to meet her demands than it did to meet anybody else's, caused a great deal of consternation, and not only amongst the rest of the Community. Sir Geoffrey Howe was reported by several newspapers to have been 'shaking with anger'

[32] *Bulletin of the European Communities, Supplement 1–1987.*

at the end of the meeting because he felt that his Prime Minister could easily have reached an agreement that would have given Britain major gains in terms of reining in the CAP and imposing binding budgetary discipline. Thatcher's reasons for not accepting the proposals were that she objected to the implicit commitment to increase EC spending overall, and that she did not believe that the Community should be given any more money until the detail of the limits on CAP expenditure had been firmly agreed.[33]

This approach lasted through another indecisive meeting of the European Council in December 1987, and finally only gave way in February 1988 at a special meeting of the European Council in Brussels. Here Thatcher surprisingly accepted a package deal that involved major concessions on her part. She achieved tight and binding controls on the rate of increase of expenditure on the CAP, and continuation of the Fontainebleau rebate mechanism, but conceded on the increase in the funds available to the Community and the change in the method of financing the EC budget, both of which would cost Britain more, and also on the doubling of the regional and social funds by 1992.

These were major concessions in return for major gains. The deal could probably have been achieved earlier, at Copenhagen if not in Brussels the previous June; in that respect there are strong echoes of the Fontainebleau budgetary settlement. Also like Fontainebleau, the conclusion of the deal did appear to indicate a British willingness to make deals, and to play the old Community game in the interest of progress on the major common objective of freeing the internal market. Yet, as Peter Jenkins warned, 'Britain's relationship with the European Community is littered with false beginnings.'[34] When the next European Council came around in June 1988 the impression of a more accommodating British attitude once more received a blow.

The Monetary Issue

The most controversial question on the agenda of the European Council meeting in Hanover in June 1988 was the role of monetary

[33] *Hansard*, 6th ser. 188 (1 July 1987), col. 493.
[34] Peter Jenkins, 'Mrs. Thatcher's Historic Compromise', *Independent*, 17 Feb. 1988.

union in the 1992 project. For the French and Germans the emergence of a single European currency was an essential complement to the freeing of the internal market. They argued that the EMS needed to be strengthened by the creation of a European central bank, and by moves to establish the Ecu as the common currency of the Community.

Just how far the British Prime Minister was from accepting the need for any strengthening of the EMS became evident in March 1988, when she clashed publicly with her Chancellor of the Exchequer, Nigel Lawson, over his policy of holding the value of the pound sterling within the range of variation that would be permissible were it part of the exchange-rate mechanism of the EMS. He had admitted to this 'shadowing' of the EMS in February, and when the pound came under upward pressure in March had been prepared to intervene to hold down its value, but the Prime Minister put a stop to that when she told the House of Commons that the fight against inflation remained the top priority, and was incompatible with 'excessive intervention' to support the pound;[35] she thereby ensured that the anticipated rise in the value of sterling beyond the EMS margins of fluctuation would occur. Much the same performance was repeated when sterling next came under upward pressure in May, provoking speculation that the Chancellor's days in office were numbered, but also provoking Sir Geoffrey Howe to state publicly his support for the full integration of sterling into the EMS.[36] However, the united opinions of both her former and present Chancellors appeared to have no effect on the Prime Minister. Far from being prepared to proceed to the next step of monetary union, which was what the rest of the Community was talking about in June 1988, Thatcher appeared to be still unprepared to take even the first step of integrating sterling fully into the EMS.

She rejected the idea of a European central bank in a statement to the House of Commons in the week preceding the Hanover meeting, arguing that the necessary corollary of a European central bank was a central European government, and she did not believe that her EC partners were ready to accept that any more than she was. In addition, she denied that there was any necessary

---

[35] *Hansard*, 6th ser. 129 (8 Mar. 1988), col. 184.
[36] In a speech in Perth, reported in the *Sunday Times*, 15 May 1988.

connection between the freeing of the internal market and the creation of a monetary union.[37]

The issue caused a straight conflict between the British Prime Minister and her German host in Hanover, with such support as was made public being all on the side of West Germany. As with the inter-governmental conference at Milan, Thatcher found herself isolated and unable to prevent the European Council from agreeing to set up a committee under the chairmanship of Delors to look into what steps needed to be taken to strengthen the EMS. The only concession to the British view was that all mention of a European central bank and a common European currency was omitted from the terms of reference of the committee; but, as Lord Cockfield told the Swiss Institute of International Relations in Zurich in October, 'no one need have any doubt about what is intended or where we are going'.[38]

Thatcher did appear to have doubts about where the Community was going. Later in October, in Italy for a meeting with the Italian prime minister Ciriaco De Mita, she told journalists:

I neither want nor expect to see such a bank in my lifetime, nor, if I'm twanging a harp, for quite a long time afterwards . . . A European central bank in the only true meaning of the term means surrendering your economic policy to that banking system that is in charge of the maintenance of the value of the currency and must therefore be in charge of the necessary economic policy to achieve that . . . So . . . what I suspect they will attempt to do is to call something a European central bank which it isn't and never can be.[39]

On this question a clear gulf seemed to be emerging between Britain and the rest of the Community. On other issues, too, differences had emerged by the time of Thatcher's visit to Italy, in particular the questions of how much central decision-making was implied in the 1992 project, and whether there would be a 'social dimension' to the project. On both topics Thatcher was apparently stung into making strong statements of position by speeches from the President of the Commission, Jacques Delors.

The Gulf Widens

The first speech of Delors to infuriate Thatcher was made to

[37] *Hansard*, 6th ser. 135 (23 June 1988), col. 1255.
[38] *Independent*, 4 Oct. 1988.
[39] Ibid., 22 Oct. 1988.

the European Parliament in July 1988. The President told the MEPs that, with the exception of Britain and West Germany, most member states had not yet woken up to the extent to which the freeing of the internal market would involve a seepage of their sovereignty to the Community. He predicted: 'In ten years, 80 per cent of economic legislation—and perhaps tax and social legislation—will be directed from the Community.'[40]

A few weeks later Thatcher, in an interview on BBC radio, admonished Delors for this statement. She said that it went 'over the top' and only served to 'frighten people'. But Delors showed himself unwilling to be browbeaten, and in September he committed what in the British Prime Minister's eyes was an even worse sin in addressing the annual conference of the TUC in Bournemouth. This time his emphasis was on the necessity for the freeing of the internal market to be accompanied by social measures. In a presentation of the issues at stake which directly challenged the view of the British Prime Minister, he said:

It is impossible to build Europe on only deregulation . . . 1992 is much more than the creation of an internal market abolishing barriers to the free movement of goods, services and investment . . . The internal market should be designed to benefit each and every citizen of the community. It is therefore necessary to improve workers' living and working conditions, and to provide better protection for their health and safety at work.[41]

Delors went on to list three principles which he said the Commission believed to be essential to the 'social dimension' of 1992: that the existing levels of social security available in member states should not be reduced by measures to free the internal market; that health and safety standards should be improved; and that there should be Europe-wide collective bargaining, with every worker having the right to be covered by a collective agreement, and with guarantees on the status of temporary work.

For this Delors received a standing ovation from the delegates to the TUC Conference, and a ringing condemnation from Thatcher when she addressed the students of the College of Europe in Bruges later in September. In particular she attacked the Commission for wanting to regulate the internal market and for wanting to centralize power in Brussels; and she specifically attacked the idea

---

[40] *Official Journal of the European Communities. Annex. Debates of the European Parliament*, 1988–9, no. 2–367/140.
[41] *Independent*, 9 Sept. 1988.

for common rules on the protection of workers as 'new regulations which raise the cost of employment'. In this speech, and again in her address to the Conservative Party Conference in Brighton in October she attempted to present the ideas of Jacques Delors as being a socialist attack on the concept of the EC as embodied in the Treaty of Rome, which she argued was a charter for economic liberty. 'Today, that founding concept is under attack from those who see European unity as a vehicle for spreading socialism. We haven't worked all these years to free Britain from the paralysis of socialism only to see it creep through the back door of central control and bureaucracy in Brussels.'[42]

However, the charge that centralized decision-making and protection for the rights of workers were socialist ideas was undermined when in October 1988 four leading Christian Democratic statesmen used the occasion of the European conference of Christian Democratic parties to line up behind Delors and in opposition to Thatcher. Helmut Kohl, Chancellor of West Germany, and Wilfried Martens of Belgium had already made personal statements in opposition to the sentiments expressed by Thatcher in Bruges, and they were now joined by Ruud Lubbers, the Prime Minister of the Netherlands, and Jacques Santer, Prime Minister of Luxemburg, in a declaration calling for a central European bank, a common security policy, European guidelines for social affairs and workers' rights, and an inter-governmental conference to consider the constitutional and legal changes needed for a European union to be achieved.[43]

This last item represented a raising of the stakes in the game that was now taking place between Britain's Prime Minister and the original members of the EC. An inter-governmental conference is a constitutional requirement for any redrafting of the Treaties that govern the EC. Britain had resisted the setting-up of an inter-governmental conference at the Milan European Council in 1984, but had lost the argument. However, the outcome of that conference, the Single European Act, had been a more modest document than some of the member states had hoped to see, and, although it represented a compromise, it was an outcome that had not displeased Britain. Yet in her Bruges speech Thatcher had appeared to repudiate the commitment in the Single European Act to a European union, presenting instead the neo-Gaullist idea of a

[42] Ibid., 15 Oct. 1988.   [43] Ibid., 20 Oct. 1988.

Europe of independent states which would co-operate closely but not submit to any central control over economic policy, nor move to any sort of political union. Now the Christian Democratic Prime Ministers counter-attacked by implicitly repudiating the Single European Act themselves in favour of a more far-reaching amendment of the treaties.

Thatcher also appeared to be prepared to go against the Single European Act on the question of dismantling customs checks at national frontiers. She insisted that such checks were necessary to apprehend terrorists and criminals, especially those attempting to transport illegal drugs, and also as a safeguard against the spread of rabies. The Commission responded to the last of these points with plans for a rabies-eradication campaign, but proposals made during the West German presidency for the problems of terrorism and drug dealing to be tackled by the formation of a European police force along the lines of the US Federal Bureau of Investigation were dismissed by Thatcher as creating yet more bureaucracy.

Of all Thatcher's objections to the Commission's plans, this is the most difficult to explain. The Prime Minister's own explanation in her speech in Bruges was that it was 'a matter of pure common sense that we cannot totally abolish frontier controls if we are also to protect our citizens and stop the movement of drugs, of terrorists, of illegal immigrants'.[44] Apart from the natural suspicion that ought to be aroused whenever 'common sense' is brought into any argument, the record of arrests of terrorists and drugs dealers appeared to show that co-operation between national police forces and excise officials was the most effective approach. Few terrorists or dealers in drugs were stupid enough to get themselves caught red-handed at routine customs checks. Here the British Government appeared to be arguing a case that went against its much-vaunted commitment to freeing the internal market, as well as going against the Single European Act.

The final point on which the British were unable to agree with the plans of the Commission was the harmonization of VAT and excise duties between the member states. Lord Cockfield, for the Commission, argued fiercely that this was absolutely necessary if a true free market were to emerge, and he proposed that all VAT be brought within two broad bands: a standard rate of 14–20 per cent and a lower rate of 4–9 per cent for 'socially sensitive items' such as

[44] Ibid., 21 Sept. 1988.

food.[45] For the purposes of the British political debate, it was the 'socially sensitive items' which were seized upon by the Labour Party, who claimed that the Government was about to allow the EC to impose VAT on food, children's clothing, and books. In the heat of the general election campaign the Prime Minister allowed herself to state categorically that she would never allow VAT to be imposed on such items. But the objections of the British went further, to the whole principle of levels of taxation being determined outside Britain.

Harmonizing VAT, and even more excise duties, would impose even larger burdens on other member states than on Britain. An existing zero-level of excise duty on wine in the Mediterranean member states made acceptance of the Commission's proposed levels politically very difficult for them. Denmark, with the highest levels of VAT, stood to lose more than Britain from bringing its existing national rates into the proposed harmonized bands. Even the French Prime Minister, Michel Rocard, expressed some hostility to the plan, although he was apparently overruled by President Mitterrand because, when the British Chancellor tabled an alternative scheme at a meeting of Finance Ministers in September, the French lined up behind the Commission's proposals— as did almost all the other member states, despite expressing some reservations about the practicalities of implementing the changes by the end of 1992. Denmark would not commit itself to accepting the Cockfield plan, but would have nothing to do with the British plan either; only Luxemburg gave any support to Lawson's alternative.

The British plan was to allow VAT rates to sort themselves out through the operation of the market. Lawson argued that after 1992 it would be illegal to put artificial obstacles in the way of cross-border shopping. In such circumstances, if rates varied considerably between member states, the states with the higher rates of VAT would have to lower them into line with those of their neighbours or see their own retail outlets suffer as people went across the border to do their shopping.

The appeal of the plan to the British was that the only part of the United Kingdom where extensive cross-border shopping was feasible was Northern Ireland, but, since British VAT rates were below those in the neighbouring Irish Republic, the benefit would

---

[45] *Bulletin of the European Communities,* 7/8–1987, point 1.2.2.

come the British way. Otherwise, cross-channel shopping trips might expand, but never to the extent of putting British merchants out of business. For Luxemburg the proposal held attractions because its very low rates of VAT already made it a considerable beneficiary from cross-border shopping. Nobody else thought it a good idea, particularly because it would ensure the harmonization of VAT and excise in only one direction, downwards, with possibly a greater loss of revenue to national exchequers than would be involved in the Cockfield plan.

Lord Cockfield's own passionate defence of the necessity of harmonization, combined with his public criticisms of other aspects of the British position, infuriated Thatcher, and in the opinion of many observers ensured that she would not reappoint him for a second term of office with the Commission. This was confirmed in July 1988, and it was announced that Leon Brittan would take Cockfield's place. Edward Heath suggested that the decision had been taken out of 'spite', and described Brittan as 'a discredited minister'.[46] Others felt that Brittan, who had been strongly suspected of shielding the Prime Minister during the Westland affair by accepting the blame for the leaking of confidential documents prejudicial to Heseltine, was being rewarded for his loyalty to Thatcher.

Ironically, Cockfield's original appointment had been seen as a reward for his steadfast backing for the Prime Minister while he was Secretary of State for Trade and Industry. His 'disloyalty' after going to Brussels was therefore harder for Thatcher to bear. Whether Brittan would prove any more reliable remained to be seen, but his address to a fringe meeting of the 1988 Conservative Party Conference was not promising from that point of view. Although applauding Thatcher's 'robust opposition to excessive intervention and unnecessary bureaucracy', he defended the idea of a further pooling of sovereignty, and held up the reorganization of the European steel industry as a shining example of the positive results that could be achieved by centralized direction.[47]

Thatcher also had to put up with Jacques Delors for at least a while longer: so pleased were the rest of the member states with his performance during his normal four-year stint as President of the Commission that at the Hanover meeting of the European Council

[46] *Independent*, 25 July 1988.   [47] Ibid., 26 Oct. 1988.

they agreed to extend his term by a further two years. He responded by replying to Thatcher's attacks on him in a speech to the European Parliament and in newspaper interviews. Although adopting a very diplomatic tone, he made it clear that he considered Thatcher's criticisms to be unfair and inaccurate, and that there could be no question of not having a social dimension to the 1992 project, of not having a European company statute, of not abolishing customs posts, for which the harmonization of taxation rates was a prerequisite, or of not including progress on monetary union.[48]

This was where the matter stood on the eve of the Rhodes meeting of the European Council in December 1988. The gap between Delors and Thatcher seemed as wide as ever. Indeed, a gap appeared to be emerging between Thatcher and Sir Geoffrey Howe, who spent time travelling around Europe trying to ensure that there was no further confrontation at Rhodes, and compounded his support for early British membership of the EMS when in November he addressed a gathering of MEPs who had met to honour Lord Cockfield, and made it clear that he personally agreed with Cockfield's opinion that the single European market was only part of the process under way.[49]

How far Howe agreed with Cockfield on what was involved in the rest of the project is less clear. Certainly there were three areas other than the freeing of the market in which Britain had expressed an interest: technological co-operation, defence co-operation, and political co-operation.

Technological Co-operation

Although theoretically committed to European technological co-operation, the British Government put itself in the position of the awkward partner on this issue in 1986–7 when it stood alone in refusing to accept the level of funding proposed for the Community 'framework programme' of research and development in high technology.

In March 1986 the Commission proposed that expenditure on this programme should be 10.3 million Ecu over five years. Britain was joined by France and West Germany in objecting to this figure, so by the time that formal proposals were brought to the Council of Ministers it had been amended to 7.735 million Ecu over four years. Still the larger member states were not prepared to agree, but when the Belgian presidency suggested a compromise figure of 6.48 million Ecu, first the French and eventually the Germans accepted it, leaving Britain isolated in opposition.

The British Minister for Information Technology, Geoffrey Pattie, refused to budge from a figure of 4.2 million Ecu as a maximum, an increase of only 10 per cent on the budget for the previous four-year period, and therefore a reduction in real terms for a budget that would now have to cover twelve rather than ten member states. This British position was maintained despite the production of figures by the Commission showing that for every £1 that the British Government paid into the research and development budget, Britain received approximately £1.25 in grants.

One possible explanation for this apparently perverse approach was that the British Treasury insisted that every pound devoted to a Community programme must be deducted from the budget of the domestic ministry involved; so the Department of Trade and Industry was simply defending the size of budget over which it exercised control, and minimizing the extent to which it was depleted by funds being channelled into the control of the Commission.[50] Geoffrey Pattie himself admitted that there was some truth in this explanation, though not much. 'These arguments do exist,' he told the *Independent*, 'but they are not forceful or central.'[51]

His own explanation was that the British Government was concerned that the programme of research should give value for money, and he proceeded to make a series of allegations about the Commission's standards of monitoring the spending of the grants given under the various schemes. However, in the face of a barrage of criticism, including some from researchers and industrialists involved in EC research projects who maintained that the monitoring and assessment procedures of the Commission were more rigorous than those operated by Pattie's own Department of Trade and Industry for projects that it funded, the Minister had to retreat, and admitted that the three main programmes under the framework— Esprit (Information Technology), Race (Telecommunications), and

[50] Quentin Peel, 'A Euro-dilemma for Britain', *Financial Times*, 30 Mar. 1987.
[51] *Independent*, 9 May 1987.

Brite (Application of New Technology)—were 'very important and valuable' and 'seem to be well run'.[52]

An alternative explanation for the blocking of the budget is that the British Government wished to use it as a bargaining counter in negotiations to achieve reform of the CAP. Indeed, this was publicly stated to be the reason, but not until the first day of the Brussels meeting of the European Council in June 1987. If it was the real reason, it would have been better to have said so from the outset, rather than to launch unjustifiable attacks on the efficiency of the Commission's monitoring procedures, which later had to be retracted. The 'bargaining-counter' explanation does not sound convincing, and seems not to have been taken seriously by other states.

It is difficult otherwise to understand Geoffrey Pattie's performance in this episode, although it is possible that the embarrassing situation in which he found himself was not entirely of his own making. *The Times* reported that Pattie was believed to be 'under strict instructions from Downing Street not to budge on the government's previous position';[53] it is feasible that the Minister was not given the reason for this instruction, and was left to defend the line as best he could.

Whatever the reasons, it is difficult to avoid the judgement that this issue was badly handled by the British Government. By the time that Britain allowed the programme to proceed, in July 1987, research teams were already having to be dismantled for lack of funds. Even then the British continued to block 6 per cent of the total until agreement was reached on other EC budgetary savings, a petty gesture presumably intended to save a little face. There is no doubt that the Government's twelve-month campaign on this issue left a legacy of bitterness in Brussels and in national capitals.

There was more British enthusiasm for the EUREKA programme. This developed from an initiative taken in April 1985 by François Mitterrand as a response to US President Reagan's SDI project. It was for a European programme of collaborative research into the non-military applications of advanced technology. Although initially cautious, from June 1985 onwards the British Government 'took an uncharacteristically prominent role in promoting the concept'.[54]

---

[52] Ibid., 9 May 1987.   [53] *The Times*, 26 Mar. 1987.
[54] Margaret Sharp and Claire Shearman, *European Technological Collaboration* (London, 1987), 70.

Three aspects of EUREKA may have attracted the British more than did the Community programme. First, as compared with the EC programme, EUREKA was more concerned with the application of technology than with pure research that might not produce practical results. Secondly, although there was some disagreement about the level of public funding, the emphasis of EUREKA, thanks to the insistence of the British Government, was more on privately funded collaborative programmes. Thirdly, EUREKA was not an EC programme. It involved West European states that were not members of the Community, and had its own secretariat rather than being under the control of the Commission.

Suspicion of allowing the Commission to become too powerful had been a strong factor motivating the Thatcher Governments to look for European co-operation to develop in other frameworks than the EC. This same sentiment had informed the British approach to the question of European defence co-operation, although here it had also been bound up with the Atlanticism of the Prime Minister.

Defence Co-operation

Defence is an area that is not covered by the Treaty of Rome and has not figured in the political co-operation procedure. It is sensitive for several reasons. First, the attempt to set up an EDC in 1950 showed that this is a matter of high politics which will not easily be taken into a process that may involve the surrender of some degree of national control. Secondly, defence is the umbilical cord that ties Western Europe to the United States and any attempt to set up a separate European defence organization might be a cause of strain within the Atlantic Alliance. Thirdly, there were states within the Community that did not wish to be dragged into the East–West confrontation, particularly Ireland, which valued its neutrality, and Greece, which under the Panhellenic Socialist Government of Andreas Papandreou had adopted a critical stance towards NATO and an accommodating stance towards its communist neighbours.

Discussion of the need for co-operation on defence dates back to events of 1980–2, when the over-reaction of the United States to the Soviet invasion of Afghanistan, and the declaration of martial law in Poland, led the EC to attempt to formulate a common

position towards the USSR, only to be frustrated by the unwillingness of some of the smaller states to become involved in the issues at
all. It was the French who first proposed the revitalization of the
WEU as a forum for the discussion of such matters. In the autumn
of 1984 the seven members (Britain, France, West Germany, Italy,
and the Benelux states) agreed to try to breathe new life into the
Union, but the British in particular expressed some hesitation, and
the first meeting in Bonn in April 1985 was a bit of a feeble affair,
at which the members were unable to agree a common position in
response to Reagan's SDI initiative.

The Reykjavik summit and the proposal from Gorbachev for a
treaty to eliminate intermediate nuclear forces gave added interest
to the experiment, though, and in a lecture to the Belgian Institute
of International Relations in March 1987, Howe called for a revival
of WEU 'as a forum for defining European defence priorities within
Nato'.[55] Although he stressed that the strengthening of the
European identity must not mean any weakening of the link with
the United States his comments appear not to have pleased
Thatcher, who publicly warned of the dangers of 'sub-structures in
Europe which could unwittingly, unintentionally have the effect of
undermining the links across the Atlantic'.[56]

Again the strong views of the British Prime Minister, forthrightly
expressed, made Britain appear to be uncooperative. Yet it has to
be stressed that, on the question of Europe developing a common
defence identity, the Irish and the Greeks had been much more
awkward than the British. Any impression that Britain was being
particularly awkward was produced by the British Prime Minister's
insistence on speaking in a way that could only make her appear to
be less concerned with European unity than with Atlantic solidarity.
There seemed to be little real difference between the British Prime
Minister and her Foreign Secretary on this matter, but Howe
managed to present the British position in a way which, while
emphasizing the importance of the Atlantic link, put the stress on
the European interest, whereas Thatcher appeared to judge the
desirability of European co-operation by whether it would strengthen the link with the United States.

[55] *The Times*, 17 Mar. 1987.
[56] Peter Jenkins, 'Brussels Haggles while Europe Yearns', *Independent*, 30 June
1987.

Political Co-operation

Britain's commitment to political co-operation was long-standing. It had played an important part in the document submitted to the Fontainebleau European Council, and had formed the major part of the Stresa paper. It was an issue on which there appeared to be accord between Britain and its partners, and some considerable progress had been made in operating the procedures of co-operation. Nevertheless, there sometimes seemed to be more difficulty in getting substantive agreements on adopting common positions. Partly this reflected the difficulty of making a rapid response to crises as they occurred when it was necessary to gain the agreement of all twelve member states. British proposals for improving the procedures were partly made with this particular problem in mind. But partly also there was a difference of perspective between the member states on many issues of international politics.

In this problem of difference of perspective the lines of division varied according to the issue. On matters relating to the Middle East, the Greeks and Italians were much more hostile to US interventions such as the Libyan bombings and the imposition of sanctions against Syria than were the West Germans, for example. But it was the British who appeared as most strongly the defenders of US policy in the region, and, while the other member states tried to accommodate their particular concerns to the formulation of joint positions, Thatcher did not. On the issue of the Libyan bombings, for example, the French refused to allow the US aircraft to overfly their airspace or to land in Corsica to refuel on the return flight. Yet France joined Britain and the United States in vetoing a motion condemning the raids in the United Nations Security Council.

Even on issues that did not have implications for relations with the United States, Britain often appeared to be the awkward partner, whereas in fact other partners also had doubts about the policy in question but were not so prepared to express them. One such issue was that of sanctions against South Africa.

This matter was raised at the meeting of the European Council in The Hague on 26–7 June 1986, immediately prior to Britain's assumption of the presidency. Agreement was reached on a joint statement in the communiqué calling on the South African Government to open genuine dialogue with 'the authentic leaders of the black population',[57] but, because of determined opposition from Thatcher, it was not possible to agree on a package of sanctions to add economic pressure to that call. Instead, Howe was asked to visit Southern Africa, in his capacity as the immediate future President of the Council, 'in a further effort to establish conditions in which the necessary dialogue can commence'.[58]

The almost universal view that Howe's mission would produce no tangible concessions from the South African Government proved correct, and most of the other member states felt that his position as a mediator had been compromised by his Prime Minister's passionate and public opposition to sanctions. However, when the question of sanctions came to be reconsidered by the EC states in September, it was West Germany that proved to be the biggest obstacle to getting more than a rather weak package accepted. In particular, it was at German insistence that coal imports from South Africa into the Community were excluded from the list.

That Britain did not emerge in September as the main barrier to sanctions owed less to a British desire to allow a common European position to emerge than it did to an earlier promise that Thatcher had made to the Commonwealth states that she would not oppose whatever sanctions the other EC member states were prepared to accept. She did, however, let it be known that she agreed with Helmut Kohl's reservations about the package; and when Howe described the agreements as being part of a concerted effort by the industrialized world to bring about change in South Africa, he received a rebuke from Thatcher.[59]

What this episode showed quite clearly was, first, that Britain was often put in the position of appearing to be the awkward partner in the Community because Thatcher was always prepared to state her strongly held opinions in a forthright manner, whereas other Heads of Government were prepared to keep quiet, even though they might share the view of the British Prime Minister, rather than risk being accused of hindering the formulation of a common European position, and perhaps also stirring up political controversy at home. Secondly, though, Thatcher's agreement to accept whatever sanctions the rest of the EC were prepared to

---

[57] *Keesing's Contemporary Archives*, pp. 34627–8.
[58] Ibid., 34627–8.   [59] *The Economist*, 20 Sept. 1986.

accept indicates that, after calm reflection, the same approach as had emerged over the inter-governmental conference on revision of the Treaties came to prevail. That is, the British Government shut up and effectively forced the other member states to show their hand. Unfortunately, in this case as in others, far more publicity went to the British Prime Minister's outspoken comments than to the West German Chancellor's quiet sabotage of the sanctions exercise.

Conclusion

Following the Fontainebleau settlement of the dispute over its budgetary contributions, the British Government appeared determined to play a more constructive role within the Community. This determination manifested itself in the papers produced at Fontainebleau and Stresa mapping out a future for the EC. The objectives pursued by Britain were: to bring the CAP under control; to promote the freeing of the internal market; to improve cooperation in foreign policy, increasingly including defence; and to avert too large a transfer of power to Brussels.

Each of these objectives was shared with some of the other member states, but a core group, embracing particularly the original six members, appeared to be committed to bringing about institutional changes to accompany economic changes, in direct conflict with the fourth British objective. Other areas of dispute that emerged were: whether the freeing of the internal market needed to be accompanied by an increase in redistributive expenditure to help the more peripheral regions and states; the role of monetary union; how far national control over economic policy would be replaced by central decision-making; the 'social dimension' of the future free market; the harmonization of VAT and excise duties in member states; and the physical removal of customs posts.

If the Prime Minister's interventions are ignored, the method adopted by the British Government in pursuit of its objectives seemed increasingly to involve playing the traditional Community game of making compromises and accepting package deals, as demonstrated most clearly at the Brussels European Council in February 1988. Opening up other modes of co-operation, as in the sponsorship of the EUREKA initiative and the reinvigoration of

WEU, contributed to the aim of keeping the power of the Commission in check. The policy of taking a back seat and calling the bluff of other member states was used successfully in the cases of the Single European Act and, eventually, of sanctions against South Africa. All of these can be considered to be examples of successful diplomatic manœuvring, involving Britain in gaining more than it conceded. They do not add up to the behaviour of an awkward partner, but to that of a normal and skilful actor in the Community game.

But, of course, the interventions of the Prime Minister cannot be ignored. Thatcher's statements, her confrontations with other Heads of Government and with the President of the Commission, grabbed the headlines in Britain and throughout the Community. They were the basis on which Britain would still have been described as an awkward partner by most of the rest of the EC at the end of the period considered in this chapter.

Various explanations for Thatcher's behaviour can be suggested: first, that her aggressive style was a bargaining technique; secondly, that it was designed purely for domestic consumption; and, thirdly, that it was simply a reflection of the personality of the lady herself.

On the first view, Thatcher raised negotiation through confrontation to an art form. By making loud public statements of her unwillingness to compromise, she extracted larger concessions from her opponents than would otherwise have been available. It can be argued on this view that the February 1988 deal was only possible because of Thatcher's uncompromising stance in Brussels the previous June. Other states were encouraged to make concessions that they would otherwise not have felt able to concede, confident that they would never have to deliver on their promises because Britain would prevent the package being accepted; they could therefore appear *communautaire* at no cost. Having thereby got the French and Germans to make concessions on agricultural reform, Thatcher gave way eight months later, leaving the French in particular totally exposed, and facing the choice of either wrecking the deal or accepting tighter limits on agricultural expenditure than they had originally wanted.

If this was a bargaining technique, though, it was a very dangerous one, and was not always used very subtly. On the issue of sanctions against South Africa, Thatcher said enough to take the obloquy before stepping back to let West Germany do the dirty work. It could have been much better here to have adopted the technique of keeping quiet from the start. And the outspokenness of Thatcher's comments in Bruges in 1988 seemed to push the Christian Democratic leaders of West Germany and the Benelux states into reopening the question of institutional reform which had apparently been resolved in a manner not unfavourable to Britain in 1985.

On the second explanation, the rhetoric was intended to throw up a smoke-screen of publicity prior to the Government taking further major steps down the road of transferring sovereign power away from Westminster. The Prime Minister on this view knew very well that the process of European integration was inexorable, and that it involved developments that were unpalatable to many of her Conservative supporters and were incompatible with her carefully cultivated image as a champion of the British nation. So, the critics were thrown off the scent by assertions that there would be no surrender, then a deal was concluded which was actually a compromise but was presented as a victory. In the case of the February 1984 settlement, the British public was repeatedly told what Britain had got out of it, and when critics attempted to point out the concessions that were involved they found great difficulty in getting a hearing, as everybody knew that Thatcher would not sell out the national interest, because she had told them so.[60]

The third explanation stresses that the Prime Minister was not one of nature's diplomats; that speaking her mind was what came most naturally to her; and that her mind was often set by deep-rooted prejudices which were resistant to rational persuasion by her advisers. Thus the pattern of confrontation followed by concession was the product of Thatcher 'shooting from the hip', after which her advisers gradually managed to persuade her to see the need for a more circumspect approach. On this view, British policy in the Community in this period was the outcome of a constant struggle between the Prime Minister and the rest of the governmental machine.

Following Thatcher's speech in Bruges, Peter Jenkins reported that the story of its genesis that was circulating in Whitehall was that the Prime Minister was inspired by her rage at Jacques Delors,

[60] This argument has been advanced by John Wyles of the *Financial Times*. See his Lombard column, 'Mrs. Thatcher's Eurobluff', *Financial Times*, 25 Aug. 1988.

which prevailed over the advice of officials 'and what ought to have been her own better judgement'.

When the Foreign Office had submitted notes for the speech they went straight into the waste paper basket. When the Foreign Office saw the next version it was considered way over the top; she considered it too wet by half. What she eventually said . . . was, I am told, considerably toned down from what she would like to have said. She was restrained from delivering a speech which, instead of merely distressing and depressing our European partners, might have done lasting damage to our national interests.[61]

It is probable that there is some truth in each of these explanations. How much is difficult to judge at the time of writing, and may not be much easier in thirty years' time when the official documents relating to British policy are available to historians.

Although there were some policy positions which in themselves upset Britain's partners, particularly the refusal to take sterling into the exchange-rate mechanism of the EMS, Britain was not quite as isolated as may have appeared from the headlines in its doubts about some of the developments within the EC which the Delors Commission was promoting. The main reason for Britain appearing as an awkward partner was the willingness of the British Prime Minister to speak out forcefully on these issues while other leaders kept a diplomatic silence. It is possible that the Community would have been less able to take decisions if the British voice had not been raised when it was, as others would have felt obliged to raise their voices if they could not have relied on Britain to do it for them. From the resulting cacophony it is quite feasible that only chaos would have emerged.

[61] Peter Jenkins, 'Thatcher Attacks her Euro-Galtieri', *Independent*, 22 Sept. 1988.

7. The Last Years of Thatcher Governments, 1989–1990

IN the course of 1989 and 1990 the world changed beyond all recognition. The collapse of communism throughout Eastern Europe left Western governments facing a situation that was unexpected and complex. In particular the rapid movement to German unity inserted a new element into the calculations of the leaders of other West European states.

Faced with the emergence of a reunited Germany, with borders that extended into Central Europe, the leaders of most member states of the EC decided that there was an even greater need to press forward to political union so as to contain the new state, but also so as to tie it into the EC and prevent it drifting eastward and concentrating on reconstructing the links that had existed between Germany and Eastern Europe before the wars.

Margaret Thatcher drew different conclusions. During 1989 and 1990 her position on further European integration increasingly came to be out of line with the positions of the other EC leaders, but also to be at odds with the position of the new Administration in the United States, and ultimately with the position of other leading members of her own Government. Thatcher was always of the opinion that, just because she was out of line with everybody else, that did not mean that she was wrong. However, her failure to adapt to the changing circumstances and thinking of the post-Cold War world proved to be the cause of her downfall.

The International Context

There can be little question about the most important international developments of 1989 and 1990. Gorbachev's policy of *perestroika* in the Soviet Union allowed the freeing up of the monolithic regimes that had existed in Eastern Europe. In the German Democratic Republic the communist regime came under pressure from popular movements, and in the course of 1989 there began a mass exodus to West Germany via the open frontiers of the Democratic Republic's neighbours, Hungary and Czechoslovakia. In the face of this challenge to its existence, the regime in East Germany began negotiations with the Federal Republic. In November 1989 it bowed to the inevitable and opened all the frontiers between East and West Germany. After that it was only a matter of time before Germany reunited.

The progress of the negotiations between the two Germanies was rapid, and left the rest of the EC out in the cold. Even France, the closest ally of the Federal Republic, was not kept informed of developments. Chancellor Kohl, seeing the opportunity to go into the history books as the man who reunified his country, seized the initiative with an energy that was surprising given his normally slow and deliberate style. The Franco-German relationship was put under considerable strain.

Obviously developments in Eastern Europe and Germany were of concern not only in the EC, but also in the United States, where in January 1989 George Bush became President. The policy of the new Administration towards Europe was clearly indicated in December 1989, when, following a summit meeting with President Gorbachev in Malta, Bush made a statement to the West European leaders in which he said, 'The events of our times call both for a continued, perhaps even intensified effort of the twelve to integrate, and a role for the EC as a magnet that draws the forces of reform forward in Eastern Europe.'[1]

This policy was subsequently elaborated in a speech by Secretary of State James Baker in Berlin in December 1989, in which he gave unequivocal support to closer European integration, said that the EC should play a central role in the shaping of the new Europe, and proposed to establish 'a significantly strengthened set of institutional and consultative links' between the EC and the United States. The phrase 'the new Atlanticism' was used by Baker to describe the relationship that he was proposing.[2]

The attitude of the US Administration was based on both economic and political considerations. The economic considerations were the legacy of the twin deficits that Bush had inherited from Reagan: a massive budget deficit and a deficit on the balance of payments. Because of these economic problems the Administration

[1] *Independent*, 5 Dec. 1989.   [2] Ibid., 13 Dec. 1989.

was looking for any opportunity to make savings; hence the willingness to allow the West Europeans the lead in stabilizing Eastern Europe. An indication of this came when the European Bank for Reconstruction and Development was set up in May 1990 to assist in the economic transition of the East European states to capitalism. It drew 51 per cent of its capital from the European Community and its member states, and only 10 per cent from the United States; in recognition of which, the presidency of the Bank went to a European, Jacques Attali, a former adviser to President Mitterrand.

The second consideration informing US policy was political. There was a strategic case for US troops not being withdrawn from Europe. Although the immediate military threat from communism had disappeared, the prospect of regional instability had increased. However, leaving US troops in the region so that they could if necessary intervene in intra-European nationalist conflicts was not a viable option, even if others could have been persuaded to pay the bills. Avoiding entanglement in European wars is one of the oldest prejudices of the US public; after all, many US citizens are descended from people who went to the United States precisely to get away from such nationalist conflicts. The idea of US lives being put at risk to sort out the old problems of the old continent was politically unacceptable.

The United States did however accept its policing role in the Middle East when on 2 August 1990 Iraq invaded Kuwait. President Bush quickly committed troops to Saudi Arabia to head off further aggression by the Iraqis (Operation Desert Shield); over the next few months the United States gradually built up its troop commitment, and eventually undertook military action to expel the Iraqi forces and restore Kuwait to its former rulers (Operation Desert Storm).

The United States led a multinational force drawn from European, Arab, and Asian states; but the largest military commitment came from the United States, which thereby demonstrated that it was now the world's only military superpower. However, the extent to which the military superpower was no longer the economic superpower that it had once been was demonstrated by the need for the US Administration to collect financial contributions from the Germans and Japanese, who were constitutionally debarred from committing troops themselves, but who ended up paying a considerable portion of the cost of the operation.

The Domestic Context

The Conservative Party went into 1989 trailing Labour in the opinion polls. Although it is not uncommon for a government party to find itself behind the Opposition in mid-term polls, there were clear signs of a revival of Labour following a highly publicized process of policy review; at the same time the policies of the Government were extremely unpopular even with Conservative voters.

The central elements of the Government's programme were the reform of the National Health Service (NHS) to introduce an internal market; the privatization of the water and electricity supply industries; and the replacement of the domestic rates with the community charge (what came to be known as the poll tax). Each of these policies was particularly associated with the Prime Minister herself, and each ran into opposition that indicated the limited extent to which ten years of Thatcherism had actually changed the fundamental attitudes of the British people.

For many people the NHS remained a symbol of all that was best about the British welfare state that Thatcher had tried so hard to dismantle. Even if she had wished to do so, she would have been unable openly to advocate a shift away from the NHS to private insurance schemes as the basis for health care in Britain.[3] Instead her Government formulated proposals that tried to introduce market mechanisms into the NHS; however, the reforms ran into opposition from the British Medical Association, which launched a campaign that included posters in family doctors' surgeries. Conservative MPs became worried as the volume of mail from constituents opposing the reforms grew to formidable proportions.[4]

At the same time, the privatization of the water supply was seen even by Conservative supporters as taking the privatization

---

[3] There had been plenty of warning signs of the unpopularity of any move to private health provision: 'A nasty storm blew up when it emerged, in 1982, that the Cabinet Office think-tank was looking at the possibility of switching from tax-based finance to private insurance. A shoal of letters flowed in when, last year, a junior health minister argued that more people should pay for their health care.' *The Economist*, 4 Feb. 1989, p. 25.   [4] Ibid., 18 Mar. 1989, p. 51.

programme too far. Water was seen as a basic human necessity that ought to be provided by the state.

But by far the most unpopular of these policies was the one most closely associated with the Prime Minister personally. While there was a widely acknowledged need for some change in the existing system of local taxation, the Government had been warned that the community charge would be difficult and expensive to collect. Nevertheless, the Prime Minister insisted that it should go ahead because it would make people more aware of the cost of local services, and therefore less inclined to vote for financially profligate local politicians.

Unfortunately, again the British people showed an attachment to a sense of social justice that pre-dated Thatcherism. Although the amounts of money involved were not large, it was widely argued that a tax which fell equally on rich and poor alike was unfair. This sense of injustice fuelled a widespread campaign for non-payment of the tax, which made the difficulties of collecting it greater than they would otherwise have been. Matters were made worse because the level at which the tax was set by many Conservative-controlled councils was much higher than anticipated, and gave the lie to the argument that it was only profligate Labour authorities who would have to impose a heavy burden on their citizens. By late 1990 Conservative MPs were becoming increasingly anxious about the unpopularity of the tax, and concerned for their seats at the next election if it were not abandoned or at least modified. Yet Thatcher continued to put her weight behind its retention.

Throughout 1989 and 1990 the Conservatives were running behind Labour in opinion polls; and after October 1989 Thatcher's popularity was trailing that of the Conservative Party as a whole, suggesting that perhaps she had become an electoral liability.[5] Labour convincingly won the elections to the European Parliament in 1989, and scored gains in local elections, and in by-elections.

Adding to the worries of Conservative MPs were economic conditions, which deteriorated at first steadily and then, in the second half of 1990, rapidly. Following boom conditions in 1987 and 1988, with growth in GDP sustained at the very high level of 5 per cent in 1987 and 4.6 per cent in 1988, monetary policy was

[5] David Butler, 'Elections in Britain', in Peter Catterall (ed.), *Contemporary Britain: An Annual Review 1990* (Oxford, 1990), 46–51, and *Contemporary Britain: An Annual Review 1991* (Oxford, 1991), 59–62.

tightened in the second half of 1988 to counteract rising inflation and a large deficit on the balance of payments. Interest rates rose to 13 per cent in November 1988, to 14 per cent by May 1989, and to 15 per cent in September 1989.

The effect of these policies was a sharper cut-back in output than anticipated in 1989, with growth of just 2 per cent; but inflation remained stubbornly high, actually rising from 7.5 per cent in January 1989 to 8.3 per cent by June; and sterling remained weak on the foreign exchanges throughout the year. Because of this, although the high interest rates were proving extremely painful to consumers and borrowers, they could not be quickly brought down. This added to the unpopularity of the Government, particularly because the high rates caused a collapse of house prices, which had artificially inflated during the boom of 1987–8, so that many householders were left with mortgages higher than the market value of their properties. Combined with lower wage settlements, higher prices, and higher unemployment, this resulted in record levels of home repossessions during 1990.

In the first half of 1990 inflation continued to be remarkably resistant to the monetary medicine, rising further to reach 10 per cent by July. Output also continued to grow at this stage, at an annual equivalent of 2.5 per cent in the first six months. Then in the second half of the year output suddenly collapsed, producing a technical recession, with negative growth in two successive quarters. Yet inflation still did not drop, because the outbreak of hostilities in the Gulf led to a rise in the price of oil, which caused inflation to push up to 11 per cent by the autumn.[6]

The Elections to the European Parliament

The European elections in Britain were marked by divisions within the Conservative Party, and the apparent conversion of Labour to being the more pro-European of the two major parties.

Divisions within the Conservative Party over the EC had been simmering since the Bruges speech. In February 1989 the Bruges Group was formed to support the principles laid down by the Prime

[6] The material in this section on the performance of the economy is based on Alan Budd and Alan Davies, 'Economic Policy and Macro-economic Developments', in Catterall (ed.), *Contemporary Britain: An Annual Review 1990*, pp. 137–45, and *Contemporary Britain: An Annual Review 1991*, pp. 156–68.

Minister in her speech. Although the membership of the Group was not drawn exclusively from the Conservative Party, the bulk of its support came from Conservatives, as did the members of the parliamentary 'Friends of Bruges'.

In May 1989 there were interventions by senior Conservative back-bench MPs which showed that the Bruges tendency was not unchallenged. Sir Edward Heath launched the first of what were to become a series of attacks on Thatcher's attitude to the EC. In a television interview in Britain, and in a speech in Brussels, he stated that the Prime Minister was trying to mislead the British people about the risk of the EC turning into a socialist superstate, and warned in the television interview that if Britain tried to hold up the development of the EC the other eleven members would go on alone, leaving Britain as a second-class member.[7] Michael Heseltine issued a similar warning about Britain being left behind by developments in the EC in a book also published in May 1989.[8]

These voices did not have much influence, though, on the tone of the Conservative campaign for the European elections, which presented the nightmare of incessant interference from Brussels in British internal affairs were it not for the sturdy resistance put up by the Conservative Government. It was a campaign that was closely associated with the Prime Minister, who was believed to have personally dictated its tone. Labour, in contrast, presented itself as a strongly pro/EC party, contrary to its previous image, a conversion that was part of the policy-review process, which had been informed throughout by pro-EC attitudes.[9]

The result of the election may well have owed more to prevailing economic conditions than to voters' feelings about the relative merits of the two major parties' policies on the EC. Nevertheless, the reversal in the number of seats won when compared with the previous election in 1984—the Conservatives then got forty-five seats to Labour's thirty-two, while in 1989 the figures were precisely reversed—and the collapse in the Conservative share of the vote from 40.8 per cent to 34.7 per cent contributed to

[7] *Independent*, 15 May 1989 and 14 June 1989.
[8] Michael Heseltine, *The Challenge of Europe: Can Britain Win?* (London, 1989).
[9] On the change in Labour's attitude see Stephen George and Ben Rosamond, 'The European Community', in Martin J. Smith and Joanna Spear (eds.), *The Changing Labour Party* (London, 1992), 171–84.

undermining the Thatcherite line, especially as opinion polls had been indicating for some months that the British public was now much more sympathetic towards further European integration than at any previous period since the 1975 referendum.[10]

A Change of Tone

At the Madrid meeting of the European Council in June 1989 Thatcher adopted a much more conciliatory tone than was normal for her. Although she registered her continued opposition to plans for a rapid movement to monetary union, and for a social dimension to the 1992 programme, she made a significant move on the question of British membership of the exchange rate mechanism of the EMS. Whereas previously she had only said that Britain would join when the time was right, she now spelt out the conditions which, when met, would allow membership to occur. These were: the abolition of all restrictions on capital movements; full liberalization of financial services; a stronger EC competition policy; the completion of the internal market; and a substantial reduction in British rates of inflation.

Some observers saw the more accommodating tone as a direct consequence of the European election result. But a change of tone by the British Government had been detectable even before the elections.

In January 1989 stories appeared in the British Press based on public hearings before a committee of the European Parliament, which indicated that fraud against the EC was widespread, particularly under the CAP.[11] The British Secretary of State for Agriculture called for action to eliminate these abuses, but no immediate attempt was made to use the revelations to attack the Commission or the EC generally.

Then, at the end of February, Sir John Hoskyns, who was believed to be close to Thatcher, used the occasion of his retirement from the post of Chairman of the Institute of Directors to launch a strong attack on the Commission in which he spoke of widespread corruption.[12] Press speculation that this was an attack inspired by

---

[10] *Independent*, 15 June 1989.
[11] Ibid., 25 Jan. 1989; *Guardian*, 26 Jan. 1989.
[12] Sir John Hoskyns, 'Why the Single Market Programme is in Trouble', *Director*, 31 (13 Mar. 1989).

the Prime Minister proved to be unfounded; indeed, Peter Jenkins reported that Thatcher had sent a personal message to Jacques Delors dissociating herself from the speech.[13] Despite a report from the House of Lords' Select Committee on the EC which criticized the failure of the Commission to deal with fraud,[14] the Government allowed the matter to drop from public view, while continuing to press for action behind the scenes.

Here was an initial indication that a new approach had been agreed within the Government to try to make peace with the rest of the EC, and to ensure that Britain was seen as a committed member and remained fully involved in the continuing discussions on the future. However, it was a change of tone rather than a change of substance. When the Delors Committee on Monetary Union reported in April 1989, proposing a three-stage process for movement to monetary union,[15] its proposals were immediately rejected by the Chancellor of the Exchequer, Nigel Lawson, who said that Britain would be producing its own proposals. And when in May the European Commission produced the first draft of a 'social charter' of workers' rights,[16] the Secretary of State for Industry, Lord Young, attacked the proposals before they had even been published, arguing that Britain had 'far too much experience of well-intentioned social legislation which had the opposite effect to that planned',[17] and the Employment Secretary, Norman Fowler, pledged his opposition to aspects of the proposals.

At Madrid Thatcher accepted implementation of the first stage of the Delors Report, involving the closer co-ordination of national economic and monetary policies, while restating that Britain was unhappy with the plans for stages 2 and 3. More significantly, she accepted that an inter-governmental conference should eventually be convened to consider what changes might need to be made to the

---

[13] Peter Jenkins, 'How Britain can Avert a Two-Tier Europe', *Independent*, 7 Mar. 1989.

[14] House of Lords, Select Committee on the European Communities, *Fraud against the Community. 5th Report, Session 1988–89*, Parliamentary Papers HL 27 (1988–9).

[15] European Communities, Committee for the Study of Economic and Monetary Union, *Report on Economic and Monetary Union in the European Community*, Apr. 1989.

[16] European Commission, *Social Dimension of the Internal Market*, COM(89) 248 final (May 1989).

[17] *Hansard (Lords)*, 5th ser. 507 (3 May 1989), col. 158.

Treaties to allow further progress. Although she ended the meeting in her not unfamiliar minority of one in opposing the social charter, her general demeanour was judged to be much more co-operative than in 1988.

The same tone persisted at the Strasburg European Council at the end of the year. Here Thatcher was outvoted on the adoption of the social charter, and on starting the inter-governmental conference on monetary union by the end of 1990; but she indicated that Britain would play its full part in the EC despite differences on policy, a statement which drew a round of applause from the other participants.

The change of tone does seem to represent agreed government policy. The departure from it in the campaign for the European elections seems to represent a badly judged tactical decision by Thatcher, and one which, by its failure, reinforced the original decision.

Political Union

In November 1989, François Mitterrand told the European Parliament that he believed the lessons of the upheavals in Eastern Europe were that the EC must strive for political unity to ensure the stability and success of the whole of Europe.[18] In January 1990 Mitterrand and Kohl jointly wrote to Charles Haughey, the Irish Taoiseach, whose country held the presidency of the Council of Ministers for the first half of the year, proposing that an inter-governmental conference be convened on political union.

The thinking behind this proposal was inspired by the rapid movement towards a united Germany. France feared domination by its enlarged neighbour, but also feared that the reunified Germany would turn its back on the process of West European integration.

The underlying concern in Paris has been lest their German partners lose their enthusiasm for closer Western integration in their fascination with national reintegration; and the response, remarkably unanimous through-out France's political leadership, has been to express acceptance of a

---

[18] *Official Journal of the European Communities. Annex. Debates of the European Parliament*, 1989–90, no. 3-383/155.

united Germany while demanding a strengthening of the European institutions within which it may successfully be contained.[19]

At the same time as wanting to tie Germany into the Western system, France also hoped to tie down the potential superpower that was emerging in the midst of Europe, and to restrain any possibility of resurgent German nationalism. This second reason was also exactly why Helmut Kohl supported the initiative. He did not want to go down in history as the Frankenstein who had created a monster. A resurgent nationalist Germany would attract suspicion and fear from its neighbours, and that would tarnish his achievement in having brought about unification.

Given its consistent record on the question of European integration, the British Government was understandably not keen on the idea of using political union as a way of tackling what they also recognized as a potential German problem. Thatcher and her Foreign Secretary Douglas Hurd both made it clear that Britain did not think an inter-governmental conference on political union was desirable, and expressed concern lest focusing on such matters should slow progress on the freeing of the internal market. Hurd did, however, say that, should an IGC be convened, Britain would play a full part in it.[20]

Hurd's statement was in line with the new, more co-operative tone of British policy within the EC. It is quite possible, though, that the Prime Minister herself was more strongly opposed to moves to political union than was the general line of the Government. Unfortunately for her, her position had been undermined somewhat by the policy of the US Administration, which was strongly stated by President Bush following his summit with Gorbachev in Malta in December 1989, in words that echoed those used by Mitterrand to the European Parliament the previous month. Although Thatcher subsequently told the Commons that the US President had telephoned her to say that his position remained one of full support for the open and liberal Europe that she also wanted to see,[21] it seemed that her inter-governmental

[19] William Wallace and Martin Spät, 'Coming to terms with Germany', *World Today*, 46 (Apr. 1990), 55–6.

[20] Thatcher's statement is recorded in *Hansard*, 6th ser. 171 (24 Apr. 1990), col. 154; Hurd's comments were made in a speech to the Institute of Political Science in Paris, reported in the *Independent*, 25 Apr. 1990.

[21] *Hansard*, 6th ser. 163 (5 Dec. 1989), cols. 152–3.

vision of the future Europe had been undermined by the US wish to see closer unity.

In the week after James Baker's speech in Berlin, in which he expanded on US policy towards Europe, the *Sunday Times* ran an article that identified a number of important advisers in the State Department and White House as the originators of this policy. Robert Zoellick, Counsellor to the State Department and a man whom Baker had taken with him from the Treasury, was identified as a leading figure in the move to encourage a more unified EC. Dennis Ross, Director of Policy Planning in the State Department, was identified as an ally of Zoellick; and in the White House, Condoleeza Rica, a Soviet specialist, and Robert Blackwill, a European specialist, were seen as sharing the same analysis. Interestingly, the newspaper, which was a supporter of Thatcher, described these people as anti-British. The evidence for this was that: 'They think the United States should concentrate on building a special relationship with the European Community in general and West Germany in particular.'[22]

Faced with implied support from the United States for the Franco-German position, the British Government was never likely to be able to block the convening of the inter-governmental conference that Mitterrand and Kohl wanted. At a special meeting of the European Council in Dublin on 28 April 1990 Thatcher spoke against the inter-governmental conference, but the meeting agreed to ask Foreign Ministers to undertake an examination and analysis of the need for possible changes to the Treaties, and to report back to the regular European Council in June, also in Dublin.[23] At this meeting agreement was reached to convene the inter-governmental conference to run in parallel with one on monetary union that had already been agreed. The decision was taken on a vote of eleven to one, with Britain voting against.

Consistently with the Government's line that it would continue to negotiate despite its differences with the other members of the EC, Douglas Hurd outlined to Parliament in June the position that Britain would be taking in the conference. It would emphasize the need for co-operation on foreign and defence policy to remain

---

[22] John Cassidy, 'Pro-German, Anti-British Group gains Influence in Washington', *Sunday Times*, 17 Dec. 1989.
[23] *Bulletin of the European Communities*, 4–1990, point 1.12.

inter-governmental in nature; and, so far as institutional changes were concerned, it would press for an increase in the powers of the Commission and the Court of Justice to ensure that member states fulfilled their obligations under EC law.[24] The latter position was in line with the findings of studies which had shown that Britain, together with Denmark, had implemented more of the agreed 1992 legislation than other member states, some of which had a poor record of doing that which they had agreed to do.[25]

Subsequently, Francis Maude, Minister of State at the Foreign Office, indicated to the Commons Select Committee on European Legislation that the Government would also be pressing for the principle of subsidiarity to be written into the revised Treaty.[26]

Subsidiarity

Both the Prime Minister personally and the Government more generally seem to have become increasingly suspicious of the tendency of the European Commission to extend its competences. Shortly before the Madrid European Council, Lynda Chalker, Minister of State at the Foreign and Commonwealth Office, told the House of Commons Select Committee on Foreign Affairs that the Prime Minister wanted to ensure 'proper scrutiny of everything that comes up . . . to see whether it should be a matter of Community competence'.[27]

It was this concern to prevent incremental extension of the powers of the central institutions that led the Government to oppose two proposals, for which it was strongly criticized. One was for an extension to secondary schools of the Lingua programme of foreign-language teaching. Although Britain stood to benefit financially from such an extension, the Government blocked it on the grounds that the EC had no treaty competence in the field of education outside of vocational training and the university sector.

---

[24] *Hansard*, 6th ser. 174 (11 June 1990), col. 23.
[25] *Independent*, 7 Sept. 1989.
[26] House of Commons, Select Committee on European Legislation, *Minutes of Evidence, Wednesday, 18 July 1990*, Parliamentary Papers HC 188–iii (1989–90), 6–8.
[27] House of Commons, Foreign Affairs Select Committee, *The Single European Act: Minutes of Evidence*, Parliamentary Papers HC 446–i (1989–90), 12.

To allow this extension would be to set a precedent that the Commission could build on in the future. The second example concerned attempts to put a standardized health warning on packets of cigarettes. Although there were already health warnings on cigarettes sold in Britain, and the EC legislation would not have affected this, the Government argued that such measures of health protection were a matter for national governments to decide.

Such an attitude actually had a good deal of support in other member states, as subsequently became apparent. What helped to mobilize this support, and indicated the extent to which the British were learning to play the game of EC politics, was the adoption by the Government of the federalist term 'subsidiarity' as the basis for their argument that only those matters that had cross-border implications should be legislated upon at EC level, leaving national governments to deal with other issues.

Sovereignty

In June of 1990, sovereignty became an issue in a way that may well have heightened Margaret Thatcher's concerns. The European Court of Justice ordered British courts to suspend the implementation of the Merchant Shipping Act 1988, pending the hearing of a case before the Court in which the rules on national registration in the Act were being challenged by Spanish fishermen, who claimed that they breached EC law.[28] The lawyers for the fishermen claimed that the livelihoods of their clients were damaged by the application of the law during the hearing of the case, and the Court agreed.

The actual circumstances of the case were less important than the principle. There was no provision in the constitution of the United Kingdom for any court to suspend an Act of Parliament, which is what the European Court was ordering. There was an outcry in the Commons,[29] but the House of Lords imposed the injunction on 7 July. It was clear that the implications of membership of the EC for parliamentary sovereignty had been severely underestimated by most MPs, and the issue raised sensitivities in a way that may have influenced Thatcher's attitude later in the year to a suggestion of a further surrender of sovereignty, over monetary policy.

---

[28] Law Report, *Independent*, 20 June 1990.
[29] *Hansard*, 6th ser..174 (20 June 1990), cols. 921–6.

Deteriorating Relations with Germany

Sovereignty also figured in the resignation in July 1990 of the Secretary of State for Trade and Industry, Nicholas Ridley, a close political ally of Thatcher. His resignation was sparked by an interview published in the *Spectator* magazine in which he said that he was not opposed to surrendering sovereignty in principle, but that he was not prepared to surrender it to the European Commission, which he described as 'seventeen unelected politicians'. However, the section of the interview that caused the real problems for Ridley and for the Government was that in which he described moves towards monetary union as 'a German racket designed to take over the whole of Europe', and just for good measure insulted the French too by describing them as 'acting like poodles to the Germans'.[30]

A further deterioration in Anglo-German relations was provoked by the publication in a British newspaper that same weekend of a leaked confidential memorandum written for Thatcher by her adviser on foreign affairs, Charles Powell, which purported to be the record of a briefing seminar on German unity involving a number of academics and journalists.[31] In the memorandum, the accuracy of which was questioned by some of those who had been present, typical German characteristics were said to include 'aggressiveness' and 'bullying'. The Germans did not take kindly to being described in these terms by a source close to Margaret Thatcher of all people. Damage limitation was difficult because the document was also published by the Hamburg news magazine *Der Spiegel*.

The Aspen Speech

In August 1990 Thatcher seems to have decided to launch a counter-attack against the foreign coalition that was undermining her position on the future of Europe. She was due to receive the Statesman's Award of the Aspen Institute, an international think-tank devoted to improving Western leadership, and to deliver a speech to the Institute in Colorado. Her speech looks as though it may have been intended to be an American Bruges speech.

[30] *Spectator*, 14 July 1990.
[31] *Independent on Sunday*, 16 July 1990.

The Bruges speech had taken the Thatcherite view of the future of Europe on to the Continent. Because of where it was delivered, it is plausible to interpret it as a direct intervention in the internal politics of other EC member states; had it been intended for a purely British audience it would not have been necessary to go to Belgium to give it. As it was, the venue could not have been better chosen to attract widespread publicity in other member states, and to provoke in those states the mobilization of political forces which also had doubts about the direction in which the EC was moving.

Aspen may have been intended to produce a similar response in the United States in opposition to the European policies of the Bush Administration. In the speech Thatcher called for a 'European Magna Carta' to be agreed at the forthcoming summit meeting of the Conference on Security and Co-operation in Europe (CSCE) in Paris. This charter would guarantee basic rights for all European citizens, including those of the Soviet Union, and would enshrine the right to 'maintain nationhood', and for people to be free from 'fear of an overmighty state'. The impression that this prospectus was directed as much against the EC as against the Soviet Union was given by passages later in the speech in which Thatcher called for the door to EC membership to be left open to the East European states, which meant that it must be a Community based on 'willing co-operation between independent sovereign states'. She asserted that the states of Eastern Europe had 'not thrown off central command and control in their own countries only to find them recreated in the European Community'.[32]

Unfortunately for Thatcher the impact of the speech was entirely lost because it coincided with the Iraqi invasion of Kuwait, and the start of the Gulf crisis. Things did not seem to be going her way: it began to look as though her luck had run out.

Agricultural Reform

While sources close to the Prime Minister were causing problems in Britain's relations with its EC partners, the general government policy of adopting a more moderated and *communautaire* tone continued to be heard from other Ministers. The difference was

---

[32] Transcript of speech given by the Prime Minister, Mrs Thatcher, to the Aspen Institute on Sunday, 5 Aug. 1990, Foreign and Commonwealth Office Press Release (undated).

highlighted over the issue of agricultural reform in the context of the world trade talks under the GATT.

Reaching agreement on a wide-ranging multilateral deal to liberalize trade was a key item of British policy. One of the main obstacles was the CAP. The United States, strongly backed by other agricultural-producing states, was demanding that steps be taken to eliminate agricultural subsidies, and particularly export subsidies. The US proposal was that all subsidies be cut by 75 per cent of their current level by the year 2000, with a 90 per cent cut in export subsidies. The EC Commissioner for Agriculture, Ray MacSharry, had suggested to the EC that it respond with a counter-proposal for a 30 per cent cut in the 1986 levels of subsidy. As 1986 had been a particularly expensive year for EC agricultural subsidies, this would amount to a cut of only 15 per cent on current subsidies. But even this modest level of reduction was not acceptable to the German, French, and Irish Ministers for Agriculture. No agreement had been reached by 15 October, the date on which the EC should have tabled its proposals.

Although Britain, together with The Netherlands and Denmark, supported the MacSharry proposals, the criticism voiced of other EC states by the British Secretary of State for Agriculture, John Gummer, was muted. He was much more critical of the United States for its failure to understand the nature of the CAP, and what the effects of its proposals would be. Not so Thatcher. In the Commons she was strongly critical of the other member states who were blocking an agreement, and suggested that agriculture, rather than monetary union, should have been the main item on the agenda of the October 1990 European Council.[33]

This episode indicated how far there had opened up a gap between the tone of the Prime Minister and that of her Government. That gap was to become fatally wide over the issue of monetary union.

Monetary Union

Throughout 1989 and 1990 monetary union was a dominant theme of discussion within the EC, and within Britain. It eventually became the issue that precipitated the downfall of Margaret Thatcher as Prime Minister.

[33] *Hansard*, 6th ser. 178 (30 Oct. 1990), cols. 873–4.

Monetary union was of great importance to the French President François Mitterrand. His commitment to it was based on the fact that the French had chosen to tie their currency to that of Germany and that, as things stood, decisions on interest rates made by the German Bundesbank simply had to be accepted by the French if they wanted to keep the link between the Deutschmark and the franc. Monetary union might look like a surrender of sovereign control over the national currency to the British: it looked to the French like an attempt to reassert some control over their own monetary policy.

Nicholas Ridley's argument that monetary union was a German plot to take over Europe had no basis in reality. The German Chancellor was less committed to monetary union than he was to progress on political union, and the German Bundesbank was definitely unenthusiastic. It was France that took the lead: the German Government went along because it wanted to keep the Franco-German special relationship working, and as a symbol of Germany's commitment to the EC.[34] It was even suggested that there was a Franco-German deal whereby French support for German unification was conditional on German acquiescence in monetary union.[35]

In the mean time the British Prime Minister continued to oppose British membership of the exchange rate mechanism, let alone movement to monetary union. Her opposition to membership of the exchange rate mechanism was partly based on the views of her personal adviser on economics, Sir Alan Walters, and her support for his publicly expressed views on the subject led in October 1989 to the resignation of her Chancellor, Nigel Lawson.

The split was brought about when Walters was critical of the exchange rate mechanism in an article for publication in an academic journal. When questioned in the Commons about Walters's position, Lawson maintained that these were 'clearly not the views of the Government',[36] but Thatcher chose not to give public backing to her Chancellor against her economics adviser.[37]

---

[34] Louis W. Pauly, 'The Politics of European Monetary Union: National Strategies, International Implications', *International Journal*, 47 (1991–2), 93–111; Wayne Sandholtz, 'Choosing Union: Monetary Politics and Maastricht', *International Organization*, 47 (1993), 1–39.   [35] Sandholtz, 'Choosing Union', p. 33.

[36] *Hansard*, 6th ser. 158 (19 Oct. 1989), col. 252.

[37] See her evasive response to direct questioning on this, ibid. (26 Oct. 1989), cols. 1044–5.

In consequence she lost them both. Lawson's resignation speech was extremely critical of the Prime Minister's handling of the monetary issue within the EC, and inflicted one more wound to her failing credibility.[38]

The Cabinet reshuffle that followed Lawson's resignation brought no respite from the pressure on Thatcher to enter the exchange rate mechanism, because her new Chancellor, John Major, declared that he too supported early entry. However, Thatcher had at Madrid stated the conditions on which entry was possible, and one of those was clearly not about to be fulfilled. Inflation in Britain was not falling and was not approaching the European average: on the contrary, it was rising and diverging even further from the average. There did not seem to be much prospect of early entry therefore in late 1989 when Major became Chancellor.

By remaining outside of the exchange rate mechanism Britain was seriously damaging its chances of being able to play a constructive and active part in the diplomacy surrounding the discussions on monetary union. When the Delors Report was published, Lawson rejected its approach based on the setting of target dates for movement between stages, and in September the Treasury produced its own plan based on the concept of a 'hard Ecu'.[39] The idea was that the European currency unit should be converted into a real currency, which would exist alongside the national currencies. Firms and individuals could decide whether to use the Ecu instead of national currencies, and if enough of them did so it would gradually displace the national currencies and become the single currency for Europe.

In the context of Thatcher's stated antipathy to monetary union by any route, this scheme was generally seen as a diversionary tactic designed to head off monetary union rather than to facilitate it. However, when John Major took over at the Treasury he launched a revised version of the scheme in June 1990,[40] and made a tour of national capitals to promote it to other Finance Ministers. There

---

[38] Ibid., 6th ser. 159 (31 Oct. 1989), cols. 208–10.

[39] For details of the plan see House of Lords, Select Committee on the European Communities, *Economic and Monetary Union and Political Union*, Parliamentary Papers HL 88–i (1989–90).

[40] For details of this scheme see House of Commons, Treasury and Civil Service Select Committee, *European Monetary Union: Minutes of Evidence, 25 July 1990*, Parliamentary Papers HC 620 (1989–90).

was some interest in the idea in informed circles in France, Spain, and other member states,[41] but it was not easy to win credibility for the plan so long as sterling was not in the exchange rate mechanism.

By the autumn of 1990 the Labour Party was advocating entry to the exchange rate mechanism, and the Shadow Chancellor, John Smith, was arguing that the increased stability that entry would give to the value of sterling would permit a reduction in interest rates of 1 per cent. To the surprise of almost everyone, that is exactly the step that the Government took on 5 October. That the decision owed something to political considerations was clear from the timing of the announcement, on the last day of the Labour Party Conference. John Major, however, engaged in an intensive series of radio and television interviews to stress that the move was taken for purely economic reasons. No doubt for him it was; after all, he and his predecessor had been advocating it for some time. On the other hand, the political considerations may well have been what enabled him finally to persuade the Prime Minister to agree to the move. There was no argument more likely to sway Thatcher than that some action would damage the Labour Party politically.

Major also took pains to deny at the Conservative Party Conference the following week that the step was a prelude to agreeing to join a monetary union in Europe. Perhaps in the context of internal party politics this statement was necessary; but in the context of the debate in the EC on monetary union it did nothing to enhance the British position.

Just how far Britain had fallen behind the pace of events in the EC became startlingly clear at the Rome meeting of the European Council on 27–8 October. Stung by criticism of their presidency of the EC in the British Press, which they believed originated in British government circles, the Italians, against the expectations of most national delegations, pushed to a vote a proposal to set a target date of 1 January 1994 for the start of the second stage of the Delors plan for progress to monetary union. Once the vote was called there was no doubt about the outcome: it was the usual eleven to one. In her press conference afterwards Thatcher could not conceal her anger at what had happened.

---

[41] Tristan Garel-Jones, 'Tories must Set Agenda for Tomorrow's Europe', *The Times*, 21 June 1993.

The End of an Era

In replies to questions in Parliament following her statement on the Rome meeting, the Prime Minister asserted that she would not 'hand over sterling and the powers of this House to Europe',[42] and that the Government's policy was to support the creation of a hard Ecu as a parallel currency, but that in her view there was little chance of the hard Ecu being widely used in place of national currencies.[43] This outburst led directly to the resignation of her Deputy Prime Minister, Sir Geoffrey Howe, who said in his resignation letter that the mood that Thatcher had struck in her dealings with the EC had made it more difficult for Britain to exercise influence in the debate that was going on about the future.[44] It was yet another blow to the authority of the Prime Minister, and one which set in train a series of events that proved to be fatal to her premiership.

On 13 November Sir Geoffrey made his resignation speech to Parliament. He launched a strong attack on the Prime Minister over her handling of relations with the rest of the EC, and blamed her for the rise in inflation because of her resistance to joining the exchange rate mechanism.[45] It was a speech remarkable for its aggressive tone from one who was noted for his mildness in political debate.

The next day Michael Heseltine announced that he would be a candidate in the annual Conservative Party leadership election which was about to take place. Normally an incumbent Prime Minister can expect to be re-elected unopposed, but Thatcher's authority had been so damaged by Howe's attack on her that the leader-in-waiting saw the best opportunity that he would have to achieve his ambition.

In the first ballot Thatcher won 204 votes to Heseltine's 152, just four short of the total that she needed to win outright on the first ballot. In Paris for the CSCE summit, Thatcher immediately announced that she would stand on the second ballot without apparently consulting Hurd, who as Foreign Secretary was with her. However, she was subsequently persuaded that she could not defeat Heseltine, and that her only hope of preventing him from

---

[43] Ibid., col. 878.   [42] *Hansard*, 6th ser. 178 (30 Oct. 1990), col. 873.
[44] *Independent*, 2 Nov. 1990.
[45] *Hansard*, 6th ser. 180 (13 Nov. 1990), cols. 461–5.

succeeding her, a thought that she could not contemplate, was for her to step down and leave the field free for her Cabinet colleagues to run against Heseltine in the second ballot. Surprisingly she took advice, and resigned her posts of party leader and of Prime Minister, reputedly commenting, 'It's a funny old world!'

Conclusion

It was indeed a funny old world at the end of the 1980s and the start of the 1990s, a world that had turned upside down; and Margaret Thatcher had failed to adapt to it sufficiently to retain her credibility as the leader of the Conservative Party. While economic conditions and the unpopularity of the community charge were clearly factors that caused many Conservative MPs to vote against her and for Heseltine, who opinion polls showed could lead the Party to another election victory, it was the EC that led directly to her downfall. With two inter-governmental conferences due to begin in January 1991, leading figures in the Party had come to the conclusion that British interests would be severely damaged were Thatcher still in charge. Her increasingly intemperate outbursts, which ran directly counter to agreed government policy on adopting a more measured and co-operative tone, made it likely that the British voice in the conferences would be marginalized, and the EC would go off again in directions in which the British Government did not wish to go. It was only by being centrally involved in the discussions, as a co-operative and reasonable partner, rather than living up to its reputation as an awkward partner, that Britain could hope to influence developments at this crucial stage in the history of the EC.

8. The Major Governments

THE Major Governments opened with an attempt to make a new start in relations with the rest of the EC, but drifted increasingly back towards the sort of hostile relations that had prevailed under Thatcher. In a context where many of the ideas of the British Conservatives about the nature of the EC were beginning to gain more widespread acceptance, the Government was in an ideal position to be at the centre of the European debate. That is the position that John Major tried to mark out for his Government in its first months. However, a combination of events in the EC itself and domestic political circumstances led to a retreat from that position to one of effective isolation and almost total lack of influence by the end of Major's premiership.

The International Context

Within months of John Major assuming office, hostilities finally broke out in the Gulf. Operation Desert Storm was a remarkably quick and, in military terms, a devastatingly successful campaign. The whole operation lasted less than six weeks from the first military action to the official declaration of the end of hostilities. The coalition led by the United States suffered less than 400 fatalities, of whom 44 were British. Iraqi fatalities were impossible to determine precisely, but ran into the tens of thousands.

The close co-operation between the United States and Britain in the Gulf temporarily breathed new life into the special relationship, but the renewed closeness did not survive the election in November 1992 of the Democrat Bill Clinton to the US presidency, particularly because Major appeared to give support to Bush during the election campaign. The Clinton administration was even more determined than Bush to concentrate on domestic issues and to insist that the Europeans sort out European problems. It also saw Germany as a more relevant partner than Britain in dealing with European problems.

In July 1994 Clinton visited Germany. Before leaving Washington he spoke of his support for a united Europe, and while in Germany he drew an explicit comparison between the relationship of the United States with Britain, which was a historic one, and that with Germany, which was more relevant to current problems because of Germany's 'more immediate and tangible concern' with the key issues in Europe, notably the problems in Eastern Europe and Russia.[1]

In August 1991, conservative forces in the Soviet Union attempted a coup against Mikhail Gorbachev. By moving swiftly to condemn the move, and to give his backing to Gorbachev, Major showed decisiveness in support of a statesman whom the British Government had strongly backed. However, the real hero of the crisis, and the person who benefited most from it, was not Gorbachev but his democratic rival Boris Yeltsin, President of the Russian Republic.

The failed August coup proved to be a turning-point. After it, Yeltsin's star rose inexorably; Gorbachev's waned. It was the starting-point of a process that culminated in the dissolving of the Soviet Union, the creation of the Commonwealth of Independent States in December 1991, and Gorbachev's resignation.

Gorbachev was a reform-minded communist and, although he tried to change the Soviet economy to make it more responsive to market forces, he tried to move cautiously, with the result that he went too slowly for some and too quickly for others. Yeltsin, however, embarked on a process of radical economic reform to turn Russia into a capitalist economy. It was a process that provoked an even stronger conservative reaction than had Gorbachev's reforms, although the experience of the failed coup meant that the army did not intervene.

While communist rule collapsed in Russia, many members of the Communist Party remained in the national parliament, which was elected before the demise of the Soviet Union. They were subsequently joined by Russian nationalists who were no friends of the Communist regime, but were prepared to ally themselves with the Communists to prevent what they interpreted as the selling out of Russia to Western influences, and the abandonment of the traditional Russian sphere of influence in the region.

The former Soviet Union had become a volatile place. As well as

[1] *Independent*, 12 July 1994.

Russia being in internal turmoil, problems arose in other former Soviet Republics, such as Georgia and Ukraine, with the suspicion never far from the minds of the rulers of these newly independent but economically weak states that the Russians were fomenting many of their troubles as an excuse to intervene, whether overtly or covertly.

The rise of nationalism in Russia accelerated applications for membership of the EU from the states of Central Europe. In April 1994 both Poland and Hungary lodged formal applications. Their governments acknowledged that their economies were not yet ready for membership, but they pleaded the need for urgency because of the increasing aggressiveness of Russia and the descent of the Ukraine into instability.[2] Eventually the EU faced applications for membership from ten states in Central and Eastern Europe: Bulgaria, the Czech Republic, Estonia, Hungary, Lithuania, Latvia, Poland, Romania, Slovakia, and Slovenia. However, while Britain and Germany strongly favoured enlargement to the East, there were serious doubts about both the economic and the political effects amongst other member states.[3]

Although in the long term the collapse of the Soviet Union seemed likely to prove the bigger problem for the rest of the world, in the short term the collapse of the former Yugoslavia was even more traumatic. The breakup of the unitary state was probably inevitable, as Slovenes, Croats, and others were determined to free themselves from domination by the Serbs. It was precipitated, though, by the insistence of the German Government at the end of 1991 that the European Community should recognize the independence of Croatia and Slovenia. This insistence was driven by a German public opinion very sympathetic to the wish of the Croats and Slovenes to break away from rule by the Serbs, who dominated the Yugoslav Government. Until December 1991 the official position of the EC was to maintain the integrity of Yugoslavia on the grounds that, as soon as its constituent republics began to break away, the process would become unstoppable and old territorial and ethnic rivalries would resurface throughout the Balkans. The British and French, who might have to commit troops if fighting

---

[2] *Independent*, 8 April 1994.
[3] See, e.g. reports in the *European*, 2–8 Dec, 1994, and the *Financial Times*, 17 Nov. 1995.

broke out and threatened to get out of control, were resistant to abandoning this position. The Germans, however, who were constitutionally debarred from deploying troops outside the borders of Germany, insisted that unless there were agreement on joint recognition of Croatia and Slovenia, they would break ranks and unilaterally recognize the independence of the two states. To maintain some semblance of a common front, the rest of the EC went along with this German ultimatum. Subsequently, war broke out in what remained of Yugoslavia between Serbs, Croats, and Muslims, and the EC proved incapable of effective action to bring this conflict on its very doorstep to a peaceful conclusion.

Nearer home, on 1 November 1993 the Treaty on European Union came into force, something of the history of which is related below; and from that point it became normal practice to refer to the organization as a whole as the European Union (EU), a convention which is adopted in the remainder of this book.

Within the EU there was a significant change of leadership in France in 1995. The socialist President, François Mitterrand, retired in April. He was suffering from prostate cancer, and died the following January. He was succeeded by the Gaullist Jacques Chirac. France already had a conservative Government, elected in March 1993; it now had a conservative President, which opened up new prospects for co-operation with the Conservative Government in Britain.

The Domestic Context

John Major's election to the leadership of the Conservative Party brought a much-needed boost to its standing in the opinion polls, but this was soon dissipated amidst continuing economic gloom. Throughout 1991 Labour and the Conservatives remained within a few per cent of each other in the opinion polls, with Labour establishing a consistent if small lead in the summer months, but the Conservatives pulling back to be running neck-and-neck by the end of the year. By-elections told a rather different story. The Government lost four in the course of 1991, two to Labour, and two to the Liberal Democrats.[4]

[4] David Butler, 'Elections in Britain', in Peter Catterall (ed.), *Contemporary Britain: An Annual Review 1992* (London, 1992), 51–4.

Major's personal popularity remained encouragingly high, boosted first by the simple fact that he was not Thatcher, and subsequently by his handling of the Gulf War, which received overwhelming support from public opinion. Major's refusal to take the triumphalist tone over the victory in the Gulf that his predecessor had taken over the victory in the Falklands undoubtedly judged the mood of the country. He easily maintained his personal standing well above that of the Labour leader, Neil Kinnock, who in some peculiar way seemed to be diminished by the departure from office of his great opponent, Margaret Thatcher.

Yet the conditions never seemed right for the early general election that the Labour Party insisted was the only proper course for the new Prime Minister to take in order to legitimate his position. The immediate aftermath of the Gulf War must have tempted Major. His personal popularity was high, and the Government ended February a clear four points ahead of Labour in the opinion polls. Yet this was still within the margins of polling error, and too close for comfort at a time when the economy was performing badly.

The recession that had started in the latter half of 1990 tightened its grip in the first half of 1991. Interest rates were high, inflation was high, unemployment was rising, and output was falling. This was no context in which to choose to hold an election. The hope was that the first signs of recovery could not be far away, and then the Government could go to the country on a rising economic tide.

Inflation began to decline in the spring, dropping to 6.4 per cent by April and reaching 4.5 per cent in the autumn. Throughout the year interest rates were edged down by half a percentage point at a time, against the background of rising interest rates in Germany, where the economy was booming and showing signs of over-heating. By the autumn British rates were down to 10.5 per cent, only one per cent above German rates. It was perhaps a tribute to the stabilizing effect of British membership of the exchange rate mechanism that such a low differential with German interest rates could be sustained without causing severe pressure on the value of sterling relative to the Deutschmark.

Despite these positive indicators, though, the economic position remained worrying throughout 1991. Unemployment rose steadily from 1.8 million at the start of the year to 2.6 million. Output fell over the year by 2 per cent; and although most of the drop was in the first 6 months of the year, there was little sign of recovery in the second half.[5]

Running out of time, and with no sign of an economic recovery on the horizon, Major went to the country in the spring. He faced one of the toughest electoral tasks of the post-war period: to try to win an election when the economy was apparently mired in recession. Yet, after a hard-fought campaign, he did it, helped by some serious misjudgements by the Labour Party.

Electoral defeat meant the end of Neil Kinnock's leadership of the Labour Party. He resigned following the defeat, and on 18 July 1992 John Smith, the former Shadow Chancellor, was elected his successor. Tragically, Smith died of a heart attack less than 2 years later, on 12 May 1994. On 21 July 1994 Tony Blair became leader of the Labour Party and of the Opposition, and set about completing the restoration of the electoral credibility of Labour that had been started under Kinnock. While both Kinnock and Smith had been capable leaders, it soon became clear that Blair was intent on giving strong and determined leadership to Labour, which transformed the image of the Party and presented the Conservatives with the serious problem of at last facing a really effective Opposition and a totally credible alternative government.

For John Major victory in the 1992 election could have meant the beginning of his real leadership of the Conservative Party. There seemed to be a chance for him to seize the moment and assert his own authority within the Party, to rout the Thatcherite tendency that had been constantly sniping at him over Europe, and to mark out his own distinctive programme for the new Government.

The problem with this scenario was that Major did not emerge from the election campaign as strong as he might have wished; he had a narrow majority in Parliament (21 seats, compared to 88 in the previous Parliament), and even if the bulk of the parliamentary party had been prepared to accept his lead the loss of just a few votes could have been dangerous. In addition, he did not have a programme that was particularly distinctive from that of the Thatcher Governments. He had, after all, been Thatcher's own chosen successor. Given the role that it had played in his predecessor's fall, his abandonment of the community charge was inevitable. But he made no attempt to stop the NHS reforms or the

---

[5] Alan Davies, 'Economic Policy and Macro-Economic Developments', ibid., 158.

privatization programme, nor was there any indication that he wished to stop them. On most policy issues, including economic policy, he was actually closer to the Thatcherite wing of the Party than to the Heath or Heseltine wing. Yet on one crucial issue Major was out of line with the supporters of Thatcher: the EC.

The problems of the Government in ensuring ratification by Parliament of the Maastricht Treaty are detailed below. Subsequently, in November 1994, it felt obliged to remove the Conservative Whip from eight MPs who voted against it during the passage of the European Communities Finance Bill. This drastic step left the Government with a very small technical majority because of its persistent loss of seats in by-elections. Throughout the period of this Parliament the Conservatives lost every by-election that was held, starting with two losses to the Liberal Democrats in early 1993, and culminating in the Wirral by-election just 2 months before the 1997 general election, where a 17.2 per cent swing gave the seat to Labour, and left the Government in a minority in the Commons, even though the Whip had by this time been restored to the rebels.

The steady erosion of the Government's majority was a direct consequence of its unpopularity. As well as its serious divisions over Europe, there were growing accusations of immoral and corrupt behaviour by Conservative MPs. Perhaps even more importantly, there was a lack of confidence in the Government's ability to manage the economy, despite the recovery from recession which saw inflation edging down, reductions in the total numbers of unemployed, and increases in real disposable incomes.

The precarious nature of its overall majority left the Government peculiarly susceptible to pressure from its backbenches. In such a situation strong leadership might have rallied the troops and pulled the Government through; however, part of the problem for the Government was the perception that John Major was not a strong leader. Not only was he facing criticism from the backbenches, which he did not seem to be able to silence: he also presided over a fractious and divided Cabinet, with Europe again forming its chief fault-line.

In an attempt to restore some semblance of authority to his premiership, on 22 June 1995 Major resigned as Leader of the Conservative Party, thereby precipitating an internal leadership election. He said, 'The Conservative Party must make its choice

... it is time to put up or shut up.'[6] John Redwood, a right-wing member of the Cabinet, put up and lost by 218 votes to 89. However, when the abstentions (8) and spoilt ballots (12) were added to Redwood's vote, one-third of the parliamentary Conservative Party did not vote for the incumbent Prime Minister to continue as its leader. Far from confirming his authority, the leadership election possibly contributed to undermining it further.

So, European policy throughout the period between 1992 and 1997 was conducted against a domestic background of an internally divided Government, with an increasingly precarious parliamentary majority, which was unpopular in the country and subject, as time went by, to scandals and misfortunes. Central to all of this was the issue of British membership of the EC/EU.

A Renewed Change of Tone

In the early months of the new Government, the change of tone that had been attempted in 1989 but had been spoiled by the increasingly hard-line statements of the then Prime Minister and her supporters, was attempted again once John Major took over the premiership. It was signalled by several Ministers.

In January 1991 the Secretary of State for Employment, Michael Howard, met in London with Vasso Papandreou, the EC Commissioner for Social Affairs, to outline the extent to which Britain could accept her proposed social directives. Howard stressed to the Press that Britain was prepared to accept almost half the proposed directives, and that it was the only member state to have implemented all 18 of the social directives already agreed. This positive tone was in marked contrast to the accusation that Howard had launched only 4 months earlier, that Papandreou was bringing the EC into disrepute with her proposals for directives on maximum working hours, rights for part-time workers, and harmonized maternity benefits.[7]

At a meeting of the inter-governmental conference on monetary union in January, the new Chancellor, Norman Lamont, stressed that the British plan for a 'hard Ecu' as a possible route towards monetary union was open to modification.[8] As the year wore on

---

[6] *Keesing's Record of World Events* (1995), 40613.
[7] *Independent*, 14 Jan. 1991.   [8] *Independent*, 29 Jan. 1991.

the British Government increasingly emphasized that monetary union would have to be preceded by economic convergence, which seemed to imply that Britain could accept an eventual monetary union. This was a long step from the position of Thatcher, who reiterated her opposition to monetary union in speeches in the United States later in the year.[9]

In those same speeches, Thatcher continued to criticize the idea that the EC should develop a security and defence dimension, perhaps by developing the Western European Union (WEU) into a bridge between the EC and NATO. Again, the line of the new Government began to diverge from that of the former Prime Minister. In February, giving the Winston Churchill Memorial lecture in Luxemburg, Douglas Hurd made a distinction between security policy, which 'goes with foreign policy', and defence, which was 'a different matter'.[10] But he also accepted that 'Europe has to take on more responsibility for its own defence' and spoke of WEU being developed into 'a bridge between the Twelve . . . and NATO'.[11]

Shortly after Hurd's lecture, the Government's renewed positive tone was underlined by the Prime Minister in a Foreword to a government White Paper which reported developments in the EC in the second half of 1990. He stated his aims for Britain in Europe as being 'to help build and shape the future Europe—and to do so with enthusiasm. We need to be right at the heart of the Community, working closely with our partners, if we are to do that.'[12]

In March John Major made a visit to Bonn in an effort to mend Anglo–German relations, which had reached a postwar low in the latter months of Thatcher's premiership as a result of the Ridley and Powell incidents. While there he made a speech to the Christian Democratic Union, the party of Chancellor Helmut Kohl, in which he repeated that he wished to see Britain 'where we belong', at the

---

[9] Mrs Thatcher was touring the United States, and other parts of the developed world, to raise money for her Thatcher Foundation. Her speeches in Chicago on 17 June and in Washington on 23 Sept. were widely reported in the British Press.

[10] Transcript of the *Churchill Memorial Lecture*, Foreign and Commonwealth Office press release, 19 Feb. 1991, 13.

[11] Ibid., 14.

[12] HMSO, *Developments in the European Community*, July–Dec. 1990, (Cmnd. 1457), iii.

very heart of Europe working with its partners with enthusiasm in building the future.[13]

How far these changes of tone represented real changes of position now needs to be examined in the light of developments in the debate on social affairs, and in the inter-governmental conferences on political union and on monetary union.

Social Affairs

The newly discovered harmony between Michael Howard and Vasso Papandreou did not last long. The emphasis that Howard put on Britain's commitment to the social dimension of the EC was simply highlighting the positive aspects of what had already been true under Thatcher. Although her Bruges speech in 1988 had convinced most people that Britain entirely rejected all social legislation, this was a misperception. The Government had always accepted that the programme to free the internal market of the EC must be accompanied by the setting of minimum EC-wide standards on health and safety at work: otherwise, employers might try to achieve a competitive advantage by reducing safety standards. All of the directives that had already been agreed were of this nature.

What the British Government did not accept was that there should be EC legislation on other matters, such as working hours and employees' rights. On these issues there was no change of policy. When Papandreou produced proposals for directives on maximum working hours and maternity rights the British continued to oppose them, and objected vigorously to the Commission's classification of them as measures involving health and safety at work, and therefore subject to qualified majority voting under the 1987 Single European Act.[14]

In the inter-governmental conference on political union, the suggestion was made in draft agreements prepared by both the Luxemburg presidency in the first half of the year and the Dutch

---

[13] John Major, 'The Evolution of Europe', *Conservative Party News*, 11 Mar. 1991, 13.

[14] *Independent*, 31 Oct. and 1 Nov. 1991. Eventually a modified version of the directive on pay for pregnant women was passed without a vote, with Britain abstaining, along with Italy. The effect of the directive was not to increase maternity pay in Britain. *Independent*, 7 Nov. 1991.

presidency in the second half of the year that social affairs as a whole should come under majority voting. This position was flatly rejected by the British.[15]

Here, then, there seems to have been little change of substance; and the reason for this can perhaps be seen in the speeches made to the annual conference of the Confederation of British Industry (CBI) in Bournemouth in November 1991, when speaker after speaker attacked the Commission's proposals as imposing unacceptable and unnecessary costs on industry that would make it less competitive in world markets.[16]

Political Union

Discussion in the inter-governmental conference on political union appeared generally to go well for the British Government. The draft Treaty produced by the Luxemburg presidency in April proposed a European Union with three pillars, of which the EC would be one. The others, which would cover first foreign policy, external security, and defence, and secondly internal security, would be essentially inter-governmental in their procedures. When the Dutch presidency produced a more federalist draft in September it was rejected by an overwhelming majority of the member states, and had to be withdrawn to be replaced with something much nearer to the Luxemburg draft.

This did not mean there were no disagreements. On the question of whether immigration should be centrally controlled, for example, the Germans were determined that it should be, the British that it should not. Eventually the British view prevailed. There was also considerable wrangling over whether the preamble to the new Treaty should describe the European Union as having a 'federal goal'. The phrase had negative connotations in Britain, and although the Prime Minister at one stage suggested that it might be acceptable were the term 'federal' clearly defined, eventually it was replaced by the phrase 'creating an ever closer Union amongst the people of Europe' so as not to offend British political sensibilities.

On the question of a security and defence dimension for the EC, the experience of the Gulf war and of the civil war in Yugoslavia

---

[15] Ibid., 24 Sept. 1991.   [16] Ibid., 5 Nov. 1991.

helped to produce a consensus that such a dimension was necessary. Although the French and Germans jointly produced a plan to put the process under EC rules, they so mishandled their case as to upset the other states.[17] A strong intervention from the President of the United States at the NATO summit in Rome in early November[18] also helped to sway the final proposals in the direction of the British view, that defence and security should not be incorporated in such a way that there would be any rupture with NATO, despite French wishes for a more independent policy.

Although these issues caused some discontent in domestic policies, especially the security and defence question, it was particularly the negotiations on monetary union that had domestic political repercussions.

Monetary Union

At a meeting of Finance Ministers in May 1991 Margaret Thatcher's old sparring partner, Jacques Delors, the President of the Commission, suggested a formula that would allow Britain an 'opt-out' clause on movement to a single currency. This suggestion was taken up in the subsequent draft Treaty presented by the Dutch presidency in early September. It proposed writing into the Treaty a right for any member to consult its national parliament before actually adopting a single currency, thus putting off the final decision until such time as the process had reached full maturity.

This procedural device proved acceptable to some of the Conservative critics of monetary union. Teddy Taylor MP indicated that it would satisfy the doubts of the Tory Reform Group, a backbench group of some seventy Conservative MPs. But Nicholas Ridley attacked the proposal in a speech to the Bruges Group, and shortly afterwards a Bruges Group memorandum was leaked to the Press which appeared to threaten a split in the Conservative Party if the Prime Minister did not veto a treaty on monetary union.

Although this memorandum was repudiated by Bill Cash MP on behalf of the parliamentary 'Friends of Bruges', the issue did not go away. Norman Tebbit joined Ridley in publicly attacking the whole

[17] Ibid., 7, 9, and 17 Oct. 1991.   [18] Ibid., 8 Nov. 1991.

concept of a monetary union, and Thatcher continued to make speeches in a similar vein.

In November 1991 the question was brought out into the open in a two-day debate in the House of Commons.[19] Margaret Thatcher used the occasion to call for a referendum on monetary union before Britain agreed to participate.[20] This intervention was unhelpful for the Government, which had already indicated that it did not intend to put the agreement to a referendum. The Prime Minister chose to interpret his predecessor's comments as a call for a referendum only at the point when the decision actually to enter the monetary union came to be made, and therefore a matter for a future parliament.

Maastricht

Britain did get an 'opt-out' clause on monetary union written into the new Treaty, but it referred specifically to Britain. This was something that the Government had hoped to avoid: it gave the impression that Britain was again the awkward partner in the Community, and it also led to the risk that industrialists would think twice before investing in Britain so long as a question-mark remained over whether the country would eventually participate in the single currency that would complete the single market. However, other member states were not prepared to accept a general opt-out provision because they feared that the German parliament, the Bundestag, might try to use it to take the Deutschmark out of any future monetary union, thus causing the collapse of the whole project.

In the event the question of majority voting on social matters became the most difficult issue at the summit in Maastricht in December 1991, and an agreement there only proved possible because the social chapter was dropped from the draft Treaty, and replaced with a protocol in which the other eleven member states committed themselves to making progress on social issues while Britain committed itself to nothing beyond those obligations already contained in the Treaty of Rome and the Single European Act.

---

[19] *Hansard*, 6th ser. 199 (20 Nov. 1991), cols. 269–389; (21 Nov. 1991), cols. 436–527.   [20] Ibid., (20 Nov. 1991), cols. 297–8.

Because of these two derogations for Britain, Neil Kinnock accused the Government of a 'double opt-out' which left Britain as a semi-detached member of the Community.[21] But Conservative backbench sceptics on Europe at first seemed prepared to accept the agreement that the Prime Minister had brought back, and immediate criticism from within the party was muted. Even Margaret Thatcher kept quiet. It was generally agreed by observers that John Major had achieved quite a diplomatic and political success, which was likely to enhance his standing in his party and in the country.

What were less noticed were the concessions that Britain had made in other directions, particularly in agreeing to an extension of the range of issues on which there would be majority voting in the Council of Ministers, and on increasing the powers of the European Parliament. There was also some doubt about whether the wording on security and defence was really more favourable to the British view than to the French view. Indeed, the agreement failed finally to settle many of the issues around which the negotiations had circled. An indication of this was the provision of a review clause to allow the whole structure of the new European Union to be looked at again in 1996.

In some ways the Maastricht agreement was a less fundamental step in the evolution of the European Community than the Single European Act which Margaret Thatcher had signed in 1986. Nevertheless, in some respects it could be interpreted as a big step toward closer European unity, and perhaps a bigger step than many members of the Conservative Party initially realized. As time passed perceptions began to change, and Major found himself having to defend the Treaty against domestic opposition which was fuelled by events elsewhere in the EC.

Defending Maastricht

In presenting the Maastricht agreements to Parliament on 11 December 1991, and again when introducing the debate on the agreements on 18 December, the Prime Minister stressed the extent to which he refused to accept what for many Conservative politicians was the unacceptable. Pressure to take decisions on

---

[21] *Hansard*, 6th ser. 200 (11 Dec. 1991) cols. 862–3.

foreign policy by majority voting had been successfully resisted; the social chapter had been taken out of the Treaty at British insistence. He explicitly linked the Treaty with the question of further enlargement of the Community, suggesting that this was imminent and would serve to dilute those elements of federalism that had crept in; and he stressed that the principle of subsidiarity—that decisions should only be taken at the Community level where a compelling case could be made that they were more appropriately taken at that level than at the national level—had been written into the Treaty as a legally binding principle.[22]

While members of the British Government were stressing in Westminster that the Maastricht Treaty was a very limited document, Jacques Delors was telling the European Parliament that the same Treaty had relaunched the Community, and was emphasizing the significance of the decision to proceed to monetary union in furthering integration.[23] These differences of presentation were representative of their different audiences, and of the fact that Maastricht was a compromise in which neither side wanted to admit its concessions. Delors tried to talk up the federalist aspects of the Treaty, not just to the European Parliament, but to the media throughout Europe. This proved to be a big mistake.

Delors' emphasis on the federalism of the Treaty caused alarm bells to start ringing in the New Year in several member states. Opinion polls showed doubts in Ireland and Denmark, but also in Germany, where monetary union was very unpopular, and even in France.

In May 1992 the British Government began to gear itself up to taking over the presidency in July with an offensive to demonstrate its firmness of purpose behind Maastricht. Tristan Garel-Jones, the Foreign Office Minister with responsibility for Europe, made a speech in Bonn giving a most positive view of Britain in Europe, saying that the British Government stood firmly by the Maastricht Treaty and warning against the dangers if it were not ratified.[24] Also in May, the Queen made her first speech to the European Parliament, an event of some symbolic significance that served to

---

[22] Ibid., cols. 859–62; (18 Dec. 1991), cols. 275–86.
[23] *Official Journal of the European Communities: Debates of the European Parliament*, 12 Dec. 1991, No. 3–412/232–6.
[24] *Independent*, 14 May 1992.

underline British seriousness about its role in the EC, but which annoyed the British Eurosceptics.[25]

When the ratification debate opened in Parliament on 20 May Major said that the Treaty marked a turning away from EC centralization, a move that would be enhanced by the imminent enlargement of the Community from twelve member states to twenty. He knew that many people feared the creation of a strong central government in Brussels with only some powers devolved to the member states, but the agreement to go for co-operative arrangements outside the framework of the EC on foreign and security policy, justice and internal matters reflected a steady diminution of 'the old tendency among some of our partners to think that action by the Community was always the answer'.[26]

A strategy was emerging in the defence of Maastricht. The Government was pressing the view on its own supporters that Maastricht enshrined inter-governmentalism and, where it did not, the British had managed to opt out. At the same time it was taking advantage of the unpopularity in other parts of the EC of Delors' federalist interpretation to push its own minimalist version. As the British presidency approached, the rejection of the Treaty by the Danish electorate in a referendum on 2 June appeared to strengthen the hand of the British Government.

Denmark's narrow referendum defeat of Maastricht (by 50.7 per cent to 49.3 per cent) sent shock waves throughout the Community. Although the Treaty could only come into effect if ratified by all twelve member states, most of the other Governments decided to press ahead with ratification as though nothing had happened; but in Britain, Parliament decided not to proceed with the committee stage of the ratification Bill, and in France President Mitterrand immediately announced that he would suspend parliamentary ratification and hold a referendum.

Denmark's action provoked a strengthening of anti-Maastricht sentiment elsewhere in the EC. Seizing on this to reinforce the British interpretation of the Treaty, Douglas Hurd told the House of Commons on 8 June that it was vitally important to allay fears

---

[25] *Official Journal of the European Communities: Debates of the European Parliament*, 12 May 1992, No. 3–418/103–4.
[26] *Hansard*, 6th ser. 208 (20 May 1992), col. 268.

throughout Europe that Maastricht would turn out to be a centralizing move,[27] a comment that was made against the background of press reports that Britain was advocating an addition to the Treaty, a declaration removing any ambiguity about it being a reversal of moves to centralization. Such an interpretation, of course, ran against the view that had been expressed by Delors to the European Parliament and the interpretation that had been put on the Treaty in some of the other member states. But the outbreak of public concern even in the core countries of France and Germany had given the initiative to the British to press their minimalist view.

However, at the same time as the Danish result strengthened the hand of the British Government in the politics of the EC, it brought problems in domestic politics, with sixty-eight Conservative back-bench MPs signing a Commons motion calling on the Government to use its presidency of the Council of Ministers to make a new start on the development of the EC. In response the Prime Minister told the Commons that renegotiation was not a practical proposition 'at the present moment'.[28]

Clearly Major was constrained in this by the unwillingness of the Germans and French to consider any change in the terms of the Treaty, although his own interpretation of it as a decentralizing document—as, in effect, a new start in itself—also made it unlikely that he would embrace the idea of renegotiating.

In the face of the rising tide of public concern throughout Europe that Maastricht was a further measure of centralization, an attempt to emphasize the decentralizing tendencies of the Treaty was made at the Lisbon meeting of the European Council in late June, when it was decided that all existing EC legislation should be examined to see whether it should be modified.[29] This was obviously an important victory for the British view that centralization had already proceeded too far, although there were dangers in reopening the question of the Commission's powers. For example, the French appear to have wanted to repatriate competition policy because they were unhappy with the way in which the British Commissioner, Sir Leon Brittan, was using the powers that he had

[27] *Hansard*, 6th ser. 209 (8 June 1992), cols. 32–9.
[28] *Hansard*, 6th ser. 208 (3 June 1992), col. 830.
[29] *Bulletin of the European Communities*, 6–1992, 1.1.

acquired to vet large-scale mergers. Nevertheless, the British did seem to have gained something here.

There was also agreement at Lisbon that work would start immediately on negotiating mandates for the members of the EFTA that had applied to join the EC (Austria, Sweden, Finland, and Switzerland)[30] and that dialogue with the countries of Central Europe would be stepped up. Again there was an apparent gain here for the British view that there should be rapid progress towards enlargement.

In the EC, gains are usually accompanied by concessions, and perhaps the concession that Major made was agreement not to undermine the Treaty or to support its amendment. He told Parliament on 25 June:

The Maastricht treaty was negotiated in good faith by all member states. I have no intention of breaking the word of the British Government that was given on that occasion, neither do I have any intention of compromising what we agreed on that occasion and wrecking this country's reputation for plain and honest dealing and good faith.[31]

As Britain assumed the presidency at the beginning of July, the domestic problems concerning the Treaty continued. Margaret Thatcher, now Baroness Thatcher of Kesteven, attacked the Prime Minister in a television interview with David Frost on 28 June. She said that Major had been wrong to agree to reappoint Delors, whom she described as a man who had increased bureaucracy, and who had chosen to go for majority voting rather than unanimity wherever he could. She also said that Major was wrong on Maastricht, which she described in a ringing phrase as 'a treaty too far', and that he was wrong on maintaining the value of the pound within the exchange rate mechanism of the EMS, because a policy of high interest rates which was right for Germany was causing high unemployment in Britain.[32]

Major counter-attacked on Lady Thatcher's call for a referendum when he reported to the Commons on the Lisbon European Council on 29 June. He vigorously defended the Treaty, dismissed calls for a referendum, and said that he was not prepared to see Britain standing on the sidelines of the EC with other countries

---

[30] Norway applied later, and the Swiss application was subsequently withdrawn.
[31] *Hansard*, 6th ser. 210 (25 June 1992), cols. 381–2.
[32] *Independent*, 29 June 1992.

making the decisions that affected the livelihood of British people.[33]

In her maiden speech in the House of Lords, on 2 July, Lady Thatcher repeated her call for a referendum in Britain on Maastricht, and made it clear that she would vote against ratification.[34] This gave an unequivocal lead to her many supporters in the Conservative Party. She also said that Britain ought to use the presidency to restate the Luxemburg compromise, and rejected comments by the Prime Minister that the Single European Act (which she had signed when she was Prime Minister) was a more centralizing document than Maastricht.

This attack on her former protégé received a strong reply only an hour later (although clearly it was not a reply in the sense that Major could have been responding directly to Thatcher's comments). The Prime Minister told the 1922 Committee of Conservative backbenchers that the Government wanted more power to remain with national governments, and for some powers to be repatriated; but this had to be done by negotiation. He added that if Britain had been negotiating from the centre of Europe throughout the previous 20 years, it might have had more influence on the development of the Community than had been the case.[35] This seemed to be a swipe at his predecessor's negotiating style: the domestic political contest was becoming heated.

After the French referendum produced the smallest of votes in favour of Maastricht (50.6 per cent to 49.3 per cent), Major called a special European Council meeting for 15 October in Birmingham to try to find a solution to the Danish problem. But the closeness of the French result put new momentum behind the opponents of Maastricht within the Conservative Party, and on 6 October at the Party Conference, Lord Tebbit (the former Cabinet Minister, Norman Tebbit) launched a stinging attack on the Government, demanding that they press home their advantage against the federalist tendency in Europe and force a renegotiation of the Treaty. He received a standing ovation from about one-third of the audience, and the reply of the Foreign Secretary, although politely applauded, was much less enthusiastically received.

[33] *Hansard*, 6th ser. 210 (29 June 1992), cols. 585 and 587.
[34] *Hansard* (Lords), 5th ser. 538 (2 July 1992), cols. 895–901.
[35] *Independent*, 3 July 1992.

Subsequently, on 4 November, the Government scraped a victory by only three votes in the House of Commons on a motion to reintroduce the Bill to ratify the Treaty. The Labour Party, despite having proclaimed itself pro-EC, decided to vote against the motion on the grounds that this was in effect a vote of confidence in the Government. Conservative backbench rebels were apparently bought off with a commitment that the third reading of the Bill would not take place until after a second referendum had been held in Denmark. Even so, there were 32 Conservative rebels at a time when the Government's majority was only 21, and the majority was only achieved with Liberal Democrat support.

Black Wednesday: Leaving the ERM

Despite the sniping from the sidelines, the British Government at this stage was conducting very successful diplomacy within the EC, taking advantage of the concerns in other member states about centralizing tendencies in order to move the Community further in the direction that it wished to see; but it was also itself suffering from the same domestic problems that afflicted the other Governments. These might have been kept in check, though, had it not been for the monetary crisis that erupted in the run-up to the French referendum.

Indications that the French might vote against Maastricht in the referendum on 20 September led to a loss of confidence by the financial markets in the ability of the exchange rate mechanism to hold together. First the Italian lira came under speculative pressure, and even a devaluation of 7 per cent did not restore confidence. The pound was next. On 16 September 1992 it was forced out of the exchange range mechanism amidst recriminations against the Bundesbank for not being prepared to give adequate support to maintaining the parity. An attempt by the British to get a general realignment of currencies within the system had failed, and the decision to float the currency was subsequently taken unilaterally by the British Government.

This whole episode caused a considerable setback to John Major's strategy. First, it ruined his economic strategy of combating inflation by tying the pound into a high parity against the Deutschmark. Second, it appeared to vindicate Baroness Thatcher's strictures against that policy, and so strengthened her position and that of her supporters in the internal debate within the Conservative Party. It also caused a cooling of the good relations with Germany which were important to success in EC diplomacy.

The Record of the British Presidency

When Douglas Hurd presented the programme of the British presidency to the European Parliament on 8 July he identified the priorities as: the completion of the internal market; enlargement, with the aim of opening negotiations with the EFTA applicants in late 1992 or early 1993; reform of the finances of the EC; international issues, especially completion of the Uruguay Round of trade negotiations under the GATT, developing relations with the states of Central Europe and the former Soviet Union, and tackling the problem of Yugoslavia; and, finally, clearing the way for the ratification of the Maastricht Treaty.[36]

In the face of its domestic political problems, it was difficult for the British presidency to take a strong line in Community affairs, and there was some criticism from other member states of self-absorption and failure to address any concerns other than those of Britain. However, by the end of the six months there were certain achievements that could be claimed in the areas identified by Hurd as priorities of the presidency.

The internal market was completed in all its essentials, with agreement on some ninety measures, a record for any presidency. Agreement was reached at the Edinburgh meeting of the European Council in December on opening enlargement negotiations with the EFTA applicants early in 1993. A new budgetary arrangement was agreed, with John Major winning plaudits for brokering an agreement between the poorer states, led by Spain, who were insisting on an increase in the existing structural funds plus a substantial cohesion fund, and the net contributors to the budget, including Britain itself, who were anxious to keep the increased cost as low as possible.

---

[36] *Official Journal of the European Communities: Debates of the European Parliament*, 8 July 1992, No. 3–420/139–43. See also Hurd's reply to a question in the House of Commons on 1 July, when he added an extra objective, to 'make progress toward limiting the scope of Community interventions'; *Hansard*, 6th ser. 210 (1 July 1992), col. 844.

On the international issues, there was little progress on Yugoslavia, but there was an acceptance at the Edinburgh European Council for the first time that Poland, Hungary, the Czech Republic, and Slovakia should eventually become members of the EC. More significant, though, was the settlement of a disagreement with the United States over agriculture that had been holding up an overall agreement in the GATT.

The GATT agreement was actually negotiated by the Commission, but the British presidency did make an important contribution by throwing its weight behind the Agriculture Commissioner, Ray MacSharry, who was negotiating seriously to get a settlement and at one point appeared to be undermined by a lack of support from the Commission President, Jacques Delors. Although French farmers reacted angrily to the agreement, and the French Government was highly critical of it, there was a feeling that this was all predictable, and that the cost of sinking an overall trade agreement would be too high for the French economy for a veto actually to be used. In any case, that would come only after the end of the British presidency.

The special meeting of the European Council in Birmingham in October failed to come up with any solution to the Danish problem, but the regular six-monthly meeting in December in Edinburgh did agree a series of opt-out clauses for the Danes which would allow them to hold a second referendum with some reasonable prospect of a successful outcome.

Overall, particularly because of the achievements at Edinburgh, the Government was able to claim a success for the British presidency despite its problems during the six months.[37]

Britain at the Heart of Europe?

The success at Edinburgh could not hide the fact that the events of 1992 had given a buffeting to John Major's strategy of putting Britain at the heart of Europe. Perhaps the most serious blow was the enforced removal of sterling from the exchange rate mechanism, particularly because it was accompanied by an unseemly public

---

[37] For two conflicting views on the British presidency, see Peter Ludlow, 'The UK Presidency: a View from Brussels', *Journal of Common Market Studies*, 31 (1993), 246–60, and Tristan Garel-Jones, 'The UK Presidency: An Inside View', ibid., 261–7.

exchange with the Bundesbank over the level of support that the German monetary authorities had been prepared to give to the British currency. Close relations with Germany had been central to Major's approach to putting Britain at the heart of Europe. Those relations were also damaged by the revelation that the British Government had only managed to obtain its majority of three on the vote to reintroduce the ratification Bill into Parliament by promising its backbench rebels that the final ratification would not take place until after the second Danish referendum. This ran counter to everything that the Government had been saying to its EC partners, and gave a signal of weakness.[38]

That this unfortunate incident did not mean any abandonment of the overall strategy seemed to be indicated by continued British willingness to compromise on what had at one time been signalled as issues of principle. In April agreement was reached on an EC Directive on a 48-hour maximum working week, which the British had previously been blocking. Although the British Government had achieved considerable concessions on the detail of the proposals, it had previously maintained that the issue should not be subject to EC legislation at all, but that principle was now allowed to drop. A month later, just before the British presidency, the Chancellor of the Exchequer, Norman Lamont, accepted that there should be an EC minimum level of VAT at 15 per cent. Again, the British Government had achieved concessions on specifics, but again the position had previously been one of principle, which was now relaxed.

Against these signs of more co-operative behaviour the Government still had to cover its back against its domestic critics. The parliamentary passage of the Treaty was not achieved until May 1993, and in the course of the remaining proceedings the Government was defeated by a combination of its own rebels and the Opposition parties on the minor issue of the composition of the British representation on the Committee of the Regions which the Treaty created. It also had to agree to hold a separate vote, after the ratification was completed, on its opt-out from the social protocol.

This vote caused the Government very serious embarrassment. An amendment by the Labour Party was tied at 317 votes for and against; the Speaker's casting vote was needed to prevent a

[38] Ludlow, 'The UK Presidency', 256.

government defeat. Then the vote on the main motion was lost by 324 to 316. Major had to call a vote of confidence in his Government for the following day in order to tidy up this last piece of Maastricht business. It was probably the most serious parliamentary defeat suffered by the Conservative Party this century.[39] Even with the Treaty having completed its parliamentary ratification, the struggle was not over. Lord Rees-Mogg decided to make an application to the High Court to have a judicial review of the Treaty to test its compatibility with the constitution. This was abandoned in early August following the effective collapse of the exchange rate mechanism. Speculative pressure finally tore the mechanism apart, and it was agreed to widen the bands of fluctuation to an almost meaningless 15 per cent. Since Rees-Mogg's primary concern was with the implications of monetary union and this development seemed to put off any prospect of rapid movement towards it, he withdrew his application.

Sniping at the Government continued into the Party Conference in September, during which Major promised the Party would fight the 1994 elections to the European Parliament on a platform of resisting centralization of power in Brussels. In the same month he published an article in which he set out the Government's objectives in the European Union.[40]

The Objectives of the British Government

In her Bruges speech of 1988 Margaret Thatcher identified five guiding principles for the future of the EC. These were: that willing and active co-operation between independent sovereign states was the best way to build a successful European Community; that Community policies should tackle present problems in a practical way; that Community policies should encourage enterprise; that Europe should not be protectionist; and that the defence of Europe should be achieved through NATO.[41]

---

[39] For a detailed analysis of the Government's problems see David Baker, Andrew Gamble, and Steve Ludlam, 'The Parliamentary Siege of Maastricht 1993: Conservative Divisions and British Ratification', *Parliamentary Affairs*, 47 (1994), 37–60.

[40] John Major, 'Raise your Eyes, there is a Land Beyond', *Economist*, 25 Sept. 1993.   [41] *Independent*, 15 Oct. 1988.

The arguments developed by John Major in his *Economist* article were remarkably similar. He said:

> It is for nations to build Europe, not for Europe to supercede (sic) nations.[42]

> Unless the Community is seen to be tackling the problems which affect [the electorates of Europe] now, rather than arguing over abstract concepts, it will lose its credibility.[43]

> I want to see a competitive and confident Europe, generating jobs for its citizens and choice for its consumers.[44]

He also called for a successful outcome to the GATT negotiations and the removal of barriers to trade with Eastern Europe;[45] and for 'common security arrangements firmly linked to NATO'.[46]

The other policy principle with which Thatcher was particularly associated, but which was noticeably not mentioned in the Bruges speech, was monetary union. On this Major stated forthrightly that in the light of the effective collapse of the exchange rate mechanism of the European Monetary System in July 1993, 'economic and monetary union is not realizable in present circumstances'.[47]

The objectives outlined by John Major in this article clearly did not differ substantially from those of the Thatcher Governments. However, by the end of 1993 the attempt to pursue them by adopting a change of tone had already been damaged by the domestic problems over ratifying Maastricht and the acrimony surrounding the departure of sterling from the exchange rate mechanism of the EMS. It became increasingly difficult for the Government to pursue normal diplomacy within the EC/EU because of the way that issues became tangled in domestic politics. A prime example of this was the dispute over qualified majority voting in March 1994.

Enlargement and the Qualified Majority

This incident in early 1994 showed how the pursuit of diplomatic objectives could easily become caught up with the need to satisfy domestic political demands. It concerned the apparently rather esoteric issue of the adjustments that would be needed to the system

---

[42] Major, 'Raise your eyes', 27.
[43] Ibid., 23.
[44] Ibid., 27.
[45] Ibid., 24 and 27.
[46] Ibid., 27.
[47] Ibid., 24.

of qualified majority voting in the Council of Ministers following enlargement of membership to take in Austria, Finland, Sweden, and as it seemed at the time, Norway.[48]

Although a keen supporter of enlargement, the British Government had, as early as 1992, put forward a paper on politically sensitive aspects of the institutional changes that might come with enlargement. This included the number of votes that would constitute a blocking minority under qualified majority voting. The British Government wanted it to be left at 23, whereas the Commission proposal was that it should be increased to 27, in line with the increase in the total number of votes from 76 to 90. At first France and Germany seemed likely to support the British position, but Helmut Kohl felt that this might damage Germany's relationship with the smaller states. The subsequent change in the German position led France to change its stance too, leaving Britain and Spain as the only two states to attach a reserve to the issue.[49] The two Goverments argued that this would allow 41 per cent of the population of the EU to be out-voted.[50]

By February 1994 it was clear to Douglas Hurd that a compromise would be necessary, and he warned the Cabinet of this; but he met opposition, including, surprisingly, from Kenneth Clarke, the Chancellor of the Exchequer, who was generally pro-European. Michael Howard, the Home Secretary, was also an advocate of a strong line, expressing concern about the possible implications for social policy. On the other hand, Gillian Shephard, the Secretary of State for Agriculture, argued that the Government should agree to increase the blocking minority on the grounds that reform of the CAP would be much easier with a higher blocking minority, which would help to get through measures to reduce subsidies on rice, sugar, tobacco, and olive oil that were opposed by Mediterranean states. She had support from John Gummer (Environment), a former Secretary of State for Agriculture, and privately from other senior Cabinet members, including the Deputy Prime Minister, Michael Heseltine.[51]

---

[48] Norway negotiated terms for entry, but did not join after the Norwegian people rejected membership in a referendum by 52.2 per cent to 47.8 per cent.
[49] *Independent*, 29 March 1994, article by Donald Macintyre and Andrew Marshall.   [50] Ibid., 15 March 1994.
[51] Ibid., 21 March 1994.

The issue first emerged into public view during a meeting of Foreign Ministers in March 1994, and led to questions in the House of Commons, in reply to which John Major said that the effects of the revised system of voting needed to be very carefully considered to ensure that democratic legitimacy and the rights of minorities were sustained.[52] At this stage the official tone was measured and diplomatic, with an emphasis on the serious arguments that lay behind the British position, rather than on its conflictual aspect. On 16 March, Douglas Hurd spoke on the subject to Conservative backbenchers. He reported that Spain had proposed a compromise: if two large states plus one small state opposed a measure, it would not be passed. He tried to play down the impression of a confrontation with Germany that some newspapers were giving, insisting that the German Government had been helpful in trying to get a compromise; and he noted that Germany would have been in a strong position to press for more votes for itself following reunification, but that it had desisted from doing so.[53]

It seems that the Foreign Secretary was trying to prevent a matter of diplomatic negotiation becoming complicated by being enmeshed in domestic politics. However, the measured diplomatic tone was soon overtaken. Because the issue fed the divisions within the Conservative Party it was used by Labour as a stick with which to attack the Government, producing a strong statement in the Commons from the Prime Minister, who said that Britain would not succumb to threats from the Commission that enlargement was being jeopardized, and that, in contrast to Labour, the Government would fight Britain's corner. He gratuitously described John Smith (who had not even asked him the question) as 'the man who likes to say yes in Europe—Monsieur Oui, the poodle of Brussels'.[54] This outburst caused concern amounting even to anger amongst pro-Europeans, and there was speculation that Major was manoeuvring for Thatcherite support in advance of a possible leadership election.[55]

On 27 March, at a meeting of Foreign Ministers in Ioannina in Greece, Hurd was presented with a take-it-or-leave-it deal which

[52] *Hansard*, 6th ser. 239 (15 Mar. 1994), col. 742.
[53] *Independent*, 17 March 1994.
[54] *Hansard*, 6th ser. 240 (22 March 1994), col. 134.
[55] *Independent*, 23 March 1994.

would raise the blocking vote to 27, but would allow a delay in any legislation that met with an objection from two large plus one small country. The delay would not be indefinite, and could be ended at any time by a simple majority in the Council. Discussions on a permanent arrangement would begin before 1996.[56] Also on 27 March, Hurd had a difficult meeting with Ministers from Austria, Finland, Norway, and Sweden who were becoming 'very angry and distressed' at the possibility that their membership might be delayed.[57]

At a Cabinet meeting on 29 March Kenneth Clarke, who had been a strong advocate of Britain remaining firm on the issue, threw his weight behind acceptance of the terms brought back by Hurd. The Foreign Secretary told Cabinet that they were the best terms that could be obtained, and that if they were not accepted and negotiations had to be re-opened the Dutch, the French, and Delors, who had all been unhappy about the concessions made to Britain, might harden their stance.

Two further concessions to the British position were reported: that the right of 23 votes to delay acceptance of a proposal would be legally binding; and that there would be no time-limit to the delay. In addition, Sir John Kerr, the British Permanent Representative in Brussels, was reported to be negotiating for a firm assurance from the Commission that no more social legislation would be slipped through under qualified majority voting, or imposed on Britain despite its opt-out from the Social Protocol. This referred to a dispute that was then running about a Commission proposal on works councils, which, it was argued, should cover Britain, despite its opt-out from the Social Protocol, because it applied to multinationals wherever they operated.[58]

On 29 March Major announced that in return for acceptance of the compromise on the size of the blocking minority, the Government had received an assurance from the Commission on social policy. Delors said that all he had done was remind the British of what was in the Commission's legislative package for 1994, and this had never contained anything that could be interpreted as smuggling in social legislation under the heading of health and safety. However, the British said that the Commission

[56] *Hansard*, 6th ser. 240 (28 Mar. 1994), cols. 635–6.
[57] *Independent*, 28 March 1994.
[58] Ibid., 29 March 1994; *Hansard*, 6th ser. 240 (29 March 1994), col. 797.

had accepted that, for purposes of the proposal on works councils, employees of a multinational who were based in Britain would not be counted as part of the total when determining liability or eligibility.[59]

Despite the Government's best efforts to present the outcome as a vindication of its stance on the issue, the general impression was that it had taken a strong line and then been forced to back down. This way of looking at the matter ignored the fact that a genuine compromise had been reached. Neither Conservative backbench Eurosceptics nor the British Press were interested in bargains and compromises: they saw everything to do with Britain and the EU in terms of winning or losing. This was not a victory, and so it must be a defeat.

The 1994 Elections to the European Parliament

In June there were elections to the European Parliament. The start of the campaign was delayed because of the death of John Smith, but when it did begin, the Conservatives ran on a manifesto entitled *A Strong Britain in a Strong Europe*, and adopted a distinctly nationalistic tone. It did not work: the outcome was little short of disastrous for the Conservatives. Their representation was cut from 32 to 18 seats, and their vote, at 27.8 per cent, was the lowest they had obtained in a nationwide poll in the twentieth century. In contrast, Labour ran on a programme that advocated a more co-operative approach to the EU, and increased their representation from 45 to 62 seats, polling 44.2 per cent of the vote, their best result in a national election since the 1960s.

Although the result could be interpreted as a rejection of their nationalist line, the low turn-out (36.1 per cent in mainland Britain) allowed the Conservatives to argue that many of their voters had simply been unable to bring themselves to vote for the European Parliament at all. This argument allowed the Eurosceptical wing of the Party to prevent a defeat in the country from being translated into a setback in internal party politics.

The campaign was also notable for an interesting development in the position of the Government. In a speech at Ellesmere Port in Cheshire on 31 May, John Major spoke of the advantages of a 'multi-speed and multi-track Europe'. He said:

[59] *Independent*, 30 March 1994.

I have never believed that Europe must invariably act as one on every issue. Trying to make every country conform to every plan is a socialist way of thinking; it's not for us. I don't happen to think that it threatens Europe if member states are free do to some things in their own way and at their own speed.[60]

The specific issue that the Prime Minister quoted was Britain's opt-out from the social provisions of Maastricht. Although this argument for the opt-out had been used before, it was the first mention by the Prime Minister of the concept of flexible integration, an idea which had already been floated by Douglas Hurd, and which was to re-emerge in a more developed form in a statement of the Government's position that the Prime Minister made in Leiden in September 1994.

Nominating the President of the Commission

Before the Leiden speech, in June 1994, there was another incident that was widely interpreted as an example of British awkwardness. At the Corfu European Council the British Prime Minister vetoed the appointment as next President of the Commission of Jean-Luc Dehaene, Prime Minister of Belgium and the nominee of the French and German Governments.

There were three candidates to succeed Jacques Delors: Dehaene; Ruud Lubbers, the Dutch Prime Minister; and Sir Leon Brittan, the British Vice-President of the Commission. François Mitterrand and Helmut Kohl agreed to support Dehaene's candidacy at a regular bilateral Franco–German summit in Mulhouse in May. Their choice was leaked to the Press by officials.

When the issue was discussed at the meeting in Corfu, Dehaene and Lubbers left the meeting to be replaced by their alternates: Willy Claes, the Belgian Foreign Minister; and Wim Kok, the Dutch Finance Minister. After presentations on behalf of each of the candidates, the Greek presidency surprised participants by calling a vote. Brittan only got the support of Britain. Dehaene was supported by France, Germany, Belgium, Denmark, Ireland, Luxemburg, and Portugal. Lubbers received support from the Netherlands, Spain, and Italy. At this point Major announced that he could not support Dehaene under any circumstances, and would

[60] *Independent*, 1 June 1994; *Financial Times*, 1 June 1994.

not agree to his nomination even if Britain were in a minority of one. This was ultimately the position that was reached.[61]

Major's exercise of the veto was widely treated in the Press as an example of British positions in the EU being driven by domestic political considerations. It was noted that Major had just suffered two reverses on European issues: he had backed down on the re-weighting of qualified majority votes in the Council, and his party had suffered a drubbing in the elections to the European Parliament. His aggressive presentation of the issue to Parliament on 27 June certainly met with approval from a majority of his back-benchers.[62]

However, the Prime Minister maintained that he had vetoed Dehaene for two reasons that had nothing to do with domestic politics. The first was that, although the British position was not intended as a personal criticism of Dehaene, he was not the right person for the job because he was not in sympathy with the deregulatory emphasis that the British Government believed was necessary for the Commission to pursue over the coming years. The second reason was that the procedures that had been followed both before and during the European Council meeting were unsatisfactory. There had not been the wide and comprehensive consultation that should have taken place. This was a lightly veiled criticism of the way in which the German and French Governments had attempted to force their candidate on the rest of the EU.[63] Both these reasons were plausible explanations of the British position.

Dehaene was from the trade-union wing of the Belgian Christian Democratic Party, and had in the past been associated with the policies that had led Belgium to have a ratio of debt to GDP of 136 per cent, the highest in the OECD; a budget deficit of 6 per cent; and some of the most generous public pension arrangements in Europe.[64] Although his Government, which came to office in March 1992, had been trying to tackle the high budget deficit,

[61] No formal record of the voting is available, but the consensus reporting was that Britain was ultimately alone in holding out against Dehaene. However, Lionel Barber, in the *Financial Times*, 27 June 1994, reported, 'Mr Dehaene secured 10 votes at the end of two ballots'.

[62] *Financial Times*, 27 June 1994.

[63] *Hansard*, 6th ser. 245 (27 June 1994), cols. 554–5.

[64] 'Financial Times Survey: Belgium', *Financial Times*, 28 June 1995.

Dehaene had not impressed Major with his commitment to the market-oriented ideas that informed British Government policy.[65] As for the other reason given by the British Prime Minister, it was not just Britain that was unhappy about the way in which the Germans and French had tried to bounce the meeting into accepting their candidate, whom they had chosen with no prior consultation with the other member states. Several governments, including those of Italy, Portugal, and the Netherlands, were reported to be unhappy at the heavy-handed way in which the Germans in particular had pushed their candidate.[66] The Portuguese Foreign Minister, Jose Manuel Durao Barraso, summed up the mood when he said that the co-operation of France and Germany was vital for the EU, but 'we do not like the way that this has been handled'.[67]

Major could be accused of having been unnecessarily adamant in his rejection of Dehaene. However, it can also be argued that he was only reciprocating the unreasonableness of Kohl, who refused to support Lubbers, and refused to say why he would not support him. The hostility of Kohl reflected the fact that Lubbers had never been afraid to stand up to the Germans in the past, and this was interpreted by Kohl as evidence that the Dutchman was 'egotistical' and 'anti-German'.[68] Although this view was expressed privately, it was no secret; and Kohl's irritable refusal to say why he would not support Lubbers was a public manifestation of his unreasonableness.

Eventually, two weeks later, agreement was reached on the nomination of Jacques Santer, Prime Minister of Luxemburg. Major described Santer as 'a healer and reconciler: the right man in the right place at the right time'.[69] When Santer said publicly that there was no difference between himself and Dehaene on the issue of European integration, sections of the British Press seized on this to argue that the veto of Dehaene had been nothing more than a gesture to the Eurosceptics in the Conservative Party. However, this interpretation ignored the reasons given by the Prime Minister for blocking the nomination of Dehaene: that he came from an

---

[65] *Hansard*, 6th ser. 245 (27 June 1994), col. 564.
[66] *Financial Times*, 27 June 1994.
[67] Ibid.
[68] *Financial Times*, 28 June 1994.
[69] *The Week in Europe*, 21 July 1994.

interventionist economic tradition and that his nomination was being forced through by the French and Germans. Santer's Luxemburg was much less regulated than Dehaene's Belgium; and the nomination had emerged as a result of wide consultation and discussion amongst all the member states. In addition, where Dehaene was seen as Kohl's protégé, Santer had a reputation for being his own man.

This episode was possibly the last straw in the deteriorating relationship between Major and Kohl, causing it finally to break down. Perhaps, though, that relationship had already broken down as a result of the German Chancellor's exasperation with Major over the ratification of Maastricht, and the British Prime Minister's exasperation with Germany over its failure to support sterling inside the exchange rate mechanism in September 1992. Whether the Dehaene episode was cause or symptom of a final irreconcilable break-down, after it there was no question of Kohl helping Major out of any future difficulties that Britain might encounter in Europe.

The Leiden Speech

The William and Mary Lecture given by the Prime Minister in Leiden on 7 September 1994 was used as an opportunity to expand on the idea of flexibility that had emerged during the election campaign for the European Parliament.[70]

Beginning from the position that trying to force all the member states into the same mould would crack that mould, John Major called for an agreement that if some states wanted to integrate more closely or more rapidly than others, they should be allowed to do so. This was not a new principle: it had been accepted in the agreements reached at Maastricht on the future single currency. On the other hand, it was important that no state should be excluded from participation in closer integration in a policy sector if it was willing and able to participate.

His second principle led Major to reject the idea of a 'hard core' Europe. This was an idea that had been advocated in a discussion paper produced by Wolfgang Schauble and Karl Lamers for the

---

[70] John Major, *Europe: A Future That Works*, Second Annual William and Mary Lecture, Leiden, the Netherlands (London, 7 Sept. 1994).

CDU/CSU parliamentary group in Germany on 1 September.[71] A similar approach, envisaging a Europe of concentric circles with France and Germany at its centre, had been outlined by the French Prime Minister, Edouard Balladur, in an interview published two days before the German paper.[72] Major referred to both interventions in his lecture, welcoming the opening of a debate but insisting that any approach that excluded states from participating in common policies in which they wished to join would be disastrous for Europe.

Despite his rejection of a hard core of member states, there was one sort of 'hard core' which the Prime Minister did advocate: that is, one of basic policies from which no state could opt out. These policies were: international trade obligations, the Single Market, and environmental protection.

Looking ahead, Major argued that bringing prosperity and stability to the states of Central and Eastern Europe was a historic task that required the enlargement of the EU. That enlargement would produce such a variety of member states in size, shape, economic and industrial profile, philosophy, history, and culture that it would require the introduction of the flexibility that he was advocating.

In the course of the lecture the Prime Minister also made an initial comment on the position that the British Government would take up in the forthcoming inter-governmental conference; but he did little more than argue that the democratic deficit should be addressed by increasing the role of national parliaments rather than further extending the powers of the European Parliament. The presentation of a more detailed prospectus had to wait a little longer.

The Inter-Governmental Conference

Throughout 1996 and into 1997 the EU was engaged in yet another inter-governmental conference. It had been part of the Maastricht agreement in December 1991 to review the Treaty again after five years. At that time nobody had anticipated the delay in gaining

---

[71] Wolfgang Schauble and Karl Lamers, *Reflections on European Policy*, CDU/CSU Discussion Document (Bonn, 1994).

[72] *Le Figaro*, 30 Aug. 1994.

ratification, which meant that the inter-governmental conference was reviewing the working of the revised Treaty only just over two years after it came into operation. In practice, by the time it started the conference was being treated as an exercise in preparing the EU for the next enlargement, to Central and Eastern Europe. The British Government decided to produce a White Paper setting out its objective in the conference.[73] The main pressure for such a statement had come from the Eurosceptic wing of the Party; but the decision was in line with the procedures of other member states. The problems in convincing national electorates to accept the Treaty on European Union had convinced most governments of the need to proceed in a much more transparent way this time.

The White Paper was presented to Parliament by the Foreign Secretary, Malcolm Rifkind, in terms that emphasized how far the British Government disagreed with what were purported to be the aspirations of federalists for further European integration. The Government wanted subsidiarity further entrenched in the Treaty; it wanted safeguards against directives being used in ways that were never intended; it wanted less EC legislation; it wanted the position of national parliaments to be strengthened; it rejected majority voting in the second and third 'pillars' of Maastricht; it rejected the absorption of the WEU into the EU; and it wanted limits placed on the European Court of Justice.[74]

However, the White Paper itself was not the negative document that the Foreign Secretary's statement seemed to make it out to be. Although all the points mentioned in his speech were present in the Paper, the tone was generally much more positive, and there were constructive suggestions for tackling problems which were widely agreed to require attention at the Conference.[75]

In one policy sector in particular, the Common Foreign and Security Policy (CFSP), the British Government's position seemed to become more central as the inter-governmental conference approached.

---

[73] Foreign and Commonwealth Office, *A Partnership of Nations: The British Approach to the European Union Intergovernmental Conference 1996* (London, 1996).

[74] *Hansard*, 6th ser. 273 (12 Mar. 1996), cols. 785–9.

[75] See the analysis in S. George, ' "A Partnership of Nations": The British Government's White Paper on the Intergovernmental Conference', *European Access*, 3 (1996), 7–9.

Common Foreign and Security Policy

Following a parliamentary debate on the Government's policy to the EU, in March 1995, the then Secretary of State for Defence, Malcolm Rifkind, launched a memorandum on defence cooperation which featured a plan for the WEU to be able to launch operations short of war, using NATO infrastructure. The operations would include peace-keeping and humanitarian measures. Rifkind said the document was intended to launch new ideas to enable Western Europe to make an even more impressive contribution to NATO.[76]

At first sight the proposals fell far short of the more ambitious schemes that had been associated with the Franco–German alliance, such as the formation of a 'Euro-corps' that would be a European joint force. Such ideas had been pushed by France particularly. However, when the British proposals were presented to a meeting of EU Foreign Ministers at Carcassonne later in March, they were generally well received as a basis for discussion within the inter-governmental conference, including by the French representative.

In fact there were already signs of a convergence of British and French positions. In November 1994 Alain Lamassoure, the French socialist Minister for Europe, floated ideas at a seminar in Paris that resembled those outlined by Douglas Hurd earlier in the year. The terminology was different: Lamassoure spoke of the need for an 'institutional revolution', and for the creation of a European foreign ministry. However, it appeared that what he had in mind was strengthening the existing CFSP Secretariat, under the close supervision of the member states, rather than any move to hand over foreign and defence policy to central institutions.[77] This reflected the French Government's concern at losing its ultimate power to control its own military interventions. The German insistence on the recognition of Croatia and Slovenia in December 1991 had started alarm bells ringing. No German lives were put at risk as a result of the policy that the German Government forced through, because Germany insisted that it constitutionally could not deploy troops outside of its own borders, while French troops were in the front line as Yugoslavia disintegrated, as were British troops.

---

[76] *Independent*, 2 Mar. 1995.   [77] Ibid., 23 Nov. 1994.

Nevertheless, so long as he remained President of France, Mitterrand argued in favour of Europe developing a defence capability independent of NATO. On this there could be no meeting of minds with the British position. However, following the retirement of Mitterrand and the election of Chirac, French policy began to shift. Where Mitterrand had rejected the American idea for Combined Joint Task Forces which would be part of NATO but could be used by the WEU, the new French Administration indicated its willingness to pursue the idea. Within the inter-governmental conference the French showed themselves to be unwilling to back proposals to incorporate WEU within the EU which, under Mitterrand, they might have championed. Instead, Chirac began to speak of re-integrating France within NATO to facilitate the emergence of a European pillar inside the alliance.

Anand Menon offered two explanations of this evolution of the French position. The first was that, in the post-Cold-War world, France had found itself having to work alongside Britain and the United States in the Gulf and in Bosnia, and had come to appreciate the effectiveness of NATO command structures and infrastructure: 'Nato is invaluable because it exists and because it works.'[78] The second was the need to cut defence budgets in order to reduce public-sector deficits. It was for this reason that Chirac abandoned conscription in favour of a smaller professional army on British lines. It also made the idea of closer collaboration with NATO more attractive, because the French forces could then use the NATO infrastructure, such things as transport to get forces to a trouble-spot, or reconnaissance aircraft, rather than having to fund a European infrastructure.

The closer relationship in this sphere between Britain and France was marked when Chirac visited Britain in October 1995 to open a joint Franco–British air-force command base at High Wycombe in Buckinghamshire. The two leaders announced that there was considerable convergence between them on strategic matters, and particularly on nuclear doctrine. Here the support that Britain gave to France over Chirac's decision to conduct nuclear tests in the

---

[78] Anand Menon, 'French Shift to Nato Hails End of the European Army Dream', *European*, 16–22 May 1996; also see Anand Menon, 'Defence Policy and Integration in Western Europe', *Contemporary Security Policy*, 17 (1996), 264–83.

Pacific, for which Chirac had been criticized by other EU partners including Germany, obviously contributed to the agreement. Officials reported that personal relations between the two men were cordial.[79] Subsequently, on the eve of a state visit to Britain, Chirac said in a Press conference that he wanted to build on the political and military relationship which the two states had developed in Bosnia. He also welcomed suggestions that Britain might join the European armaments agency that was planned by France and Germany.[80]

The fact that there was a Franco–German agreement to set up a joint armaments procurement agency for European weapons indicates how important it is not to overstate the extent to which France's position had moved away from Germany and towards Britain. The agreement had been reached at a bilateral summit meeting in Baden-Baden on 8 December 1995. Its stated aim was to ensure that all the members of the Euro-corps were e ipped with the same weapons, although to many observers it s .ned that an unspoken aim was to build a European defence industry that could compete with the United States.

Why was Britain interested in such an agency, given the British Government's advocacy of close defence links with the United States, and its tendency in the recent past to buy US weapons? A clue was given on 13 December 1995, when Dick Evans, the chief executive of British Aerospace, called for moves to rationalize the European defence industry in the light of the merger of US firms, the emergence of Lockheed Martin, and the proposed link-up between Boeing and McDonnell Douglas. He called for governments to encourage strategic alliances between European firms, and for European weapons procurement to be opened up to European-wide competition. Although he did not want to see a 'fortress Europe', he argued that US firms should not initially be allowed to compete because they would simply dominate.[81]

Britain joined the procurement agency in November 1996. Although Defence Secretary Michael Portillo, a known Eurosceptic, emphasized that this did not prevent Britain from buying American armaments in future if they offered better value for money, he also

[79] *Financial Times*, 31 Oct. 1995.
[80] Ibid., 14 May 1996.
[81] Ibid., 14 Dec. 1995.

said that he shared the goal of a strong defence industrial base in Europe.[82] The move put Britain nearer to the heart of Europe in terms of the debate on the future for security and defence.

Monetary Union

An area where Britain was not at the heart of the debate was the single currency. Because of the opt-out negotiated at Maastricht it was difficult for the British Government to make its voice heard in the debate about the nature of the future monetary union. Nevertheless, Chancellor Kenneth Clarke indicated in February 1995 that Britain would take a constructive role in preparing for the single currency; and to a large extent that proved true. However, this contribution was made against a democratic background of increasing demands for the Government to end its non-committal stance and to reject membership of the monetary union, or at least to commit itself to holding a referendum before taking any decision to rescind its opt-out and enter a future single currency.

For a long time these demands were resisted, perhaps because of Clarke's opposition to them within Cabinet. In June 1995 Douglas Hurd told the Commons Foreign Affairs Select Committee that the Government did not rule out a referendum on the issue, but he vigorously denied a newspaper report that he had told a backbench committee that the Prime Minister favoured a referendum.[83] The official position was not to take up a position. Eventually, though, this had to be abandoned, partly perhaps because of pressure from Conservative backbenchers, but also to undermine Sir James Goldsmith, who was threatening to run Referendum Party candidates in all constituencies in the next general election. Goldsmith was likely to appeal more to Conservative than to Labour voters, and might take enough votes to affect the outcome in a close-run election. Although he was demanding a more fundamental referendum, on British membership of the EU, the promise of a referendum on the issue of the single currency gave some defence for Conservative candidates.

---

[82] Ibid., 12 Nov. 1996.
[83] *Independent*, 22 June 1995.

Mad Cows and Englishmen

The difficult relationship of the British Government with its partners in the EU was made even worse during 1996 by a bitter dispute over Bovine Spongiform Encephalopathy (BSE), colloquially known as 'mad cow disease'. This disease of cattle was apparently rare in other European states, but much more prevalent in Britain,[84] and was believed to result from the practice of feeding cows with animal offal.

On 20 March 1996 the Government announced that eating beef from cows affected with BSE could, in some instances, lead to the development of a related disease, Creutzfeld-Jacob Disease (CJD), in humans.[85] It had always previously denied this. The announcement led to a panic reaction across Europe. Bans were imposed on the import of British beef into most EU member states, although such unilateral action was illegal under the rules of the CAP.

Franz Fischler, the Agriculture Commissioner, wrote to Douglas Hogg, the British Minister for Agriculture, criticizing him for not alerting the Commission to the new evidence in advance of the announcement, so that measures could have been taken to co-ordinate the reaction. Fischler subsequently proposed a worldwide ban on the export of British beef, a measure which was blocked in the College of Commissioners by the two British Commissioners, Sir Leon Brittan and Neil Kinnock. John Major apparently telephoned Jacques Santer, furious at the proposal, which he said was not justified by the available scientific evidence.[86] However, the ban was imposed on 27 March.

When it was not lifted despite the British Government agreeing to a plan to eradicate BSE, John Major announced in the Commons on 21 May that the Government would not agree to any measure that required unanimity until progress was made on lifting the ban; that it would not facilitate progress in the inter-governmental conference; and that it would ensure that the issue of the ban on British beef dominated the forthcoming European Council meeting

---

[84] The problem was apparently less in other European countries, but there was also suspicion that its extent had simply been neither acknowledged nor reported. See the intervention into the House of Commons debate by Barry Field MP, *Hansard*, 6th ser. 274 (20 Mar. 1996), col. 381.

[85] Ibid., cols. 375–6 and 387.

[86] *Financial Times*, 25 Mar. 1996.

in Florence.[87] The decision of the Ministers of Agriculture was a direct response to the failure of the EU's Veterinary Standing Committee to agree to a Commission proposal for a partial lifting of the ban. Major accused some member states of bad faith in voting against the proposal in the Standing Committee after private assurances had been given that they would vote for it; it subsequently appeared that he was referring to Germany and Spain. Major had reached an understanding with Kohl which had not been honoured, in contrast with the position of Chirac, who had delivered on his promise to support the lifting of the ban.[88]

Eventually the crisis was resolved, and the British policy of non-cooperation lifted, following agreement at the Florence European Council in June 1996. However, in the meantime the issue had inflicted untold damage on the credibility of John Major's Government in the EU, and had fed the growing anti-European frenzy of Conservative backbenchers.

A Far Better Thing?

Despite widespread predictions that John Major would fight the election 'on an anti-federalist ticket—suitably tinged with a genteel xenophobia',[89] the EU was not a particularly significant issue in the general election. The campaign was fought much more on the issue of so-called 'sleaze', a term that covered a multitude of sins and alleged sins, but particularly focused on allegations that Conservative MPs had accepted cash in return for asking parliamentary questions on behalf of the Al-Fayed brothers, the owners of the Harrods store. Nevertheless, as a measure of how important the issue remained in the Conservative rank and file, over 100 Conservative MPs defied the official party line on the single currency, which was that a decision had yet to be made, and declared themselves against British membership.

As the campaign progressed, with opinion polls predicting a large Labour victory, attempts were made by the Eurosceptics to shift the

---

[87] *Hansard*, 6th ser. 278 (21 May 1996), cols. 99–100 and 103.
[88] *Financial Times*, 23 May 1996.
[89] David Marquand, 'Commentary: Tweaking the European Nerve', *Political Quarterly*, 66 (1995), 3.

focus to the EU and to persuade the Prime Minister to fight an overtly anti-European election. Many Conservative backbenchers blamed his refusal to do this on the inlfuence of Kenneth Clarke.

Whether an aggressively anti-EU campaign would have succeeded is very doubtful, given the deep unpopularity of the Government and its experience in the 1994 European election. In any case, the Labour Party resolutely refused to fight on that ground, constantly retreating to positions that were practically identical to those of the Government. The only result of a more aggressive rejectionist stance by the Conservatives would have been to make the bargaining position of any future British Government impossible in the post-election EU. John Major was constantly accused throughout his period in office of bowing to pressure from his backbenchers on Europe. In the general election he was accused of bowing to the pressure from his Chancellor of the Exchequer. It is possible, though, that he did not fight on an extremely anti-EU platform because he was not prepared to sell out the national interest for the sake of a possible victory at the polls. If so, it was a far better thing that he did than he was given credit for.

Conclusion

John Major began his premiership with the aim of putting Britain at the heart of Europe. He ended it with his Government as isolated as ever his predecessor's had been. The most common interpretation of what went wrong is that a Prime Minister with a small majority in Parliament chose to accommodate the anti-European elements within his party rather than confront them. On this view, the Government's stance within the EU was 'a foreign policy dictated by the Euro-sceptic wing of the Tory party.'[90]

The influence of domestic politics on the policies of British Governments within the EC/EU has been a consistent explanatory theme of this book, and it would be absurd to deny the effect of considerations of internal party management on the Major Government. The scale and intensity of rebel Conservative activity between 1992 and 1997 was very significant, not just in terms of

---

[90] Philip Stephens, 'Major Plays Safe by Denying Dehaene', *Financial Times*, 27 June 1994.

parliamentary behaviour, but also in terms of publicity; and it increased in salience as the Government's majority shrank. However, there are other explanations of Britain's position in the EU which should not be ignored. Two in particular are worth mentioning: the British Government's view of the nature of the EU; and the personal factor.

The continuity between the vision of the EU held by Thatcher and that presented by Major is outlined earlier in this chapter in the form of a comparison of Major's article in the *Economist* with Thatcher's Bruges speech. A case can be made for saying that the Government did have a clear, coherent, and positive vision of the future of Europe, and that that vision, rather than short-term considerations of party management, informed the positions that it adopted in EU negotiations, whether on social policy, monetary union, or the CFSP. Britain's awkwardness in this sense reflects the differences between that vision of Europe and the Franco–German vision. Indeed, if the issue is seen as being mainly about economic liberalism versus state-interventionist policies, the British position could be said to have become more central to the EU throughout the Major period.

The bitter tone adopted by the Prime Minister in some of the later disputes, especially over the presidency of the Commission and the beef crisis, can perhaps be explained by his personal sense of having been frequently let down by other European leaders, and especially by the German Chancellor. Before becoming Prime Minister, with the exception of a very brief spell as Foreign Secretary, John Major had spent the whole of his ministerial career in the Treasury. His contact with the EC had been through the Council of Economics and Finance Ministers, or Ecofin, as it is known. This manifestation of the Council is particularly liable to adopt a collegial, problem-solving approach to the issues before it; politics are less evident than in other Councils. The gradual erosion of the Prime Minister's positive attitude towards the EU may have been related to his growing disillusionment with the political games that other leaders were prepared to play. A man of good faith himself, Major found it difficult to deal with what he saw as frequent examples of bad faith by his fellow heads of government.

A combination of factors, rather than any single one, contributed to frustrating the aim of the Prime Minister to put Britain at the heart of Europe. How far the explanation lies in factors that were conjunctural, and how far in those that were structural, is an important question; on its answer depend the prospects of Britain ever being able to make an effective new start in its relations with the EU. It is this question which is addressed in Chapter 9.

9. Conclusion:
Still Awkward after all this Time

ON the face of it, little changed in the relationship between the British Government and the rest of the EC in the period covered by this book. John Major's Government could still be described as an awkward partner. Yet changes did take place in the underlying fundamentals of the relationship which suggested that the condition might not be inevitable, that Britain had at least the opportunity to be seen as a less awkard partner. This was partly due to changes in Britain, and partly to changes in the EC.

There were several reasons for Britain's reputation for awkwardness: domestic political constraints on the positions that British Governments could adopt; real problems for the British economy in adjusting to membership, especially the problems of Britain's contributions to the common budget; an awkwardness on the part of British negotiators in handling the terminology of political debate that had developed among the original members; and an instinct of many leading British political figures to look first to the United States for partnership. If we examine each of these factors in turn, we can see where the deep structures were changing, even if the surface relations remained static.

Domestic Political Constraints

Not even the Heath Government made any real effort to convert the British people to Europeanism, and the need to win elections in a political culture that was, for much of the period under review, sceptical of the benefits of being linked to the rest of Europe led easily to anti-EC rhetoric from politicians of both the leading parties. This in turn tended to reinforce rather than undermine attitudes based on generations of imperialism, of Britain looking to the wider world and treating Europe with disdain, of negative attitudes to the French that became embodied in popular culture, and, since the early twentieth century, of fear of and mistrust towards the Germans.

Domestic electoral constraints eased throughout the period of British membership, and even began to move in favour of a more accommodating British position. Slowly, without prompting from politicians, public attitudes to the EC changed in Britain. Public-opinion polls showed a steady increase in pro-EC attitudes, particularly among a new generation who had grown up not knowing the imperialist Britain of the past, and for whom membership was a fact of their whole lives.[1]

By the end of the period under review there was some evidence that this gradual change in attitudes had started to feed through to politicians. The recognition that anti-EC sentiments did not strike a chord with younger voters was evident in Douglas Hurd's comments to the CBI Conference in Glasgow in November 1990 when he said, 'We have to make a success of Britain in Europe. Our younger generation requires this.'[2]

Coming immediately after Margaret Thatcher's remarks about never surrendering sovereignty to Brussels, this could be seen as a rebuke to the Prime Minister, whose normally sound political judgement already seemed to have been clouded by her instinctive anti-EC prejudices when she insisted on the Conservative campaign for the 1989 elections to the European Parliament being conducted on a strongly anti-Brussels platform. The victory for the Labour Party in these elections was due to much more than the contrast in the tone adopted by the two parties on the attitude that Britain should adopt towards the EC. Nevertheless, Labour's strong showing amongst younger voters in those elections augured badly for the long-term electoral position of the Conservatives; and Labour's tone on the EC fitted more easily than Thatcher's with the attitudes expressed by younger voters in opinion polls.

The problem for John Major was that the general attitude of the public was not reflected in the attitudes of members of the Conservative Party, where older prejudices held sway, reflecting the age profile of party members as well as the reinforcement of those attitudes given by their espousal in the statements of Margaret

---

[1] Neill Nugent, 'British Public Opinion and the European Community', in Stephen George (ed.), *Britain and the European Community: The Politics of Semi-Detachment* (Oxford, 1991), 172–201.
[2] *Independent*, 6 Nov. 1990.

Thatcher both throughout her time as Prime Minister and in her attacks on the Treaty on European Union during the ratification debate. This gave a lead to backbench Conservative MPs to attack their own Government for appearing to have abandoned the Thatcher line on the EC. With a dwindling parliamentary majority, Major had to make certain concessions to what became known as the Eurosceptic position. These included fighting the 1994 elections to the European Parliament on a similar platform to that of 1989, with even more disastrous results.

Economic Problems and Adjusting to Membership

There were real economic problems for Britain in adjusting to EC membership, problems that were reflected in the difficulties over British contributions to the common budget. The CAP, the only substantial common policy of the EC when Britain joined, did not particularly benefit Britain; while the basis on which the contributions were calculated penalized Britain because it conducted more of its trade outside of the EC, and so had to pay import levies on the goods it brought into the EC.

While the budgetary settlement at Fontainbleau cleared up the immediate issue of dispute, the basis for the imbalance was being steadily eroded anyway. First, the CAP was in the process of radical reform by the late 1980s, reform imposed by the demands of the outside world that the EC stop subsidizing its agricultural production and exports. Second, over the period since membership the interdependence of the British economy with the rest of the EC increased dramatically. In the mid-1960s the twelve states that comprised the EC between 1986 and 1995 accounted for less than 20 per cent of Britain's total trade; by 1986, following the accession of Spain and Portugal, around half of Britain's total trade, both imports and exports, was with the rest of the EC, and by the end of the 1980s Germany had overtaken the United States as Britain's leading trading partner.[3]

The arrival of the Mediterranean member states changed the pattern of alliances on budgetary issues. These states were successful in demanding a large increase in the structural and

[3] For detail on the effects on Britain, in the legal, political, and social areas as well as the economic, see Simon Bulmer, Stephen George, and Andrew Scott (eds.), *The United Kingdom and EC Membership Evaluated* (London, 1992).

cohesion funds to allow them to strengthen their economies, which in turn led to an alignment on the budgetary issue of potential contributing and recipient states in which Britain was on the same side as Germany, France, Denmark, The Netherlands, Belgium, and Luxemburg. In this respect changes in the EC had put Britain into the position of a much more normal member state.

However, some economic differences remained. The 50 per cent of trade that Britain did with the rest of the EC was still a smaller proportion than that of other member states. Also, the British economic cycle was in closer synchronization with that of the United States than with that of the rest of the EC. This is one reason why the pound ran into such severe problems within the exchange rate mechanism in 1992; and why it would have been necessary for any British Government to exercise caution before committing itself to membership of the single currency.

Becoming communautaire

Adjusting to the EC's ways was difficult for both British politicians and officials.

For the politicians one difficulty was in the difference between the British adversarial political system, in which the government of the day usually had a majority in Parliament and could get its own way, and the system of compromise to which European politicians were accustomed. Coalition governments are the norm in most other member states of the EC, so their politicians expect to have to compromise and are adept at it. British politicians have only slowly got used to this way of working. Margaret Thatcher never adapted her approach, and John Major found the cutting of deals increasingly tiresome and frustrating.

A second problem was that both politicians and officials had difficulty in presenting British national interests in a way that did not appear to be against the common EC interest, whereas the French were always adept at wrapping pursuit of their national interest in a *communautaire* vocabulary. A sign that some adjustment had been made here was the adoption by the British in 1990 of the term 'subsidiarity', part of the terminology of European federalism and of Christian Democracy, as the basis for their campaign to limit the extent of interventions in national affairs by the Commission. Subsidiarity was embraced with enthusiasm by other member states, especially the French, who immediately after the ratification of the Treaty on European Union, which made subsidiarity a part of the constitutional basis of the EC, set about scrutinizing the whole of *acquis communautaire* to identify powers that had been transferred to the EC in the past and which ought to be repatriated under the subsidiarity principle.

At the same time the other members of the EC gradually adjusted to the British approach. Alan Butt Philip and Christina Baron, in a study of the implementation of EC legislation, suggested that the frequent awkwardness of the British in negotiations owed a good deal to the attitude of the national administration to enforcing the legislation once it had been agreed. They argued that those closer to the decision-making centres of the EC understood this better than most of the public, either in Britain or in the other member states.

It is understood that the British will be demanding in negotiation in order to ensure that an acceptable position is eventually reached, because whatever decision is finally reached will be enforced throughout the UK with the same rigour as is applied to UK domestic decisions. The principle of not agreeing to any proposal unless certain it can be implemented, which many seem obstructive in Britain's European partners, is a product of the UK administration's legalistic attitude to enforcement.[4]

With the agreement of a host of legislation designed to create the single European market, there was growing awareness after 1992 that consistent implementation was necessary if the single market was to be a reality. In this context, the British (and Danish) position on agreeing to legislation and implementing it was becoming more normal.

Atlanticism

A factor often overstated but not to be ignored in explaining Britain's awkwardness was the natural instinct of many leading political figures to look to the United States for partnership, and to regard with suspicion what were perceived as the federalist designs of Europeans. Federalism was seen not only as a threat to British

---

[4] Alan Butt Philip and Christina Baron, 'United Kingdom', in Heinrich Siedentopf and Jacques Ziller (eds.), *Making European Policies Work: The Implementation of Community Legislation in the Member States*, ii. *National Reports* (Brussels, 1988), ch. 10.

sovereignty, but also as an attempt to undermine US hegemony in the capitalist world, and as part of an overall conception of the EC that was inherently protectionist against the rest of the world.[5]

Strangely, the position of the Heath Government, which appears not to fit this pattern, can be seen as a precursor of the position that gradually developed in the British approach. Heath was as committed as any British Prime Minister to the defence of global internationalism in economics and to ensuring global stability in the arena of high politics. In the context of the growing absorption of the Nixon Administration with the narrowly defined national interest of the United States it was not clear that these objectives could be achieved by a close alliance with the United States. The alternative, which was pursued by the Heath Government, was to use the EC as a vehicle for achieving them.

That approach was abandoned by Wilson, Callaghan, and Thatcher, all of whom were instinctive Atlanticists. However, there were signs even under Thatcher that the British Government would not always align itself with the United States against the EC. The incident over the US ban on the export of equipment to the Soviet Union for the Siberian gas pipeline was a case in point.[6]

Given the position of both the Bush and Clinton Administrations on the need for Europe to take responsibility for its own affairs, the reluctance of the United States to involve itself in world-policing operations, and the murmuring of protectionist tendencies within the US Congress and the Democrat Party, the Major Government in the early 1990s moved towards the same position on the EC that Heath had mapped out over 20 years earlier, only to be blown off-course by domestic and personal factors.

The Future

Despite the obvious awkwardness of the Major Government in its relations with the EC/EU in its final years, developments suggested that the British position would not need to alter too much to be central to the European debate on the future.

---

[5] These arguments are developed fully in Stephen George, 'Nationalism, Liberalism and the National Interest: Britain, France, and the European Community', *Strathclyde Papers on Government and Politics*, 67 (Glasgow, 1989).
[6] See Ch. 5 above.

The problems in achieving ratification of the Treaty on European Union throughout Europe had shown public scepticism about the federalist aspirations of some of their leaders; in particular, the European project of Mitterrand in France appeared to have failed, and Gaullist nationalism to have reasserted itself. In addition, enlargement to bring in Austria, Finland, and Sweden increased the number of states that were in many respects close to the British view of what degree of European integration was acceptable.

Enlargement also complicated the process of alliance formation, which had already become more complex as a result of the spread of qualified majority voting to more areas of policy. While the Franco–German alliance remained powerful, it could no longer dominate proceedings; a more co-operative tone from Britain would have been welcome by other member states, which were often unhappy about the extent to which the French and Germans tried to dominate.

Although the Franco–German alliance was still alive and well, it came under strain throughout the 1990s, particularly over French reluctance to accept a GATT deal (where the Germans were closer to the British than to the French), and on the question of intervention in Yugoslavia (where the French were closer to the British than to the Germans). Without trying to break apart the Franco–German alliance, British diplomacy under the Major Government aimed at becoming involved in discussions with both partners on matters of common interest, and this was beginning to work before the dialogues were drowned out by unhelpful noises from the domestic arena and the unhappy incidence over BSE.

Predictions of a new start for Britain in Europe had too often proved unfounded for them to be asserted with any confidence in 1997. Yet the underlying situation seemed promising for a Government that was not hindered by the problems that afflicted John Major, for putting Britain at the heart of the debate about the future of Europe.

Bibliography

ALBERT, ERNST, 'Britain again at the European Crossroads', *Aussenpolitik*, 25 (1974), 146–57.

ALLOTT, PHILIP, 'Britain and Europe: A Political Analysis', *Journal of Common Market Studies*, 12 (1975), 203–23.

ASHFORD, NIGEL, 'The Conservative Party and European Integration, 1945–1975', Ph.D. thesis (Coventry, 1983).

BAILEY, RICHARD, *The European Connection* (Oxford, 1983).

BAKER, DAVID, GAMBLE, ANDREW, and LUDLAM, STEVE, 'The Parliamentary Siege of Maastricht 1993: Conservative Divisions and British Ratification', *Parliamentary Affairs*, 47 (1994), 37–60.

BALFOUR, NANCY, 'President Nixon's Second Term', *World Today*, 29 (1973), 98–107.

—— 'President Ford and Congress', *World Today*, 33 (1975), 89–92.

BARKER, ELISABETH, *Britain in a Divided Europe* (London, 1971).

—— *The Common Market* (rev. edn., Hove, 1976).

—— *The British between the Superpowers, 1945–50* (London, 1983).

BARRACLOUGH, GEOFFREY, *An Introduction to Contemporary History* (Harmondsworth, 1967).

BILSKI, RAPHAELLA, 'The Common Market and the Growing Strength of Labour's Left Wing', *Government and Opposition*, 12 (1977), 306–31.

BLAKE, DAVID, 'Now the EEC can really Start to Shape its Policies', *The Times*, 9 June 1975.

BRANDT, WILLY, *A Peace Policy for Europe*, trans. Joel Carmichael (London, 1969).

BRETT, E. A., *The World Economy since the War: The Politics of Uneven Development* (London, 1985).

BRISTOW, S. L., 'Partisanship, Participation and Legitimacy in Britain's EEC Referendum', *Journal of Common Market Studies*, 14 (1976), 297–30.

BUDD, ALAN, and DAVIES, ALAN, 'Economic Policy and Macro-economic Developments', in Peter Catterall (ed.), *Contemporary Britain: An Annual Review 1990* (Oxford, 1990), 137–45.

—— —— 'Economic Policy and Macro-economic Developments', in Peter Catterall (ed.), *Contemporary Britain: An Annual Review 1991* (Oxford, 1991), 156–68.

BULMER, SIMON, GEORGE, STEPHEN, and SCOTT, ANDREW (eds.), *The United Kingdom and EC Membership Evaluated* (London, 1992).

BURBAN, JEAN-LOUIS, 'La Dialectique des élections européennes', *Revue française de science politique*, 27 (1977), 377–406.

BURGESS, SIMON, and EDWARDS, GEOFFREY, 'The Six plus One: British

Policy-making and the Question of European Economic Integration, 1955', *International Affairs*, 64 (1988), 393–413.

BUTLER, DAVID E., 'Public Opinion and Community Membership', *Political Quarterly*, 1 (1979), 151–6.

—— 'Elections in Britain', in Peter Catterall (ed.), *Contemporary Britain: An Annual Review 1990* (Oxford, 1990), 46–51.

—— 'Elections in Britain', in Peter Catterall (ed.), *Contemporary Britain: An Annual Review 1991* (Oxford, 1991), 59–62.

—— 'Elections in Britain', in Peter Catterall (ed.), *Contemporary Britain: An Annual Review 1992* (Oxford, 1992), 51–4.

—— and KITZINGER, UWE W., *The 1975 Referendum* (London, 1976).

BUTT, RONALD, 'Mrs. Thatcher's Modern Europe', *The Times*, 5 July 1984.

BUTT PHILIP, ALAN, and BARON, CHRISTINA, 'United Kingdom', in Heinrich Siedentopf and Jacques Ziller (eds.), *Making European Policies Work: The Implementation of Community Legislation in the Member States*, ii: *National Reports* (Brussels, 1988), 637–713.

CALLAGHAN, JAMES, *Time and Chance* (London, 1987).

CAMPS, MIRIAM, *Britain and the European Community, 1955–63* (London, 1964).

CARLTON, DAVID, *Britain and the Suez Crisis* (Oxford, 1988).

CASSIDY, JOHN, 'Pro-German, Anti-British Group Gains Influence in Washington', *Sunday Times*, 17 Dec. 1989.

CASTLE, BARBARA, *The Castle Diaries, 1974–76* (London, 1980).

—— *The Castle Diaries, 1964–70* (London, 1984).

CHARLTON, MICHAEL, 'How and Why Britain Lost the Leadership of Europe (I): "Messina! Messina!" or, The Parting of the Ways', *Encounter*, 57/2 (Aug. 1981), 8–22.

—— 'How (and Why) Britain Lost the Leadership of Europe (II): A Last Step Sideways', *Encounter*, 57/3 (Sept. 1981), 22–35.

—— 'How (and Why) Britain Lost the Leadership of Europe (III): The Channel Crossing', *Encounter*, 57/4 (Oct. 1981), 22–33.

Commission of the European Communities, *Bulletin of the European Communities* (Brussels), various editions.

—— *Social Dimension of the Internal Market*, COM(89) 248 final, May 1989.

—— 'White Paper: Growth, Competitiveness, Employment', *Background Report*, 10 Dec. 1993, ISEC/B35.

COSGRAVE, PATRICK, 'Heath as Prime Minister', *Political Quarterly*, 44 (1973), 435–46.

—— 'Where is our European Policy?', *Spectator*, 15 Nov. 1975, p. 622.

CRAWFORD, MALCOLM, 'The Billion Pound Drain: What it Costs us to be in Europe', *Sunday Times*, 23 July 1978.

DAHRENDORF, RALPH, 'The Foreign Policy of the EEC', *World Today*, 29 (1973), 47–57.

DAVIDSON, IAN, 'The Ludicrous Oil Crusade', *Spectator*, 1 Nov. 1975, p. 564.

DAVIES, ALAN, 'Economic Policy and Macro-economic Developments', in

Peter Catterall (ed.), *Contemporary Britain: An Annual Review 1992* (Oxford, 1992), 158–70.

DAWKINS, WILLIAM, 'EEC Decision-making Reforms Impede Research Funds Accord', *Financial Times*, 10 Feb. 1987.

EDEN, ANTHONY, *Memoirs: Full Circle* (London, 1960).

EDWARDS, GEOFFREY, and WALLACE, HELEN, 'EEC: The British Presidency in Retrospect', *World Today*, 33 (1977), 283–6.

EL-AGRAA, ALI M., *Britain within the European Community: The Way Forward* (London, 1983).

European Communities, Committee for the Study of Economic and Monetary Union, *Report on Economic and Monetary Union in the European Community*, Apr. 1989.

FOREIGN AND COMMONWEALTH OFFICE, *A Partnership of Nations: The British Approach to the European Union Intergovernmental Conference 1996* (London, 1996).

FRANKEL, JOSEPH, *British Foreign Policy, 1945–1973* (London, 1975).

FREEDMAN, LAWRENCE, 'The Case of Westland and the Bias to Europe', *International Affairs*, 63 (1986), 1–19.

GAMBLE, ANDREW, *Britain in Decline: Economic Policy, Political Strategy and the British State* (London, 1981).

—— *The Free Economy and the Strong State: The Politics of Thatcherism* (London, 1988).

GARDNER, NICK, *Decade of Discontent: The Changing British Economy since 1973* (Oxford, 1987).

GAREL-JONES, TRISTAN, 'Tories must Set Agenda for Tomorrow's Europe', *The Times*, 21 June 1993.

—— 'The UK Presidency: An Inside View', *Journal of Common Market Studies*, 31 (1993), 261–7.

GARTHOFF, RAYMOND L., 'The NATO Decision on Theater Nuclear Forces', *Political Science Quarterly*, 98 (1983–4), 197–214.

GEORGE, STEPHEN, *The British Government and the European Community since 1984* (London, 1987).

—— 'Nationalism, Liberalism and the National Interest: Britain, France, and the European Community', *Strathclyde Papers on Government and Politics*, 67 (Glasgow, 1989).

—— *Politics and Policy in the European Community* (Oxford, 2nd edn. 1991).

—— (ed.), *Britain and the European Community: The Politics of Semi-Detachment* (Oxford, 1991).

—— 'A Partnership of Nations: the British Government's White Paper on the Intergovernmental Conference', *European Access*, 3 (1996), 7–9.

—— and ROSAMOND, BEN, 'The European Community', in Martin J. Smith and Joanna Spear (eds.), *The Changing Labour Party* (London 1992), 171–84.

GILL, STEPHEN, 'American Hegemony: Its Limits and Prospects in the Reagan Era', *Millennium: Journal of International Studies*, 15 (1986), 311–36.

GILPIN, ROBERT, *The Political Economy of International Relations* (Princeton, NJ, 1987).

GIRLING, J. L. S., 'Carter's Foreign Policy: Realism or Ideology?', *World Today*, 33 (1977), 417–24.

GOODHART, PHILIP, *Full-hearted Consent: The Story of the Referendum Campaign—and the Campaign for the Referendum* (London, 1976).

HAAS, ERNST B., *The Uniting of Europe: Political, Social and Economic Forces, 1950–1957* (2nd edn., Stanford, Calif., 1968).

HAVINGHURST, ALFRED F., *Britain in Transition: The Twentieth Century* (4th edn., Chicago, 1985).

HAWORTH, DAVID, 'The Odd Man Out of Europe', *New Statesman*, 24 Oct. 1975, p. 494.

—— 'Not a Year for Europe', *New Statesman*, 2 Jan. 1976, pp. 4–5.

—— 'Six Wasted Months', *New Statesman*, 8 July 1977, p. 42.

HEATH, EDWARD, *Old World, New Horizons: Britain, the Common Market, and the Atlantic Alliance* (The Godkin Lectures at Harvard University, 1967; London, 1970).

—— *A British Approach to Foreign Policy* (Leeds, 1976).

HENDERSON, NICHOLAS, 'Britain's Decline: Its Causes and Consequences', *The Economist*, 2 June 1979, pp. 29–40.

HESELTINE, MICHAEL, *The Challenge of Europe: Can Britain Win?* (London, 1989).

HM Government, 'Europe—The Future', *Journal of Common Market Studies*, 23 (1984), 74–81.

HMSO, *Britain and the European Communities*, Cmnd. 4289 (London, 1970).

—— *The United Kingdom and the European Communities*, Cmnd. 4715 (London, 1971).

—— *Developments in the European Community, July to December 1990*, Cmnd. 1457 (London, 1990).

HOLMES, MARTIN, *The Labour Government, 1974–79: Political Aims and Economic Reality* (London, 1985).

—— *The First Thatcher Government, 1979–1983: Contemporary Conservatism and Economic Change* (Brighton, 1985).

HORNSBY, MICHAEL, 'Why Britain seems to be Doing Better from the EEC than Anyone Imagined', *The Times*, 14 May 1976.

—— 'Tough Bargaining Day ahead for Britain's Negotiators in Europe', *The Times*, 31 Dec. 1976.

—— 'How Britain Loses out when they Balance the Books in Brussels', *The Times*, 11 Aug. 1978.

HOSKYNS, SIR JOHN, 'Why the Single Market Programme is in Trouble', *Director*, 31 (13 Mar. 1989).

House of Commons, Treasury and Civil Service Select Committee, *European Monetary Union: Minutes of Evidence, 25 July 1990*, Parliamentary Papers HC 620 (1989–90).

House of Lords, Select Committee on the European Communities, *Fraud against the Community. 5th Report, Session 1988–89*, Parliamentary Papers HL 27 (1988–9).

—— *Economic and Monetary Union and Political Union*, Parliamentary Papers HL 88–i (1989–90).

HUTCHINSON, GEORGE, *Edward Heath: A Personal and Political Biography* (London, 1970).

JENKINS, PETER, 'Brussels Haggles while Europe Yearns', *Independent*, 30 June, 1987.

JENKINS, PETER, 'Mrs Thatcher's Historic Compromise', *Independent*, 17 Feb. 1988.

—— 'Thatcher Attacks her Euro-Galtieri', *Independent*, 22 Sept. 1988.

—— 'How Britain can Avert a Two-Tier Europe', *Independent*, 7 Mar. 1989.

JENKINS, ROY, 'Europe's Present Challenge and Future Opportunity', The First Jean Monnet Lecture, delivered at the European University Institute, Florence, 27 Oct. 1977, *Bulletin of the European Communities, Supplement 10–1977*, pp. 6–14.

—— (ed.), *Britain and the EEC* (London, 1983).

JOWELL, ROBERT, and HOINVILLE, GERALD (eds.), *Britain into Europe: Public Opinion and the EEC, 1961–75* (London, 1976).

JUDGE, DAVID, 'The British Government, European Union and EC Institutional Reform', *Political Quarterly*, 57 (1986), 321–8.

KITZINGER, UWE, *The Second Try: Labour and the EEC* (Oxford, 1968).

—— *Diplomacy and Persuasion: How Britain Joined the Common Market* (London, 1973).

KREILE, MICHAEL, 'West Germany: The Dynamics of Expansion', *International Organization*, 33 (1977), 775–808.

KRIPPENDORF, EKKEHART, and RITTBERGER, VOLKER (eds.), *The Foreign Policy of West Germany: Formation and Contents* (London, 1980).

KYLE, KEITH, 'Making a Dog's Breakfast of Community Business', *The Times*, 31 May 1977.

LAMBERT, JOHN, 'European Ideals Fade in the Oil Scramble', *Sunday Times*, 27 Jan. 1973.

L'EBRELLAC, PASCAL, 'British Attitudes towards European Union since 1979', MA thesis (Canterbury, 1988).

LEIGH, MICHAEL, 'Germany's Changing Role in the EEC', *World Today*, 31 (1975), 488–97.

LOPEZ, DOLORES, 'The Conservative Government and the European Community, 1979–1984', M.Sc. dissertation (London, 1984).

LUARD, EVAN, 'Western Europe and the Reagan Doctrine', *International Affairs*, 63 (1987), 563–74.

LUDLOW, PETER, *The Making of the European Monetary System: A Case Study of the Politics of the European Community* (London, 1982).

—— 'The UK Presidency: A View from Brussels', *Journal of Common Market Studies*, 31 (1993), 246–60.

LYNE, RODERIC, 'Making Waves: Mr. Gorbachev's Public Diplomacy, 1985–6', *International Affairs*, 63 (1987), 205–24.

MACMILLAN, HAROLD, *Riding the Storm, 1956–1959* (London, 1971).

MAJOR, JOHN, 'The Evolution of Europe', *Conservative Party News*, 11 Mar. 1991.

—— 'Raise your Eyes, there is a Land beyond', *The Economist*, 25 Sept. 1993.

—— *Europe: A Future That Works*, Second Annual William and Mary Lecture, Leiden, The Netherlands (London, 7 Sept. 1994).

MARQUAND, DAVID, *Parliament for Europe* (London, 1979).

—— 'The EEC: Britain's Schizophrenia', *Listener*, 101 (1979), 408–10.

—— 'Commentary: Tweaking the European Nerve', *Political Quarterly*, 66 (1995), 1–4.

MCGEEHAN, ROBERT, 'A New American Foreign Policy?', *World Today*, 33 (1977), 241–3.

—— 'American Policies and the US–Soviet Relationship', *World Today*, 34 (1978), 346–54.

MENON, ANAND, 'French Shift to Nato Hails End of the European Army Dream', *European*, 16–22 May 1996.

—— 'Defence Policy and Integration in Western Europe', *Contemporary Security Policy*, 17 (1996), 264–83.

MERLINI, CESARE (ed.), *Economic Summits and Western Decision-making* (London, 1984).

MIDDLEMASS, KEITH, *Politics in Industrial Society* (London, 1979).

MONNET, JEAN, 'A Ferment of Change', *Journal of Common Market Studies*, 1 (1962), 203–11.

—— *Memoirs*, trans. Richard Mayne (London, 1978).

MORGAN, KENNETH O., *Labour in Power, 1945–1951* (Oxford, 1984).

MORGAN, ROGER, 'Can Europe Have a Foreign Policy?', *World Today*, 30 (1974), 43–50.

MORSE, EDWARD L., *Interdependence and Foreign Policy in Gaullist France* (Princeton, NJ, 1973).

—— 'Crisis Diplomacy: The Demise of the Smithsonian Agreement', *World Today*, 39 (1973), 243–56.

MURRAY, IAN, 'How Sir Geoffrey Reversed Roles', *The Times*, 23 July 1984.

NOEL, EMILE, 'Reflections on the Community in the Aftermath of the Meeting of the European Council in Milan', *Government and Opposition*, 20 (1985), 444–52.

NUGENT, NEILL, 'British Public Opinion and the European Community', in Stephen George (ed.), *Britain and the European Community: The Politics of Semi-Detachment* (Oxford, 1991), 172–201.

OECD, *OECD Economic Surveys* (Paris), various editions.

OVERBEEK, HENK, *Global Capitalism and Britain's Decline* (Amsterdam, 1988).

OWEN, DAVID, 'Britain and Europe: At Sixes and Sevens, between Nine and Twelve', *Encounter*, 62 (Jan. 1979), 20–6.

PARFITT, TREVOR, 'Bad Blood in Brussels', *World Today*, 33 (1977), 203–6.

PAULY, LOUIS W., 'The Politics of European Monetary Union: National

Strategies, International Implications', *International Journal*, 47 (1991-2), 93–111.

PEEL, QUENTIN, 'After the EEC Summit: Why it all went Wrong', *Financial Times*, 1 July 1985.

—— 'Mrs. Thatcher Finds the Middle Ground', *Financial Times*, 4 Dec. 1986.

—— 'A Euro-dilemma for Britain', *Financial Times*, 30 Mar. 1987.

PELKMANS, JACQUES, and WINTERS, ALAN, *Europe's Domestic Market* (London, 1988).

PIERCE, ROY, VALEN, HENRY, and LISTHAUG, OLA, 'Referendum Voting Behaviour: The Norwegian and British Referenda on Membership in the European Community', *American Journal of Political Science*, 27 (1983), 43–63.

PIERRE, ANDREW J., 'What Happened to the Year of Europe?', *World Today*, 30 (1974), 110–19.

PINDER, JOHN, 'Pragmatikos and Federalis: Reflections on a Conference', *Government and Opposition*, 20 (1985), 473–87.

PINDER, JOHN, On European Money: A Sovereign Remedy', *Encounter*, 68/3 (Mar. 1987), 42–6.

PORTER, BERNARD, *Britain, Europe and the World, 1850–1982: Delusions of Grandeur* (London, 1983).

POWELL, ENOCH, 'The One Stark Fact that Goes beyond Butter Mountains and Bureaucrats', *The Times*, 4 June 1975.

RIDDELL, PETER, *The Thatcher Government* (Oxford, 1983).

ROTH, ANDREW, *Heath and the Heathmen* (London, 1972).

SAMPSON, ANTHONY, *Macmillan: A Study in Ambiguity* (London, 1967).

SANDERS, DAVID, WARD, HUGH, and MARSH, DAVID, (with FLETCHER, TONY), 'Government Popularity and the Falklands War: A Reassessment', *British Journal of Political Science*, 17 (1987), 281–313.

SANDHOLTZ, WAYNE, 'Choosing Union: Monetary Politics and Maastricht', *International Organization*, 47 (1993), 1–39.

SCHAUBLE, WOLFGANG, and LAMERS, KARL, *Reflections on European Policy*, CDU/CSU Discussion Document, Bonn, 1994.

SCHMIEGLOW, HENRIK, and SCHMIEGLOW, MICHELE, 'The New Mercantilism in International Relations: The Case of France's External Monetary Policy', *International Organization*, 29 (1975), 367–92.

SCHWEIGLER, GEBHARD, 'A New Political Giant? West German Foreign Policy in the 1970s', *World Today*, 31 (1975), 134–41.

—— 'Carter's *Détente* Policy: Change or Continuity?', *World Today*, 34 (1978), 81–9.

SEERS, DUDLEY, and VAITSOS, CONSTANTINE (eds.), *Integration and Unequal Development: The Experience of the EEC* (London, 1980).

SEGAL, GERALD, 'Unanswered Questions at Wilson's Summit', *Spectator*, 26 July 1975, pp. 108–10.

SERFATY, SIMON, 'The Kissinger Legacy: Old Obsessions and New Look', *World Today*, 33 (1977), 81–9.

SERRE, FRANÇOISE DE LA, *La Grande-Bretagne et la Communauté Européenne* (Paris, 1987).

SHANKS, MICHAEL, 'The EEC Budget Crisis: Is our Oil the Answer?', *The Times*, 29 Nov. 1979.

SHARP, MARGARET, and SHEARMAN, CLAIRE, *European Technological Collaboration* (London, 1987).

SHLAIM, AVI, JONES, PETER, and SAINSBURY, KEITH, *British Foreign Secretaries since 1945* (Newton Abbot, 1977).

SHONFIELD, ANDREW, 'Can the Western Economic System Stand the Strain?', *World Today*, 32 (1976), 164–72.

SIEDENTOPF, HEINRICH, and ZILLER, JACQUES (eds.), *Making European Policies Work: The Implementation of Community Legislation in the Member States*, ii: *National Reports* (Brussels, 1988).

SMART, IAN, The New Atlantic Charter', *World Today*, 29 (1973), 238–43.

SMITH, DAVID, 'Growing Trade with our Partners in Europe', *The Times*, 4 Feb. 1987.

SMITH, M. H., and CAREY, R., 'The Nixon Legacy and American Foreign Policy', *Yearbook of World Affairs*, 32 (1978), 23–42.

SPANIER, DAVID, 'Why Mr. Heath is Pleased with Britain's Start in the EEC', *The Times*, 3 Dec. 1973.

SPERO, JOAN EDELMAN, *The Politics of International Economic Relations* (3rd edn., London, 1985).

STATLER, JOCELYN, 'British Foreign Policy to 1985: The European Monetary System: From Conception to Birth', *International Affairs*, 55 (1979), 206–25.

STEED, MICHAEL, 'The Landmarks of the British Referendum', *Parliamentary Affairs*, 30 (1977), 130–3.

STEEL, DAVID, *A House Divided: The Lib–Lab Pact and the Future of British Politics* (London, 1980).

STEPHENS, PHILIP, 'Major Plays Safe by Denying Dehaene', *Financial Times*, 27 June 1994.

TALBOT, ROSS B., *The European Community's Regional Fund* (Oxford, (1977).

TAYLOR, STEPHEN, 'EEC Co-ordination for the North–South Conference', *World Today*, 33 (1977), 433–42.

TSOUKALIS, LOUKAS, *The Politics and Economics of European Monetary Integration* (London, 1978).

TUGENDHAT, CHRISTOPHER, 'Out of Step to a United Europe', *The Times*, 21 Jan. 1986.

VERRIER, ANTHONY, *Through the Looking Glass: British Foreign Policy in an Age of Illusions* (London, 1983).

WALLACE, HELEN, 'The British Presidency of the European Community's Council of Ministers: The Opportunity to Persuade', *International Affairs*, 62 (1986), 583–99.

—— 'British Policy Acquires a European Dimension', *Revue française de civilisation brittanique*, 4 (1987), 147–54.

WALLACE, WILLIAM, 'British External Relations and the European Community: The Changing Context of Foreign Policy-making', *Journal of Common Market Studies*, 12 (1974), 28–52.

—— 'Europe: The Changing International Context: Implications for British Policy', *World Today*, 31 (1975), 177–213.

—— (ed.), *Britain in Europe* (London, 1980).
—— and SPÄT, MARTIN, 'Coming to Terms with Germany', *World Today*, 46 (Apr. 1990), 55–6.
WHITEHEAD, PHILIP, 'Dithering over Direct Elections', *New Statesman*, 4 Mar. 1977, 275–6.
WILSON, HAROLD, *Final Term: The Labour Government, 1974–6* (London, 1979).
WYLES, JOHN, 'EEC Summit—President Mitterrand's Exocet', *Financial Times*, 7 Dec, 1983.
—— 'Mrs. Thatcher's Eurobluff', *Financial Times*, 25 Aug. 1988.
YOUNG, JOHN W., *Britain, France and the Unity of Europe* (Leicester, 1984).
YOUNG, SIMON Z., *Terms of Entry: Britain's Negotiations with the European Community, 1970–1972* (London, 1973).

Newspapers and News Periodicals Consulted

Economist; *Financial Times*; *Guardian*; *Independent*; *Keesing's Contemporary Archives*; *Le Monde*; *New Statesman*; *Spectator*; *Sunday Times*; *The Times* (London).

Index

CPSIA information can be obtained
at www.ICGtesting.com
Printed in the USA
FFHW022245050319
50870317-56287FF